MW01170196

ALL THAT

WE ARE IS

SPACE &

STARDUST

ALL THAT WE ARE IS SPACE & STARDUST

RYAN FARLEY

Copyright © 2024 by Karen Farley

All rights reserved. No part of this book may be reproduced
in any form or by any electronic or mechanical means,
or the facilitation thereof, including information storage
and retrieval systems, without permission in
writing from the publisher, except by a reviewer,
who may quote brief passages in a review.

Library of Congress Cataloging-in-Publication Data

Farley, Ryan
All That We Are Is Space & Stardust / Ryan Farley
Karen Farley, editor

ISBN:979-8-9885320-2-6 (paperback)
ISBN: 979-8-9885320-3-3 (digital)

TABLE OF CONTENTS

Preface

There are fundamental truths that recur over the ages. I would never pretend that these are my ideas. They are the ideas of the cosmos, but I came to them, as so many have before me, on my own terms. And, although at the center these ideas are the same elementary ideas, they have over the ages found unique expression in different human lives and in different cultures, voiced in the spirit of the times or shaped by the approach of a given person or in the context of one tradition or another. So this is my expression of these central ideas, which I came to on my own terms as a young man. Over the years, however, I have learned that they are core truths that have been expressed over and over again. Here it is my turn to be the storyteller.

Ryan Farley
December, 2022

Introduction

This book is a take on the mind-body problem, not a rigorous scientific/philosophical take, although it pulls on those things. It gets at what we all know to be true, what fits with our experience. We are all researchers, and we collect data about consciousness by living our lives.

This book talks about what it always keeps coming back to for me. It *is* the solution to every problem, breaking down dualism and finding connection, which turns out never to be connection because there was never any separation ... and yet, there is somehow? It's as if the universe has made a movie, and we are all the actors.

It makes me focus on the idea of "masks." I'm thinking of a woman I met when she was in hospice, who told me all of her secrets because she needed to tell them to someone before she died, finally taking the mask off for the first time. I got to see her "real face," the face of God under her mask.

Now, we can't just say, "My experience is true and that's that," because we know one's perceptions can be faulty, but we *can* say, "My experience serves as data in a rational scientific process based on the collection of all experiences." So let's merge the conscious experience into the scientific model. Frankly, it's already in there, and trying to artificially extract it to find the "truly objective" is hopeless, even kind of stupid if you think about it, as mind and subjectivity are woven into literally every moment of every human's life throughout all of time.

Rather than focusing on the duality of the mind-body problem, we must focus on life itself, on the intuition of interconnectedness that we all feel in our mind and body, perhaps what we call "soul." We all feel the oneness and hear the whispers. As Oprah says, "Life whispers to you all the time, if you're paying attention... And really hearing those whispers is one of the most integral pieces of the puzzle."

If there is oneness, we must acknowledge that the mind-body problem is no problem at all, but a problem we've created as dualists by separating two things that are one, just as we've separated free will and determinism, outer and inner, and so many other apparent opposites.

In the film "Keeping the Faith," Edward Norton's character, Father Brian Finn, says that "faith is not about having the right answers. Faith is a feeling. Faith is a hunch, really. It's a hunch that there is something bigger connecting it all... connecting us all together. And that feeling, that hunch, is God."

Ryan Farley
December, 2022

PART 1

OBSERVATIONS

MEDITATIONS

JEWELS IN THE
NET OF INDRA

The Reality Underlying Perceived Reality

The philosopher and mathematician Pythagoras suggested that all things in human experience can be understood and represented mathematically. He also believed that the human soul could be purified through mathematics and escape the cycle of reincarnation in which impure souls are trapped. As I thought about this, I thought of two movies, which began a whole tangent of thought.

In both *Pi* and *The Matrix*, the protagonist is on a quest to see the mathematical and symbolic structure underlying reality. (In *Pi*, the narrator actually references Pythagoras.) The ability to see "the pattern" in *Pi* or "the code" in *The Matrix* is associated with some sort of religious experience. In *Pi*, the theme of Judaism suggests that the narrator is searching for the Kabbalah's mystical, unmediated contact with God—he wants to stare directly into the sun. In *The Matrix*, Neo's first vision of the code frees him from death; he then returns and uses his ability to see the code in order to liberate those who are trapped in the mechanical reality of the matrix.

I cannot help but compare the ideas of Pythagoras and the themes in *The Matrix* to Buddhist philosophy. The goal of Buddhism is to free oneself from the cycle of rebirth (*samsara*) by achieving enlightenment, which is liberation from belief in individual being and the factors of personal existence. Except for the earliest schools of Buddhist thought, which emphasized the search for *nirvana*, the true goal is to then return to *samsara* as an enlightened Bodhisattva, with the ability to see through the illusion of the ego and help to liberate other sentient beings whose minds are deluded. Buddhist and Christian themes do arise in *The Matrix*; Neo's experience is akin to enlightenment or the love of Trinity (the holy trinity), but they are not quite the same.

In the most evolved forms of Buddhism (most apparently Zen, but also foundational to Tibetan (Vajrayana) and Indian (Madhyamaka and Yogacara) doctrines), enlightenment is attained by freeing oneself from conceptualization, that is, by ceasing to hold to fixed views and concepts. It is often described as a state of objectless awareness. The idea is that, without any objects in your consciousness, you cease to have self-awareness, just as you cannot see your face without a mirror. In Zen, this state is called No-Mind.

Consciousness, in any scientific sense, requires an object and a perceiver organism, but this presents two huge problems in Buddhist philosophy. The first is: how is such a state of mind as non-conceptualization or No-Mind even possible? Would one not be dead or comatose? The second is: how, then, can Buddhas speak words, teach the Dharma, and posit philosophical arguments? Of the many responses to this question, one of the most prominent is that Bodhisattvas can see concepts without being attached to them. The Bodhisattva can see through concepts to their true, original nature, and he resides in the place where all things always already are, the void (*sunyata*). Many texts say the Bodhisattva comprehends both existence and non-existence, both the conception of reality and its inherent emptiness—he sees the world as "code." Maybe in terms of a materialist philosopher—who holds that matter and physical processes comprise the whole of reality—the Bodhisattva sees the atoms and the space in between. I don't know, but it makes sense with where I'm going... stars in the sky.

Ralph Waldo Emerson wrote an essay called "The Poet." In Emerson's view, the Poet is the "enlightened" man, so to speak. He is in touch with original nature and goes with the flow, rather like being with "the Force" in *Star Wars* or "being with the Tao," using the Taoist principle of *wu-wei*, or "effortless action." The Poet is able to be the author and composer of reality because he is one with Nature—he is the "Namer." Emerson says the Poet understands that we "are symbols, and inhabit symbols" (Ralph Waldo Emerson, "The Poet," in *Ralph Waldo Emerson: Essays and Lectures*, 456). He sees that all the elements of reality are symbols of Spirit, which is where the Poet resides. It is who the Poet truly is—to him, he is a symbol of nature in a world of natural symbols; his face is the face of Spirit itself. Let's say that this is because he uses his Jedi power of *wu-wei*, of being with the spirit of nature.

The idea that we are composers of our reality is present at the personal level, too. Art is a great example, the making of meaning in general— "play," as D.W. Winnicott would call it. When I was seven or eight I used to sneak out at night to go look at the stars—we had just begun to study them in class. I made giant maps and xeroxed them to make many blank maps. I drew a bunch of different possible connect-the-dot pictures with my own constellations marked on them, and I wrote short little stories about the constellations I named. Once I was taught what the names of the constellations actually *were*, the project seemed somehow less interesting, because I now had a preconceived picture of the stars and constellations.

I see that childhood project as an example of how we invent reality, of how our conceptualization of things informs our experience. Freedom from fixed conceptions allows us to reinvent reality. I see the stars metaphorically as symbols or units of the true structure underlying reality, the heavenly fires that fuel our little world, that we draw pictures with, creates stories for, and invent.

Plato's goal was to get to this realm of ideal forms. His head longed to be up in the clouds, in ideal-land where everything is perfection. (The ideal of circles/spheres and the realm of heavenly bodies recurs in so many of the world's cosmologies. It seems to relate to the idea of the "unit" that is the basis for a pattern of reality, much as Emerson describes the structure of reality as "circles within circles" in his essay, "Circles." This reminds me of the stars.)

For Plato, we are souls imprisoned in bodies, trapped in a cave where we only perceive shadows of the real and imperfect reflections of reality. We must escape the cave in order to see the world of "Perfect Forms." I meant, we must escape the matrix, no wait, *samsara*. Alright, they are not all the same, but I am just going to string all these threads together, leaving aside their discrepancies. "Shadows of the real, imperfect reflections of reality" is a totally Buddhist description and seems somewhat consistent with all these ideologies. Perhaps Plato's world of Perfect Forms could be roughly similar to seeing the code underlying the mechanical reality of the matrix. These various accounts seem like they could be different interpretations by different thinkers from different cultures, approaching through various disciplines what is basically the same phenomenon or idea, the notion that there is a true reality underlying perceived reality, a numinous reality behind phenomenal experience, and that we have access to this true nature. Pythagoras had a mathematical mind, so he gives a mathematical interpretation of this reality. Emerson had a literary mind. The legendary Buddhist sage Bodhidharma had no-mind.

I once heard a wonderfully insightful comment about Raphael's painting, *The School of Athens*, regarding the hand positions of Plato and Aristotle—Plato pointing up to the sky, Aristotle lowering his hand down as if to touch the earth, gestures which correlate with their respective philosophies. This was a great interpretation. However one wants to describe it, it seems that there are two basic ways of talking about the phenomenon I've been talking about. The first is to say that we live in a shadow of reality, a world of imperfect forms, and that we must leave this place in order to go to some heavenly realm. The second is to say that the real world is the ideal world, that the stuff we touch and smell is unified with divinity and nature, that we live not in symbols of spirit, but in manifestations of spirit itself.

Zen, for example, claims that our minds are already one with the enlightened Buddha nature, but we just don't realize it right now. In this view, we do not have to die to reach the world of perfect forms because we are there right now—this is it, but only if you have "Buddha vision" (and we all do). They say the Buddha "reached the other shore without leaving this one." That is, having crossed the ocean of existence, you have reached the other shore, but there is no individual as such who has "gone beyond." There is neither a shore here nor one there; it is merely a manner of speaking to say that you have crossed over. The two shores, the ideal and the formal/material, heaven and earth, are the same shore. In fact, there is no ocean separating the two realms because there is only one realm. Thus the Bodhisattva comprehends forms and emptiness. To follow my metaphor, the world of forms is the everyday world and emptiness is the ideal/ultimate nature in which the world of forms appears as "code"—concepts/symbols, circles/spheres, numbers, stars, atoms, particles, dharmas (which are like the Buddhist equivalent of quantum processes), or whatever system one uses to describe this underlying force, structure, pattern, or nature of reality.

Zen texts are not designed to posit a view of reality; they are designed to persuade one that everything is relative and dependent, and there is no set view of reality. They are designed to induce us to abandon fixed conceptions, and to appreciate the freedom of the mind. This seems similar to Socrates' goal. Socrates argued to expose the assumptions underlying people's beliefs. He wanted to break down people's views of reality.

Let me share a little conversation I just had with Socrates, in my notebook:

Socrates: The true philosopher does not fear death; their soul is freed by death to bask in true wisdom.

Me: Do you fear death, Socrates?

Socrates: No, I know something—I am a true philosopher.

Me: What is wisdom? What do you know?

Socrates: I know nothing except the fact of my own ignorance. I know nothing but the fact that I know nothing; neither I nor anyone else has any wisdom at all.

Me: Then how, Socrates, do you know that your soul gets to the afterlife to bask in wisdom? Have you yourself made an assumption? Only by faith could you believe this to be true. Have you spent your life unearthing people's beliefs so that they must turn to faith?

This is the goal of Zen masters, who test one another constantly to make sure that they do not rely on beliefs and are not attached to a fixed conception of reality. Teachers use many tactics to free their student's minds, including perplexing koans, arguments that posit logical paradoxes, direct contradiction of their own teachings, and strange questions that either force the student to think outside the boundaries of the ordinary, or else have no answer, or else are questions for which the correct answer lies not in the student's answer, but the fact of his answering. Lin-Chi, for example, is famous for striking students to help them realize momentary consciousness without conceptualization; he recalls being struck as a student and writes: *"Thinking of it now, I wish I could get hit once more like that"* (*The Zen Teachings of Master Lin-chi*, Burton Watson (trans.), 16). He teaches:

> The fault lies in the fact that they don't have faith in themselves! If you don't have faith in yourself, then you'll be forever in a hurry trying to keep up with everything around you, you'll be twisted and turned by whatever environment you're in and you can never move freely. (*The Zen Teachings of Master Lin-chi*, Burton Watson (trans.), 23)

Striking students was a way to bring students back to the immediate experience, to bring idealistic students, whose heads are stuck in the clouds among abstract ideas of divinity, back to earth. Once a student asked him how deep the river of Zen flows, and Lin-Chi threw him off the bridge into the river below. This is a perfect illustration of a thinker who sees the divine nature of earthly experiences, who sees eternity in the mundane and ordinary.

Basically, the idea is that if you can free yourself from your current beliefs and conception of reality, you will see that reality is some sort of code, a code that is then interpreted by your mind, yielding a given worldview and belief system. Then you are free to reinterpret and reinvent reality. But there is something more that I talk around and cannot pin down... something about the experience of this freedom or whatever that produces an understanding of the way things are, the course of nature, contact with God, or something like that. Is it possible that if we let go of what we think of as knowledge, there is some deeper knowledge that resides within us and is part of our very nature, knowledge which could inspire our thoughts and actions with the resonance of truth?

Emerson, for example, describes the natural world as symbolic, which may lead one to misinterpret his ideas. When Emerson says that elements of the world are symbols, he means that symbols are actually real things, that we actually live in our conceptions, which are the manifestations of

Nature, unfolding itself through the human soul (i.e., the true Poet in us all). He writes in his essay "Nature":

> But when, following the invisible steps of thought, we come to inquire, Whence is matter? and Whereto? many truths arise out of the recesses of consciousness. We learn that the highest present is the soul of man, that the dread universal essence, which is not wisdom, or love, or beauty, or power, but all in one, and each entirely, is that for which all things exist, and that by which they are; that spirit creates; that behind nature, throughout nature, spirit is present; one and not compound, it does not act upon us from without, that is, in space and time, but spiritually, or through ourselves: therefore, that spirit, that is, the Supreme Being, does not build up nature around us, but puts it forth through us, as the life of the tree puts forth new branches and leaves through the pores of the old. As a plant upon the earth, so a man rests upon the bosom of God; he is nourished by unfailing fountains, and draws, at his need, inexhaustible power. Who can set bounds to the possibilities of man? Once inhale the upper air, being admitted to behold the absolute natures of justice and truth, and we learn that man has access to the entire mind of the Creator, is himself the creator in the finite. This view, which admonishes me where the sources of wisdom and power lie, and points to virtue as to
>
>   "The golden key
> Which opes the palace of eternity,"
> [Milton, *Comus*, II, 13-14]
>
> carries upon its face the highest certificate of truth, because it animates me to create my own world through the purification of my soul. (Ralph Waldo Emerson, "Nature," Chapter VII, "Spirit," *Ralph Waldo Emerson: Essays and Lectures*, 41-42)

Emerson was still an idealist; he wanted to "inhale the upper air." It is interesting to think of Walt Whitman as trying to be Emerson's Poet, as trying to live in the world and see "eternity in men and women," and each blade of grass, and Whitman says as much in the 1855 Preface to *Leaves of Grass*. (Walt Whitman, "Preface," *Leaves of Grass* (1855), 9)

I think science is a form of art, or art is a form of science. One can appreciate beauty from an artistic perspective, a scientific perspective, or any other perspective. Creativity and art are entirely about finding new ways to see the world and appreciating new perspectives on the ordinary or extraordinary. The scientist is doing something much like the artist, looking at the world and forming an interpretation of it. I think that the world is a toy, and all the ideas and concepts available to us are toys. Seeing that the elements of reality are there for you to "play" with, that you are not attached to a specific view, is what I am talking about. Science is one way to do this; so is art, so anything that you want so long as it helps you draw your picture and give your interpretation of the way things are, so that I can read it.

I see my childhood loss of interest in the constellations as a result of holding to one fixed conception of the patterns in the sky. I could still create my own constellations even though I know the constellations taught in astronomy. In other words, scientific knowledge only limits creativity and art if you let it, if you refuse to look at other possibilities. Religious doctrines can have much the same effect. Many people I know are Christians but can't explain why—they hold to a fixed conception of God and this seems to limit their creativity and their ability to experience the world from other perspectives. If a scientist only saw flowers scientifically, and could not simply look at a flower for what it is, they would be like the scientists Whitman was writing about, stuck in their lecture hall unable to look at the stars in silence. So long as a scientist can see the world's beauty on "many levels," as the physicist Richard Feynman puts it, he will be able to see beauty in the aesthetic qualities of the flower as well as his scientific conception of the flower. Science ought to be about questioning our conception of reality, just like art and religion should be.

Constructing the Self

Only to the extent that we expose ourselves over and over to annihilation can that which is indestructible be found in us. (Pema Chodron, When Things Fall Apart: Heart Advice for Difficult Times, *9)*

I do know that that which is in us is indestructible. It is love; it is compassion for myself and every other being; it is being fully present with the truth, meeting the pain and fear, and accepting impermanence. It is opening when I want to shut and leaning in when I want to run away. It is making friends with myself. Light shines through us as though your body means nothing to the light. Remember: "Deep in their roots, all flowers keep the light." (Theodore Roethke, *Straw for the Fire: From the Notebooks of Theodore Roethke*, 40)

When we fail at this, fall short, or cause pain to others, it's easy to be consumed by guilt, to see our own guilt reflected by the world. It's easy to cover our world with it, so that our mind paints it into everything around us. The mind is good at this, painting reality, narrating a story to fit events, constructing its own world. Painting is like play, so play is constrained by the reality limit. But it's interesting when we start painting the world with our negative emotions, because it infiltrates our motives, our understanding of the world. It's a shadow power that affects us negatively but remains unseen, hidden behind the story, like what's behind love... Negativity can hollow out love, be it guilt, jealousy, pain, or any other negative emotion. At the same time, perhaps love can be found beneath guilt or grief, part of their foundations, but this is the conundrum of negative emotions.

The self is constructed as well, seeming to be a locus for all our experiences of our world to revolve around, but as this extends, the more things we say are true about it, the more often we are wrong, because those things are always transient, always changing. We find ourselves drawing lines that aren't really there, separating the self from its extended aspects, like the imagination, or the fact that it is many different things and not a monolith. It is always in flux and can't be defined or pinned down. It is like the Greek ship, the ship of Theseus, a thought experiment regarding a vessel that makes journey after journey, having a plank replaced here and then there as it is used, until finally over time the entirety of the ship has been replaced. The thought experiment asks whether, after this total replacement, the ship is still the same ship? Philosophers compare the Greek ship to the construction of an identity over time, a thing that is always changing, always in flux. In the words of Roman emperor and Stoic philosopher Marcus Aurelius:

> Keep in mind how fast things pass by and are gone—those that are now, and those to come. Existence flows past us like a river: the "what" is in constant flux, the "why" has a thousand variations. Nothing is stable, not even what's right here. The infinity of past and future gapes before us—a chasm whose depths we cannot see. So it would take an idiot to feel self-importance or distress. Or any indignation, either. As if the things that irritate us lasted. (Marcus Aurelius, *Meditations*, Gregory Hays (trans.), Book Five, paragraph 23)

Dream yourself into existence, rather than simply being born into it and molded by those around you, by your parents, the opinions of others, or society's norms and stigmas. Not everyone will see what you see. Be the person who brings your own inner vision to the world and shares it with the hopes of healing the diseases you see in your fellows, in society at large, and in this modern world with its materialism and greed, its loss of not just God but spirituality, morality, and faith along with it.

When you see the theoretical in the world and see its possibilities, have faith in them, in your capacity to see the world as you do. Trust in your mental capacity, your brand of consciousness and mode of experiencing and awareness of things seen and not seen, your particular state of consciousness. What comes out in your dreams? How do you interpret or make meaning of the world, of your self or the Self, of your mind or of the nature of Mind?

Although the mind is social and shared through social consciousness, through language, memes, and zeitgeist, and although the mind is collective and hidden in the roots of trees or the mycelium or the patterns of energy and reality—a wave brought from the "depths of the ocean," which I mean metaphorically to be from the universe at large, your mind is also particular. It is a part of the Mind, but it is also your mind. It is one transmitter/receiver in the network, one jewel in the net of Indra, which Francis Cook describes:

> Far away in the heavenly abode of the great god Indra, there is a wonderful net which has been hung by some cunning artificer in such a manner that it stretches out infinitely in all directions.... [T]he artificer has hung a single glittering jewel in each "eye" of the net, and ... the jewels are infinite in number. There hang the jewels, glittering like stars.... If we now arbitrarily select one of these jewels ... we will discover that in its polished surface there are reflected all the other jewels in the net.... Not only that, but each of the jewels reflected in this one jewel is also reflecting all the other jewels, so that there is an infinite reflecting process occurring. (Francis H. Cook, *Hua-yen Buddhism: The Jewel Net of Indra*, 2)

It is your duty to see all the other jewels and to reflect to all the other jewels what you see, as refracted through your mind and imagination. The light that is in your eyes shines on you, but also shines within you, bearing on how you receive the light but also on how, in receiving it, you reflect and create a new light of your own, perhaps based on the particular cut of your own prismatic nature, with its unique contours. It is your duty to share your light with the world, whether through a work of art like a book, visionary painting, or some other modality. You have a knowledge and vision that should not die with you. Though it may "die" with you in some sense, or though you may not finish your work, remember that your true work of art is your life, so practice everything you do. Your life is largely determined by the work of art that is your conscious experience, which you can craft by giving the mind a proper diet of information and by exercising the mind and developing the right "neural network," be that network just the neurons in your brain or in the world at large, i.e., your brain (your conscious experience as partly determined by your subconscious), your relationships with people (social consciousness), the world at large (reality-mind merger), or your intimate connection to the whole of reality (non-dual consciousness).

So practice living and practice consciousness. You inevitably create ripples that live on through your effects on the world and the people you touch in your daily mode of life, acting with compassion, and choosing your words and expression with care. So make these ripples carefully and well. However the light enters your eyes, or wherever it penetrates any of your perceptive and receptive capacities, sensory or mental, it shapes your particular vision.

As Emerson says, "the act of seeing and the thing seen, the seer and the spectacle, the subject and the object, are one." (Ralph Waldo Emerson, "The Over-Soul," *Essays*, Vol. 1, Ch. 9, par. 3)

Representational Theory of Mind

The mind can only be known by what it sees, and can only know of itself if one of the things that it sees is a representation of itself: a word, the pronoun "I," self-awareness, a reflection, an image in the mirror, an object that reflects back a self.

Where Is My Mind?

Where is my mind? The answer to this question begins with the representational theory of mind, the idea that we mentally symbolize external things and concepts and analyze situations through these symbols. "[T]he basic notion of a *representation* involves one thing's 'standing for,' 'being about,' 'referring to or denoting,' something else." (Robert Schwartz, "Representations," in *A Companion to the Philosophy of Mind*, Samuel Guttenplan (ed.), 536) Some examples are:

> ...Icons, Indices and Symbols. Icons are signs that are said to be like or resemble the things they represent (e.g. portrait paintings). Indices are signs that are connected to their objects by some causal dependency (e.g. smoke as a sign of fire). Symbols are those signs that are related to their object by virtue of use or association; they are arbitrary labels (e.g. the word "table"). (Robert Schwartz, "Representations," in *A Companion to the Philosophy of Mind*, Samuel Guttenplan (ed.), 536-7)

So important are representations to the human mode of thought that "the importance and prevalence of our symbolic activities has been taken as a hallmark of being human." (Robert Schwartz, "Representations," in *A Companion to the Philosophy of Mind*, Samuel Guttenplan (ed.), 536)

We only know the mind as reflected in these concepts by means of self-consciousness. Self-consciousness has been called a "paradox" because it refers back to itself, or, as José Luis Bermúdez states in *The Paradox of Self-Consciousness*, because "[a]ny theory that tried to elucidate the capacity to think first-person thoughts through linguistic mastery of the first-person pronoun will be circular, because the explanandum is part of the explanans, either directly ... or indirectly...." (16). In other words, it will be circular because the thing to be explained is part of the information used in the explanation itself.

Experience is just a relational property between outside and inside. Guttenplan explains this diagrammatically, "Experiencing → consciousness." (*A Companion to the Philosophy of Mind*, Samuel Guttenplan (ed.), 8) Differences in perception are simply differences in position relative to an environment or object. Like our minds, any position in space-time can only perceive things in three dimensions, so our mind can only experience by its perceptual faculties, like sight, sound, and touch.

The "Holy Communion"

In a mystical experience, however, the theater of the mind is expanded, and we experience a "holy communion" where inside and outside are connected intimately, so the mind is not just in our heads, but spread over the world, and connected to many things, including a social network.

Therefore, in a mystical experience everything is one, and the mind is much deeper than we think, a part of the universe and connected to it intimately.

Such mystical experiences make us ask questions like, "Where does our mind go after death?" Or, "Can mind be a property of light in electrical impulses as standing in relation to other things?" And, "Is something like enlightenment possible?"

Indeed, altered states of consciousness, psychedelics, and mystical experiences seem as real as normal experiences when we are in them, so after such experiences we question again, "What is reality in relation to the mind?"

These are the sorts of questions we *should* be asking, rather than questions about qualia, that is, the subjective component of experiencing phenomena, or "what it is like" to have an experience, i.e., "what it is like" to taste a strawberry, "what it is like" to hear a symphony, "what it is like" to smell a rose. Talking about qualia and "what it is like" is simply creating a problem, because in doing so we have split mind and world apart, when in reality they are one, as mystical experiences reveal. In this act of splitting one thing into two, we've created a problem that doesn't exist, just like the imagined problem of free will and determinism.

The problem arises when we create this split, place our focus on the two instead of on one unity, on the nondual solution to all problems, on our connection to all that is or ever has been, space-time, and all of it.

But we must not forget that we view the world symbolically through the representational theory of mind. If we were to obliterate the representational theory of mind, can we know things in the world differently? Is eliminating the representational theory of mind more than just eliminating a philosophical theory, but rather eliminating our own personal theory of mind, allowing us to directly relate to the world instead of relating to it through our own symbols? If so, eliminating representational theory of mind could, in a sense, be a spiritual practice.

Buddhism and Representations

Buddhism also grapples with the issue of representations. In *On Being Buddha*, Paul Griffiths argues that there is nothing "that it is like" to be Buddha. (Paul Griffiths, *On Being Buddha: The Classical Doctrine of Buddhahood*, 190) According to Griffiths, being Buddha is like being a rock; it has no subjective character, no "what it is like." Claiming that Buddhahood has no subjective character is to say that Buddhahood is not a conscious mental state.

In my view, Buddha can have all forms of consciousness of things and can also have *almost all* forms of consciousness of facts. Indeed, the only fact that Buddha must not be aware of is the fact that "*I* am the one experiencing these experiences." He can know that the representation referred to as "Siddhartha Gautama, the Buddha" is having these experiences, as long as he does not know that *he* is Siddhartha Gautama. He must only remain unaware of that one simple fact, the fact that "I am me," but this may be the most central fact in our conception of the world and the most difficult fact to disregard in living one's life.

The Mind

Meditation on the Nature of Mind

Every tree, some living centuries or millennia, yearly sprouting countless leaves, each falling and dying, is the rebirth of such leaf-corpses littering the earth, buried and decomposed, as well as blades of grass by the thousands, swarming systems of microorganisms, each of countless atoms and particles. Countless lives, innumerable forms, this is the meaning and vastness of the infinite. This is the number of forms being recycled, their transmutation, sometimes in harsh circumstances, being worn and decaying to destruction, sometimes in favorable circumstances, thriving and growing for a short time. Even millennia are like flashes of lightning, one drop in the vast ocean, and all this on one tiny planet that is like a grain of sand on the beach or a speck of dust on the ground in the vastness of the cosmos. And in this, to be a human, with the time, capacity, and opportunity to contemplate this vastness, is indeed a precious gift, like an alpine flower clinging to a mountainside in tough conditions, growing in a place it seems it shouldn't, tenuous, like a candle blowing in the wind, a bubble on the breeze, one brief opportunity to realize our place, to witness our nature, in whatever way we can.

By seeing the world, by travel, bearing witness to many passing phenomena and moments in time, by contemplation and staring upon a single flower ("observe with the patience of watching a flower grow" (GZA, "Crash Your Crew")), by whatever means we have the gift to pursue. But ultimately, to see a thing for what it is, to see things as they are, to see the surface of things clearly but also to see beneath the surface into their nature, the shared nature of which we are all parts, our nature. I must suppose that the most expedient way to see into what we are is to examine one's own mind, to be it and understand it, to realize the nature of mind and consciousness, this brief flicker of light, this spark, to be this mind fully, but also to understand what it is to be this mind, to stare into the candle's flame until you are fully fire, merge, then float away like an ember spat into the wind and transformed, falling to the earth as a speck of dust, or a raindrop falling from the sky and returning to the ocean.

To watch the candle, to burn, to be and know this luminous mind. To know the nature of life before it ends.

The Dance of Mind and Matter

Life is a marriage of mind and matter. The world is not created by the mind, as some solipsists—who believe that nothing truly exists beyond the self and the self's own experiences—would have you believe. (Sometimes solipsists love the idea that quantum mechanics shows that the mind creates reality by observing it, which seems to put too fine a point on the role of observation in quantum mechanics.) And the mind is not created by the world, as is believed by purist, fundamentalist materialists and physicalists, who hold that matter is fundamental, and that mental states and consciousness are purely the result of the nervous system and the brain.

The interaction of mind and world is a dance. It is like The Force in *Star Wars*. The Force has its own flow, and we can tune into that flow. When we do, things tend to happen "for us," almost like luck. But when we tune in, we can also bend that flow so that our influence bends events. For example, we might reach out to community, and by reaching out, we tune in and perhaps community begins to surround us. But as we join in that community, we can become involved and become an influencer in the community, someone who sways the actions the community might take (internal force) or the events that happen to the community (external force) because of those actions, or simply because of its disposition to experience things in a new way, to see things in a new light.

This most definitely does not mean that if a meteor were to fall from the sky and land on our little community, our singing kumbaya would change the reality that we will all be crushed or vaporized or what have you. But singing together may make it a peaceful experience, like the musicians on the deck of the *Titanic*, one where we celebrate being together for a brief shared moment in time that like all things passes transiently.

With the community example, we can already see the barriers of individual minds, a collective of minds, and the flow or force of the environment starting to blur and break down. But in the case of the meteor, we can see that we do not "create" reality, but we can change how we experience it, what we do about it, and in so doing, change how it happens.

... there is
nothing either good or bad but thinking makes it
so.
(William Shakespeare, *Hamlet*, Act II, Scene 2)

Regarding the physicalist viewpoint, we are ignoring the point that mind is capable of interacting with the world in a way that is somehow different from the pure cause and effect of two rocks colliding. Now I know the physicalist will hem and haw, and say that it is all the sum of a large interaction of causes and effects in an equation that we just can't comprehend yet, but in principle could comprehend with the right mathematics. But before we get into it, I might suggest that the physicalist's belief in this principle is an argument based on something they've observed scientifically, and the aggregate of these observations suggests some large web of causes and effects, but their belief that this will always be true at the large scale is still simply faith in the principles they believe in, although we can hopefully all agree that the scientific and rational exploration of reality is the most accurate and sophisticated means at our disposal.

But let me ask: what do we know about the mind? Where is the mind for starters? Conscious experiences themselves cannot be located in the brain, and they clearly involve influences from the physical environment. But they also appear in many other forms, such as the altered states of psychedelics, dreams, meditation, near-death experiences, peak experiences, flow experiences, and so on. If we are to understand those states of mind, should we not embark on an exploration involving observation and recording the actual scientific effect of these altered states on the brain?

And this is where the mind gets interesting. We can study neuroscience and cognition and behavior, but these are all external approaches to the mind. When we look at the Turing test evaluating a machine's ability to exhibit intelligent behavior comparable to that of a human, or even the behaviors of beehives or communicating fungi in a mycelial or mycorrhizal network, we can find cases where what we see on the outside suggests the presence of a mind or "inner" life. So if we are to take consciousness seriously, we must investigate these conscious experiences with the same rigor as we do the external facets of mind. Moreover, we may well need to expand the "external" facets to include the brain, the environment, and perhaps even quantum mechanics, if Roger Penrose is on the right track in his belief that quantum mechanics and the collapse of the wave function within components of brain cells plays a significant role in human consciousness. The point is, we don't know.

What I do know is what I get from living life as a conscious being. And I do not allow my "principled" idea of what reason should be to pull me away from seeing what reason actually is. For example, if I see that my mood changes with the weather, we might all be certain that the weather changed and made me feel like I was in a bad mood. But haven't we all had an experience where we got into a bad mood and then the weather changed? Aphex Twin fans remember his Houston concert, during which he began a piece with a fierce, driving beat that seemed to call down a drenching downpour, described by one fan as weather manipulation by audio, or the moment when Aphex Twin took over the weather.

There is some truth to the notion that mind creates reality. That truth has multiple aspects. For example, our attention determines what we focus on in the world and, therefore, what we experience to a large degree. Over time, this focus becomes our diet of thoughts: what we choose to read, what we expose ourselves to, what makes up our memories. The memories create a whole "story" of who we are, especially given our notion of the self, that who we are now is the person who is fixed at the present point in the ever-evolving story of "me."

What Is Mind Anyway?

Standard accounts of mind posit dualism or materialism: either that, ontologically, there are mental and physical substances that are distinct (dualism), or that there is only physical substance and minds are also physical (materialism). Modern materialist theories generally aim to place mental phenomena in a physical, causal framework, that is, they attempt to explain how mental phenomena are produced by neuronal interactions, synaptic patterns, electrical frequencies, chemical reactions, or other physiological processes. Often these causal chains are very explicit—the presence of a and b in the brain cause mental state type c… stuff like that. Also, the explanations or "psychophysical" laws that are suggested will always directly connect the mental to some physical phenomenon. For example, early attempts to explain consciousness focused on patterns of electrical signals in the pre-frontal cortex. This theory is not widely accepted anymore, but the point is, from a quantum point of view, mental phenomena are always explained in terms of macroscopic physical phenomena. Certain rare theories have suggested that mental information is encoded at a quantum level or is a result of quantum processes.

I try to imagine what the mind is on a quantum scale and what the nature of these electrical signals involved in brain processes are. If these are macroscopic events composed of microscopic interactions, then what of this? How important are quantum processes in shaping the nature of such signals? Also, if there is a "microscopic level" of quanta and a macroscopic level of brain-matter, where do mental phenomena really fit into the physical hierarchy? Should they even be distinguished from electrical signals in the brain or certain brain processes? Are they a substance of their own (probably not), and if not, *how* are they a part of whatever substance or process they are a part of? In other words, from the point of view of physical science, how could you fit mental events into the picture? These are questions that future study of mind at the quantum level must answer.

Doctors and scientists ignore the subjective nature of mind, while others ignore its objective nature. We truly need to think of them as two sides of the same coin, becoming one single perspective. And that one perspective is shared by all of reality, and yet it is dualistic, too. The two truths. But of these, we easily fall into the relative and ignore the ultimate. We also ignore the far-reaching potential of the mind, like the aspects of mind seen when taking psychedelics. The only other thing that seems infinite and full of possibility besides the universe is the mind with its infinite imagination.

Mind is the force that goes through it all. Anything can manifest in the space of mind, and everything does manifest in the space of mind. Everything we ever experience, or that anyone has ever experienced, happens in the space of mind. It is like space, present everywhere but something that cannot be touched or "captured." (As the musician GZA says in "Amplified Sample," "You remain stuck trying to figure the shape of space.") And yet everything that happens, happens in it.

Does space have form? Does space exist both when there is stuff filling it and when there is not? My body versus the empty space around it—both are in space. Even though one is filled by me, it is still part of the fabric of space-time. In this example, it turns out form and emptiness are one. This is just like thought and mind. There is mind-space and then there are its contents, but these are both part of one fabric.

The "mind-space" can fit into any cup or container. It is the color of each moment. It is each consciousness, each body; it is like water in that it pours from the source into each cup, then, when the cup breaks, it returns to the great ocean.

And water is life. It's in everything, the river systems that people drink from and the veins of a person. And again the pattern of rivers and veins, so similar, match the "pattern of life."

Consider the duality of looking at yourself in the mirror, how the eye sees itself, how the mind knows itself as experiencing subject. This is the absent and storied "witness" through which the narrative and story of our lives is written through the reflection of our own thoughts and experiences. We think that the contents of the mind-space are what define us, but the "mind," the experiencing "I," the seeing "eye," the space between things in which all experience happens, can only be whatever it sees. As Walt Whitman put it:

> There was a child went forth every day,
> And the first object he looked upon ... that object he became
> (Walt Whitman, "There Was A Child Went Forth," in *Whitman: Poetry and Prose*, 138)

Mind is spread out over the world, in the world, and throughout the world. Body is inseparable from the world, part of a continuous physical process, one continuum. Mind is the same. So holding on and staying inside this body resists the natural tendency for mind to diffuse throughout and over the world. The mind-body connection is a oneness. So your mind is the thing trying to hold on and stay inside the body, even though its nature is to expand and merge with the larger world. In the same way, body is trying to hold itself together as a discrete entity, a configuration of physical matter, even though its tendency (i.e., entropy) is to diffuse throughout the world, merge with the continuum of which it is a seamless part, totally indistinguishable and inseparable (in one sense, though body in another sense has identity, is identifiable, and is separate, a discrete thing).

It is all one continuous process. So much emphasis has to be placed on the word process rather than a static object, because a static object has discrete parameters. It's like identifying an electron from a wave. By viewing something as a static object, you are trying to pinpoint it, catch it, cut a slice out of space-time (noting the time aspect in particular), when in reality, that slice can't be removed. So to view something as static is to view it out of context. You can't pinpoint a thing, and you can't catch it. As soon as you realize conceptually that the moment is happening, it's gone.... What's a good metaphor for this? It's like trying to catch a small feather from the air, where the act of grabbing it causes an air current to push it out of your hand; or maybe it's like catching a bubble from the air, where catching it pops it, or even like catching a bubble underwater, where catching it turns it back to water and makes it no longer a bubble at all, hence rendering it uncatchable.

Then consider self-consciousness, the search for you, how you know you. It is a search, not a found thing. It's a continuous feedback loop, where knowing "you" is just a matter of you being in the process continually. You know that you're there simply by being there:

> ...the simplest form in which the wordless knowledge emerges mentally is the feeling of knowing—the feeling of what happens when an organism is engaged with the processing of an object— and that only thereafter can inferences and interpretations begin to occur regarding the feeling of knowing. (Antonio Damasio, *The Feeling of What Happens*, 26)

The sense of self, "the feeling of what happens," is constantly being built into consciousness by experiencing, by being. The act of experiencing is how we come to know "being" as a state. The "knowledge" and conceptual identification of the self is secondary or ancillary, rather than a fundamental aspect of mind's nature. It can be removed, as wheat is separated from chaff. The "knowledge" of the self is not built into the nature of being or knowing and is not fundamental to mind's nature. By this I mean that the being in question really is a floating mind. So there is the continuum of being known, or being mind-in-the-world, and then there is this appendage (and, in a spiritual sense, a residual, vestigial appendage at that) that is hanging out there. That residual appendage is the conceptual knowledge of oneself as an entity, and the long, exhausting, pluralistic narrative that cascades from the conceptual identification of oneself as an entity, from the conceptual identification of the self. To make the self vestigial through spiritual practice, that is, to make it a small remnant of its former self, makes the self vestigial in the evolutionary sense of being no longer spiritually useful.

Meaning and the World-Mind

We must start our search for what is meaningful in life with the mind. The mind is the narrator, the storyteller that interprets events and weaves meaning into our lives, but it is also the locus and essence of human existence. When we ask what we are fundamentally, we are the witness and the contents that are witnessed.

> [T]he supra-individual Witness is that which is capable of observing the flow of what is—without interfering with it, commenting on it, or in any way manipulating it. The Witness simply observes the stream of events both inside and outside the mind-body in a creatively detached fashion, since, in fact, the Witness is not exclusively identified with either. In other words, when the individual realizes that his mind and his body can be perceived objectively, he spontaneously realizes that they cannot constitute a real subjective self. (Ken Wilber, *The Spectrum of Consciousness*, 261)

The mind is also the meeting point; the place where an individual (insofar as we are individuals and not fundamentally connected) connects with the world and with other minds.

But when we try to look at the mind itself, when we try to witness the Witness, we cannot find it, as an eye cannot see itself without a mirror. Seeing the subject as that subject is impossible. In a famous Buddhist story, the second patriarch asks Bodhidharma:

> "Please, Master, quiet my mind." Bodhidharma says: "Bring your mind here and I will quiet it for you." The patriarch says: "I am searching for my mind but, in the end, cannot apprehend it." Bodhidharma says, "My quieting of your mind is over." (Jeffrey Broughton, *The Bodhidharma Anthology*, 88)

Interestingly, seeing another's subjectivity also appears to be impossible. Perhaps we look at the brain first, but we cannot find in the brain the actual experiences, the phenomenal consciousness that is human experience. We can see the functions that structure that experience, memory recall, choices and decision-making, and so forth, but we cannot find the essence, the sense of "what it is like" to be a being and to have experiences. For example, Thomas Nagel in his essay, "What Is It Like to Be a Bat?" says that to gain such subjective knowledge of a bat:

> [i]t will not help to try to imagine that one has webbing on one's arms, which enables one to fly around at dusk and dawn catching

insects in one's mouth; that one has very poor vision, and perceives the surrounding world by a system of reflected high-frequency sound signals; and that one spends the day hanging upside down by one's feet in an attic" because to truly understand it, he needs "to know what it is like for a bat to be a bat." (Thomas Nagel, "What Is It Like to Be a Bat?" in *The Philosophical Review*, Vol. 83, No. 4, 439)

Nagel concludes that such subjective knowledge is impossible for someone who is not a bat, but that "[w]e can be compelled to recognize the existence of such facts without being able to state or comprehend them." (Thomas Nagel, "What Is It Like to Be a Bat?" in *The Philosophical Review*, Vol. 83, No. 4, 441)

So then, where is the mind? The mind perhaps is spread over the world rather than localized in a single space. We know, as Descartes may have, that the subject exists, but this is all we can be sure of, yet certainly the solipsistic, self-centered view that there is nothing beyond the individual consciousness, that the world and all other beings are figments of our mind, cannot be the whole story.

Is this provable? No. But my philosophy is guided as much by faith as by logic and reason. To take the solipsistic point of view just does not *feel* right. This feels true in the same way that the idea of God, something bigger connecting it all, connecting us all, is real and feels true by faith, while logic and reason tell me that the gods as personified by man—regardless of the deity's name—do not stand the test. We could explore many lines of thinking here, e.g., if God is omnipotent, can s/he microwave a burrito so hot that s/he cannot eat it? Such paradoxes and fallacies abound in these rigid conceptions of God. Inasmuch as there is a god that is not purely man's creation, that is, of man's making of meaning, we must imagine that God is veiled in mystery and beyond our conceptions.

My faith then guides me to feel a connection to the world and to my fellow beings. Why? Because I have felt this connection so many times, in meditation, in looking at an awe-inspiring landscape or the night sky that makes me forget myself, my ego, to feel a love with someone that is so wondrous that the experience is clearly shared and not from me alone. Sometimes this feels almost telepathic in nature. I've felt these connections in the use of psychedelic consciousness medicines that can often make the experience of oneness and the dissolution of the ego tangible, and I feel them in music and song where we are all immersed in a shared rhythm, where our voices are joined in a choir and are indistinguishable from one another.

Thus, I find myself compelled to believe that the mind is indeed spread over the world. It is not just in my brain; it is in my body, in the flowers and mountains and skies that my eyes see, in the common language and shared thoughts of my fellow beings. And if indeed the mind is spread over the world, then so are its substrates. Although many memories, such as memory recall, reside in the brain, those memories came from somewhere: from the bee that stung me, from the brush of your hand, from the wind in my hair—all parts of the mind. As the Zen koan says, "Not the wind, not the flag; mind is moving." (Ekai, *The Gateless Gate*, N. Senzaki (trans.), 29)

This mind, then, is the space of holy communion; it is the meeting of mind and world, mind and other beings, and they meet in such a way that they are one. When we experience, we do not separate out the witnessing subject from the surrounding flowers and landscapes, we are simply immersed in the whole experience, all of it as one thing, one moment. Here we are connected to all, to God and our fellow beings who are also connected to it, as though we are all plugged into the same source, the same power, the same light and energy, so much so that it is better to call it mind-world.

If we are this intimately connected with all things, then so must be the substrates. The roots of the mind run deep, in the same way that some forests appear to be comprised of so many individual and separate trees, yet we may find they share a root system, as with Utah's "Pando," the largest living organism in the world, consisting of over 47,000 individual quaking aspen trees sharing a single root system that is over 80,000 years old. Our minds are like this forest. In fact, I might not say "our minds" but rather "our mind," as I may not say "our bodies" but rather "our body." For our body is the world and not ours alone. It is shared, microbes live inside it. Its parts come and return from the earth so many times, constantly in flux, and not only from the earth but from stars. We are star stuff, and all that we are is space and stardust. This flux happens throughout our lives and certainly at our death, which cannot be an end, but more of an transformation. So we are a forest, and for now, you may be a tree. We are a field, but for now you may be a blade of grass, as Whitman might have said. We are an ocean, though for now you may be a wave, soon to crash and return to the ocean. We are a cosmos, yet for now we are a mind, originating from, always connected to, and always returning back to the cosmic sea and its mysterious depths.

The mind runs so deep that we cannot see the bottom. But if there is a unifying force in the world of a human being's mind, it comes from those forces that give me a sense of unity—awe, wonder, inspiration, love, surrender, immersion, forces that dissolve us into the force that runs through all, "[t]he force that through the green fuse drives the flower." (Dylan

Thomas, "The Force that Through the Green Fuse Drives the Flower," in
18 Poems by Dylan Thomas, 13) We all feel alone, and as much as it's true
that we are all connected, there is a very real—albeit temporary—sense
that our current nature is that of being individual, separated, disconnected,
cut off, alone. We feel that we are born alone and die alone, and spend
many a lonely night between the two, wondering if anyone understands
us, if anyone really loves us, if we are alone in a cold, uncaring universe
that has no sympathy for our pain, suffering, and loneliness, and no desire
to understand us. We often feel as though even our fellow beings do not
understand us, cannot really empathize with us in any real sense.

So we must find this meaning by looking for connection, through love
and not hate, through unity and not division. We must tell our story not as
individuals but as partners, as friends, as tribes, as cultures, as a species,
and even as the story of the cosmos itself. And we look to the mind for all
these meanings:

> I embrace my desire to
> Feel the rhythm
> To feel connected
> Enough to step aside and
> Weep like a widow
> To feel inspired
> To fathom the power
> To witness the beauty
> To bathe in the fountain
> To swing on the spiral...
> Of our divinity and
> Still be a human
> (Tool, "Lateralus")

The mind is infused in this spiral of the Milky Way in which we walk.
Everything must have its reference. As the eye cannot see itself without
a mirror or the mind without its contents, so we would not know what
connection is without being separated, as we would not know up if there
were no down, and would not know love if there were no loneliness. As we
make meaning, so does God; after all, we are one. We are God's witnesses
and he is ours.

For it is the nature of nonduality, the state of absolute unity, to include
every possibility, every possible phenomenon, by definition. If so, then
one phenomenon it must contain is duality, the existence of opposites,
such as love and hate, black and white, up and down, as well as the tension
between these opposites. This tension is critical, as the psychologist C. G.
Jung said:

The ego keeps its integrity only if it does not identify with one of the opposites, and if it understands how to hold the balance between them. This is possible only if it remains conscious of both at once, however, the necessary insight is made exceedingly difficult not by one's social and political leaders alone, but also by one's religious mentors. They all want decision in favour of one thing, and therefore the utter identification of the individual with a necessarily one-sided "truth." (C. G. Jung, *Collected Works 8*, para. 425)

This is the nature of things. But when you are telling yourself your story in front of the campfire some night, in the dark under the stars, just try to remember that your story is the story of all, a thread in the whole tapestry.

This perspective is in accord with the Buddhist concept of tendrel, which states that all phenomena have an interdependent and interconnected nature, and no phenomenon exists independently. It also similar to the Hindu image of the net of Indra, which I picture as resembling the stars in the night sky:

Far away in the heavenly abode of the great god Indra, there is a wonderful net which has been hung by some cunning artificer in such a manner that it stretches out infinitely in all directions.... [T]he artificer has hung a single glittering jewel in each "eye" of the net, and ... the jewels are infinite in number. There hang the jewels, glittering like stars.... If we now arbitrarily select one of these jewels...we will discover that in its polished surface there are reflected all the other jewels in the net.... Not only that, but each of the jewels reflected in this one jewel is also reflecting all the other jewels, so that there is an infinite reflecting process occurring. (Francis H. Cook, *Hua-yen Buddhism: The Jewel Net of Indra*, 2)

This moment of nonduality is the holy communion, for what Christians call the Christ body is the world, as well as the air we taste and the food we eat, and we meet all that in the present moment. It is also the moment where we are directly unified with God, where consciousness touches the greater reality. So it is this holy union that we live in.

Here we find another path. If we can learn to be with all states, not dread them too much nor love them so much we cannot bear their parting, learn to be with them and let them go, then perhaps we can find an end to suffering. For seeing is becoming. Consciousness is the merger of mind and moment oneness, so "seeing" a moment means becoming the moment, as with water, "You put water into a bottle and it becomes the bottle." (Bruce Lee, in *Tao Te Ching: Power for the Peaceful*, (M. Mullinax (trans.), 46)

We can touch and look from above at something smaller than we are, shake hands with a rabbit, for example, but the rabbit will experience it in a proportionally different way, almost as if a three-dimensional creature were shaking hands with a two-dimensional creature. The two-dimensional creature would not experience the sphere, but only the circle.

So it would be when we shake hands with God (i.e., through life experiences, moments, and things). This is us touching God, but we only experience him as a three-dimensional creature would a four-dimensional creature, or a multi-dimensional one. Nonetheless, our mind experiencing the world is shaking hands with God: the Holy Communion.

Each of us has our own observable universe, our own "bubble" of the known, and it's only when these individual universes overlap that we directly know about the other. On the scale of the species, this happens to us through astronomical observations of the universe, where we would have a different "known universe" if we were on a different world. But it also happens at the level our individual minds, for each individual's "known worlds."

Each universe bubble is also a moment in space-time. It is the now, and it is consciousness: the phenomenal, experiential aspect of consciousness, beyond word and concept, that provides an authentic connection to the greater whole. So it is the present moment, the consciousness moment that we dig into, where we find our connection to it all, to us all, because we can share a moment... and in fact the moment often doesn't mean anything unless it's shared. And this sharing can become so deep that it becomes one experience, inseparable as voices joined in song or musicians playing one sound together, literally connecting them in a musical moment, a circle, such as two people in love or a moment with a friend, when two people are literally doing the same thing and feeling the same moment, taking the words out of each other's mouths... How often have you said to someone, "I knew that's what you were going to say!" Or consider the moment you feel someone looking at you and you turn your head and look back at them, eye to eye. This is connection. That consciousness moment is at its root the holy communion.

Phenomenology vs. Materialism

What are these two, exactly? Phenomena are the structures of consciousness resulting from an individual's perception (as opposed to the thing being observed), while materialism holds that matter is fundamental, and that mental states and consciousness are the result of the nervous system and the brain.

Phenomenology versus materialism. Somehow, it always seems to come down to these two.

In the mind-body problem, the problem of qualia, or where we locate experience in the brain or at least the physical world, is central.

Or in the phenomenology of near-death experiences, there seem to be cases where the experiences happen even though the brain is dead, although I suppose it's possible that the experience happens during the brain's dying moments and just seems to stretch on beyond brain death to the experiencing subject. Either way—this is where the rub is—we are faced with the problem of reconciling phenomenal experience with a materialistic world view.

One must think we are (as always, like with free will and determinism) creating an irreconcilable dichotomy and then wondering how they can be reconciled, that is, how a question framed in an unsolvable form can be solved. Generally, when faced with an unsolvable question, we're asking the wrong question or starting with the wrong framework, e.g., an absolute materialism or absolute determinism.

Thomas Nagel in his essay, "What Is It Like to Be a Bat?" argues that the subjective character of experience, that is, what it is like to be a conscious organism, is what makes the mind-body problem a truly difficult one. In other words, we have first-person access to conscious states that are necessarily subjective. These states are known only through subjective experience and, therefore, cannot be studied objectively. Since physical science is based upon the observation of objective reality, it seems impossible to provide a physical account of subjective experience. Though one could study brain states, one can never objectively study the subjective experience caused by brain states.

Nagel uses the example of a bat to illustrate this point. In asking, "What is it like to be a bat?" Nagel claims that, since his imagination is informed entirely by his experience, it is limited in the types of things it can comprehend. (Thomas Nagel, "What Is It Like to Be a Bat?" in *The Philosophical Review*, Vol. 83, No. 4) In other words, because of the way a human being is wired, there are certain things that the human will never be able to understand consciously. Amongst these things are the subjective states of a bat, whose sensory input relies on echolocation and various non-human abilities. Even if we could enable a human to experience echolocation and if we developed some way to transfer or duplicate the bat's experience into the human brain, to enable someone to actually experience being that bat, the subject experiencing this would effectively be that bat (at least in the subject's mind) and this subjective experience would come no closer to being objectively observable.

According to Nagel, this example shows that there are certain subjective, phenomenological aspects of mind that cannot be reduced to physical properties. This does not necessarily mean that materialism is false; Nagel is not adopting dualism. Since physical theories of mind can only rely on objective explanations and since Nagel has demonstrated that subjective phenomena cannot be objectively explained, it seems to follow that there can be no completely comprehensive physical explanation of mind. Nagel recognizes that these are the implications of his argument, yet he takes a less assertive approach to the issue, hesitating to say that physicalism is certainly false.

I see physicalism as an accurate and useful approach to the study of mind, provided that a given physicalist recognizes that subjective phenomena cannot be objectively observed. To approach the study of mind under the premise that it is physical, it should only be realized that what is being studied is not the subjective mind itself, but rather the brain (along with any physical processes or other things that may contribute to the production of consciousness). It seems that there is an explanatory gap between subjective states and physical states that materialist theories of mind cannot cross, but there is no gap if materialists recognize the limits of their investigation.

To me, the truly interesting and ironic paradox that is attached to materialism centers around subjectivity. If one views this problem as an idealist—one who sees reality as a product of mind—might view it, then saying that physical theories cannot account for subjective phenomena is ridiculous, because all "objective" phenomena can only be studied, observed, or known subjectively. Thus, there is no longer a question of how to resolve the physical and the mental. Instead, the question posed by Nagel's bat problem becomes: "How can one know about or explain the existence of what appears to be another subjective mind?" If one does not want to be an extremist, claiming that one's own subjectivity is the only real subjectivity, then one must face the problem of explaining how other subjectivities could exist. Interestingly, aside from positing some sort of subjectivity-transcending state of consciousness, the only possible answer to this question would be to posit the existence of an external reality in which various subjective minds could be grounded, link to something common, and interact.

The "hard problem" facing materialism is resolved only by subjective idealism, which reveals that the reason why we cannot physically locate and objectively study an actual subjectivity is that objective reality exists within and is thus limited to our own subjectivity. The best way to study a bat's subjectivity would be to study how the subject formulates objective reality within its experience, and, using that information, attempt to recreate, interpret, understand, or possibly even experience the bat's experience. Similarly, the only answer to an equally difficult problem with idealism is provided by materialism, which shows that the existence of multiple subjective realities is possible because they can be located in the context of a physical world. This is strange; external reality is idealism's ghost, in that it cannot be certainly observed, just as subjectivity is materialism's ghost. Subjectivity appears somehow to be physically vacant or non-extended (as Descartes would say), yet the entire extendedness of physical reality (insofar as we will ever know) exists only in the subjective mind.

This seems to suggest that there are two distinct areas to be studied and that a dualistic approach to the mind-body problem must be adopted, but I, like Nagel, want to cling to unified theory of mind and body despite logic suggesting otherwise. I would suggest (though there is certainly no way to prove this) that mental and physical reality are unified. Physical reality exists in the mind and the mind exists in physical reality; in fact, they are not separate realities at all. I would not claim that external reality cannot be known in the mind because I would not hold the view that external reality is actually external to or separate from subjective reality. I would not even claim that other subjectivities cannot be known. I believe that it is somehow plausible for me to be the bat. On a more simplistic level, can I know other subjectivities by communion through language, etc.? Nor would I claim that a subjective mind cannot be understood from the vantage point of physical reality (if one could ever achieve such a vantage point), as no subjective mind is separate from the whole of reality (including physical and mental phenomena). I agree with Nagel that it is still possible for physicalism to investigate subjective states, somehow, although this method will involve a more complete understanding of how the whole of physical reality relates to those subjective states.

In other words, I believe an explanatory gap between physical and subjective states is not a gap at all.

Theory of Mind

I recently listened to the Counting Crows song, "Time and Time Again," and the lyric:

> I wanted so badly
> Somebody other than me
> Staring back at me
> But you were gone....

It made me think of a Latin phrase, *incurvatus in se*—I'm probably butchering the theological background of that term, because I just learned it—but it means "to be turned inward on oneself."

So to return to the lyric: you want someone other than you staring back at you so that you're not turned inward on yourself. In my view, concepts are mirrors, so in order to have self-awareness, you need something mirroring the self, because the eye can't see itself, and the mind can't see itself. You need something reflecting back. And in the case of the mind, that reflecting something is a theory of mind, a concept of mind, which is the capacity to understand other people by ascribing mental states to them. At a minimum you need a concept of self, however you want to get into that. Nonetheless, this concept of self is a concept, in the end. We can get down further, below the level of concept, with some additional thinking, and say that it's a self in relation to experience, but then we're talking about phenomenal consciousness, the consciousness of phenomena, such as having the experience of encountering an actual table versus merely being aware in the mind of the concept of a table. But regardless of this, really for mental self-awareness you need the concept of mind, a theory of mind.

At some point in our lives we all come to the idea of radical solipsism. It probably comes to us young, when we're first encountering others. According to cognitive theorists, as infants we're in this magical world where mom just appears and she's part of our mind. Then we grow and develop, and we learn there are other people, and finally we develop a theory of mind that we can attribute to others. First we might develop self-awareness, and then we can attribute self-awareness to others.

Take movie *The Matrix*, for example, or take Descartes. If the cognitive theorists are right, we all get this idea at some point: what if our brain is a cog in a machine, or what if we're the only thing that exists and there's absolutely nothing outside of our own mind, that all of the people and all of the things I encounter are just illusions inside my mind? This is the inner world concept of mind, the Cartesian theater, which was the label the philosopher Daniel Dennett applied to Descartes's view. According to Dennett, the Cartesian theater is a small theater within the mind, like a movie screen. We're inside our own mind, watching a movie theater in which everything around us is going on. You can't technically disprove this idea. There are influences that occur that we can't see, but we know them by their effects. Thus they are theoretical entities, but from that we can infer that there is something outside of the mind. Being a solipsist—believing that the bubble enclosing you is the only bubble—is a desperately lonely place to be, especially if you want somebody other than yourself staring back at you.

So if your theory of mind is your own self-awareness, your concept that you're a living mental creature, a consciousness and a mind—then, now that you've got that concept, you can say, "I'm a mind in relation to X," in relation to external object X, or "I am mind in relation to this table." Is the table inside the mind? Perhaps it's a solipsistic world, and it is inside the mind, but nonetheless, I've got this concept of an inner world now, which may contain, ironically, the entire outer world, but this inner world stands in relation to "table." So I've got this second-order awareness, this self-consciousness, that's different from just plain consciousness which we might imagine in a low-level animal scurrying about, reacting to its environment with no awareness that it is a mental entity specifically. Maybe it has awareness of its body and its actions, and how the sensations that it gets through its body cause movements and reflexes. But once we have this second-order awareness of being a mind in relation to objects in the world, having that viewpoint, we can start to know things about the self: we can start to tell our story, we can start to know we're going to die, all these different things. But it's not just mind in relation to X, in relation to the table or an external object; it's also mind in relation to Y, and Y stands for another human being as that being is in our solipsistic world. Now the irony of this other human being is that we see it with our eyes and they see us with their eyes, and their self-concept is of an I and ours is of an I. So to make that less complicated, we infer that they're a mental being, we infer that we're a mental being, and we can look at each other and interact.

But what's scary is that if we're playing with this solipsist idea, or just playing with the idea that our world, the world in our mind, doesn't reach that far, doesn't quite reach far enough to conceive that each of us is a mental being, for example, that my color blue is different from your color blue. Language is a great example, because the meaning of the word "fire" definitely means something different to me than it does to you, based on our prior experiences with the word "fire": our concepts of fire, perhaps the time we were burned by the frying pan at grandma's, or the time that someone we loved was trapped in a fire and terribly hurt, or whatever. Or it could be memories of a campfire and singing songs with dad. But we know what fire is, and we can relate around the concept.

I recently learned a new word, the word "sonder." One of its meanings is "the emotional feeling that a passerby has an inner life that's as vivid and rich and complex as our own," which is attributing to them a theory of mind. We start to think about other people as mental beings as we grow up, but, because we're still kind of growing out of our solipsistic phase of development, we're still growing out of our conception of mind as being an inner world. In other words, at that stage we don't know for sure that there's another mind in there, in that inner world. We can't be that other mind, we can't experience it, and we can't tap into it.

Some materialists use a behaviorist approach to attempt to infer others' thought processes, but I don't like the rigidity of the behaviorist approach. I like there to be a spiritual kind of connection where you just know, or a psychological connection, or where we are related to each other through love, through all these different emotions, through shared experiences where we share concepts and share language. It can be a very intimate and complex experience that really can go beyond explanation. If I have those experiences, I don't have to be lonely, because I've found these other human beings, and I want someone other than me staring back at me.

I stumbled across another word that sheds light on this: "opia," as in myopia. Generally, -opia is a suffix to a word that describes the condition of the eye, like myopia or anopia. But it also has another meaning, which is the emotional feeling that you get when you're staring into someone else's eyes, and it's both vulnerable and intrusive at the same time. The way I read that definition—and you could probably take it a few different ways—is that you're reaching in and intruding, but they're reaching in and you're vulnerable because you're looking each other directly in the eye. And it's kind of an awkward feeling, as it's described in the dictionary, and we all know it. But it can also be a highly connected feeling with someone special. But typically, that's not how it works. Typically, we look each other in the eye for a moment and whoops! It gets awkward and we look away and pretend we're looking at a tree or something. But that's not cool, especially if we want to connect.

How do we get from this inner world to the next person, where we're sharing experiences, sharing language, sharing ideas, sharing touch, sharing feelings? How do we get from the inner world to really getting to them, getting to the other person, getting to the "what it's like to be them" quality? How do we get to the "what it's like" quality, their inner world that we know through the sonder? How do we get to the realization that they have a rich and complex inner life? We often get really mixed up trying to do this. Our solipsistic world tends to get muddy and slippery, and it has tentacles or roots that reach out into the outside world, like the river and the land maybe. So it is with other people, as we get closer and closer.

But we also run into this really tricky thing called "projection" in which, when we're trying to connect their inner world to ours, we lose track. It becomes really blurry at that point; we're getting really slippery. We don't know whether we're putting ideas into another's mouth or not. For example, we meet someone who seems insecure. Are they genuinely insecure? Or is it our own insecurity we're seeing in them? You don't really know until you talk about it, and even then there's subtext and emotions to wade through, and it just takes so long to get to know someone, and throughout that process we've got opia, the emotional feeling that you get when you're staring into their eyes.

I'll call it young love, but when I was sixteen I met a girl and was just struck. And I wasn't struck because she was a beautiful young lady. I was struck because we could stare into each other's eyes without flinching. And I found that when you're able to do that, you're able to really connect, so that you're sharing a moment very deeply. And because the moment is simplified, it just becomes something as simple as just quietly staring. No mind, no concept, just staring. At least that's how it was for me. It could have been different for her. For her it could have been, "Why is this creep just staring at me?" I don't know.

Then when you mix in the phenomenon of projection, then we have to wonder. Do we fall in love with the person, or with the projection of the person? Are we dreaming of the person we wish them to be? In order to know them, do we have to get to know them day by day, hour by hour, minute by minute over time, sharing experiences, developing our own little language the way couples and close friends do, where we've got our own inside jokes, maybe our own song that we share, our own little expressions that we've gotten used to? It's a great thing to connect like that, and to build that connection up with all these levels, first behavioral and verbal, and then emotional and physical levels, and soon enough, you get to where you can predict what the other person's going to say. You know them pretty well, and you have a pretty good idea what's going on in their head, but you still always wonder.

I don't know, because I haven't gotten there with someone yet. I got pretty close, but I never got all the way, and you know, with this person that I got so close to, the opia—and in fact it was probably myopia, in the sense that I was concentrating on my experience of the connection—it wasn't quite there. So I didn't get this chance to really just stare someone in the eye, which is something I always loved to do, and just stare and be comfortable staring and see if you can sort out whether there's just like real connection, whether it's sharing on this sort of alternate level where there's really no boundary or discrimination, where our self-concepts are suspended and merged into one experience.

We can look at this from a Buddhist perspective and imagine zazen, Zen meditation, sitting at the wall. We're doing wall-staring with zazen now, and the difference between us and the wall breaks down, because our self-concept is suspended, and our concept of wall is suspended, and all our discriminations and judgments and thoughts and narratives and stories we tell are all suspended, and we can really connect with each other.

In the end, if we're going with Buddhism, there's the conventional and the ultimate layers of reality, and conventionally we're two people talking and looking into each other's eyes, dreamily, but in the ultimate layer, there is no discrimination. We are, in fact, one. There's no specific entity; there's no unique mind. It's all one continuum, one process, a process that didn't even arise to begin with, so it's not even really one. It's nondual. It never became one because in a dualistic world, when there's one, there's something that's not one. So it's just not two, is the best our human language can do with it, so I think that there's really something to this ultimate connection. It's just that we end up letting our projections and our own conceptual thinking get in the way, our narratives, like, "Wow, she's the one for me. She's so dreamy; I'm looking into her eyes and, you know, she likes skiing, too," as if that would affect it!

But then we can just share a moment in silence, especially those key moments in life. I felt that when working as a hospice nurse, and I loved it, because when somebody's on their death bed, there's nothing to fight about with their consciousness and their thought processes. They can just be, sometimes. Or that moment when two people are just struck by awe and wonder with nothing to say, where you know exactly what the other person's thinking and feeling, because you're sitting next to each other on a bench, just completely blown away by this massive mountain or by subalpine wildflower meadows. And you can look into each other's eyes, and it's unspoken. The unspoken word that's been heard. Those are those moments where we can feel nondiscrimination and nonduality.

My favorite painting is a painting by Alex Grey called "One," where two people's eyes are staring directly into each other, and they're part of a web of eyes that connects to more eyes in kind of a jewel-net-of-Indra kind of way, where we've got all these jewels that are connected by light, basically. Alex Grey uses strands of fiery energy, but it's light. It's light in darkness, layering through with galaxies in between, and all these eyes connected by the fire, and in the center two people staring into each other's eyes. And those two people aren't just connected as two people; they're like godheads in the sky and the universe, like stars staring into each other's eyes.

Experience

Am I the Buddha? The Question of Phenomenal Experience

Am I the reincarnation of the Buddha? Yes, we all are. But the prefix "re-" is misleading, because there was never a time when I was not the Buddha. And the term "incarnation" is misleading because all incarnations, embodiments, entities are illusions. Incarnations are not even themselves. They are like waves from the ocean, so it is right to say they are the ocean. It is like a wave of light from a star. Our body is the universe; it is the vast light and emptiness. They are like the figments of a dream. The figments of a dream are real in a sense, but where are they? Where do we locate them ontologically? We would like to say they are in the mind, yet we cannot find them there.

Experiences, too, are like this. Objectively and from the viewpoint of physical science, we have nowhere to locate phenomenal experiences. We can locate objects (albeit mind-dependently), or so we think. We can identify the brain and all its electrochemical processes. But where is the experience? Nowhere. Even if we could locate them in energy and electricity, they would not appear as themselves, of their nature, in *propria persona*. For experiences to appear in their real nature, as they truly are, they must be experienced, for that is what makes them experiences.

Subjectively, we can locate them, but in a subtle and fleeting way. What was it to be there as you were just a moment ago? Now, that experience is a memory, dark and hazy as a dream just as you are waking. When you wake up, it is to a new moment, maybe spent trying to discern again what it was to be in that last moment. We don't even know what it is to be in this moment. We are just in it, and by the time we've realized it, cognized it, identified it, had the secondary experience of recognition of it (as in sensation vs. perception or non-conceptual vs. conceptual), the moment itself, the experience, is gone, and we're left with the idea of it, a memory made real only by being associated with a feeling that we can't quite put our finger on, as though we're grasping at illusions, snowflakes, or bubbles, and trying to hold them in the palm of our hand. They are figments, appearances of clear light in dark emptiness, with the feel of a dream, hazy light floating through the empty mind as clouds, blown by on a breeze. The sun shines through them, and they take fleeting shapes, barely discernible, identifiable only for a moment. We could see a face in a cloud, look away and back again, only to have lost track of it, never to find it again. Images of a dream are barely discernible, sensed and felt but not known, like a flicker in the corner of our eyes. We turn to look, but they are gone, and we are left only with the feeling that we have experienced them. They are hazy, like nebulas and colorful gasses floating through the vast, dark expanse of space. They are the clear light of the void. We feel the light there but only barely; it is so subtle.

The merger of the mind-world is the nature of experience.

As the philosopher Alan Watts said, "I am what is going on." That is, we have the problem of dividing things in two, creating the insuperable problem of how to put them together again. If a problem is insuperable, be suspicious that the question is framed poorly.

Why is there self and world, when the self is equipped with so many ways to sense and interact with the world? Why is there mind and body? When you take a thing out of its context, you have changed it, and it not the thing it is anymore—you hypostasize it. So how then could you ever understand what it really is, how it works, and how it fits into the larger context of existence?

This is why we cannot find phenomenal experience.

Nonduality

Opposites

Let's start with opposites, with trying to find a place in nature where something can exist without its opposite. Without north there is no south; without up there can be no down; without light there can be no darkness or shadow. In order for there to be a thing, there must be that which is not that thing. For example, Michelangelo's sculpture of David is defined by its shape but also defined by its negative space, the space which it is not. (Consider the statement, probably apocryphal, that Michelangelo is said to have made to Pope Julius II when he was asked how he carved the statue: that he studied the marble for a long time, then slowly cut away all the parts that were not David.)

So in order for there to be a thing, there must be that which is not that thing. Everything has the space which it is, surrounded by space which it is not, and they are fundamentally dependent on each other. For each thing, there is its opposite.

There is also projection upon others, what our mind projects and reflects back like an echo, what the witness sees and reflects back like a mirror. We move from love to personification, anthropomorphism, faces in the clouds, ancestors watching over us, and then our intentional explanations of theoretical entities, like Santa Claus. Eventually our projections produce a celestial being with white hair and a beard, seated upon a throne, but this is less divinity than a sort of god delusion, getting stuck on a symbol that is not the divine at all. We progress from there to the narrative meaning of life, to silence and to introspection.

All this projection on others, on the universe, and on ourselves, is based on the subject-object relation or the dualist mode—but with so many projecting and being projected upon, it becomes an infinite net that seems to surround us. But in the end, there is no subject option—no dualism.

Everything and Nothing

At fourteen, these were my philosophical ideas on what I labeled "the nature of life, death, and everything in existence." I began with the question, "What do the blind see?" and continued:

This statement is most simply answered by the word "nothing," but this is encumbered by questions, of which the most prominent is, "What color is nothing?" This again is meant as a statement, rather than a question, because it is meant less to inquire and more to perplex and inspire thought. The immediate response to this might be "black." This, unfortunately, defeats the earlier statement that the blind see nothing, because black must inevitably be called "something," even if it is only empty space (such as the space in between stars and planets), and so must white, or any color in the known spectrum. The argument might then progress to the statement, "Nothing is in fact something," which would seem to defeat my argument, because if nothing is something, then it is possible to candidly call black (being something) the possible color of nothing. My statement has been defeated, but, as I said before, the purpose of my statement was not to inquire, but to inspire thought. Therefore, in the defeat of my statement, the statement has actually accomplished its goal. Hopefully the statement has distinguished between two nothings: the nothing in terms of empty space and blackness, and the true lack of any remote form of presence whatsoever, which is a nothing that cannot be called something, as the other nothing can.

I would now propose that the universe is truly nothing (the true nothing of lack of any presence), and that, metaphorically, people who see nothing (the truly blind) in fact see the truth. This also leaves us with the equation: everything = nothing. That is, the universe is nothing, while at the same time still being something, which comes from the scientific idea that a particle may become a wave, that is, an object may be itself or be a void of nothing, and furthermore that the object may transpose between the two states. Particles assume the form of something when a human being or a form of conscious life is aware of them, and they assume the form of nothing, or a wave, at other times. If everything has a flip-side of nothingness to it, then nothing is a component of everything, and so we could say that nothing = everything. However, quantum physics suggests that the universe is aware of its own existence, and, therefore, objects must always be present (unless the universe is creating the illusion). Due to the mathematical proof that a = a, everything = everything and nothing = nothing. Now we have our four most important equations, where everything = e and nothing = n:

1. everything = nothing or e = n
2. nothing = everything or n = e
3. nothing = nothing or n = n
4. everything = everything or e = e

I called my theory "ultra-dimensions," seeing it as representing an infinite number of dimensions such as length, width, depth, and time, but also seeing that for each dimension there is an opposite, creating billions of paradoxes, just as the paradox presented when something is nothing and something at the same time. As I saw it, all of the universe functioned in this fashion, and for every dimension, there were infinite branches, which have branches, which have branches, and so on. It seemed a very reasonable thought due to the beautiful interaction of the four equations. I wrote:

If e = n, then everything has a flip-side of nothingness to it, and therefore creates a paradox. If n = e, then the same phenomenon is present. If n = n and e = e, then everything is itself, but at the same time everything has a paradoxical opposite. This is hard to imagine, but trying to be aware of every nerve in one's body helps one to imagine it as a confusing koan in the meditation style of Buddhist monks, and also helps one to research the nature of the universe.

I ended with the line, "If I were to tell you that you will exhale your soul, would you stop breathing?"

When I was older, I studied philosophy, including Buddhist philosophy, which has a great deal to say on the nature of being and non-being, duality and nonduality. I studied Buddhism's "Heart Sutra," which said:

... form is no other than emptiness,
emptiness no other than form.
Form is exactly emptiness, emptiness exactly form.

This sounded familiar: the infinite potential of emptiness, or nothing, from which the imagination can render infinite forms, just as the multitude of things in the universe sprouted from the singularity that burst into all possibilities in the big bang (which is the perfect metaphor for the infinity of thoughts coming from the infinite potential of the voidness of non-dual mind). The non-dual mind is not an infinity, but an absolute zero, a total nothingness that yields the space for everything that can potentially be, which by the imagination is infinity.

Everything/Form = nothing/emptiness
Nothing/emptiness = everything/form
Everything/form = everything/form
Nothing/emptiness = nothing/emptiness

Emptiness and form are the terms that Buddhism used; everything and nothing are the terms that I used at fourteen, before I knew much of anything about Buddhism.

Once I was exposed to Buddhist thought, I began to see the influences of Buddhism everywhere. In the film *The Matrix*, I heard a young boy tell the protagonist Neo:

Boy: Do not try and bend the spoon. That's impossible. Instead ... only try to realize the truth.
Neo: What truth?
Boy: There is no spoon.
Neo: There is no spoon?
Boy: Then you'll see, that it is not the spoon that bends, it is only yourself.

Now I could compare that to the Zen koan that said, "Not the wind, not the flag; mind is moving." (Ekai, *The Gateless Gate*, N. Senzaki (trans.), 29)

There is no dichotomy. All is non-dual, and so there is no problem, no mind versus body, no free will versus determinism, no pairs of opposites. There is only one. In the West, William Blake understood it:

To see a World in a Grain of Sand ...
And Eternity in an hour"
(William Blake, "Auguries of Innocence,"
in *William Blake: Poems*, 37)

He saw how this moment contains all moments, is eternal, and yet is right here, right now. The transcendentalist Ralph Waldo Emerson saw it, too:

We live in succession, in division, in parts, in particles. Meantime within man is the soul of the whole; the wise silence; the univer-sal beauty, to which every part and particle is equally related; the eternal ONE. And this deep power in which we exist and whose be-atitude is all accessible to us, is not only self-sufficing and perfect in every hour, but the act of seeing and the thing seen, the seer and the spectacle, the subject and the object, are one. We see the world piece by piece, as the sun, the moon, the animal, the tree; but the whole, of which these are the shining parts, is the soul. (Ralph Waldo Emerson, "The Over-soul," in *Ralph Waldo Emerson: Essays and Lectures*, 386)

How can I explain this? Let's start with the flame and the mind, meditating on a burning flame. So, stare at the candle. The candle is both the object of perception and … much more. The candle is out there in the world, but it is also in your mind.

As the wind blows, the flame moves. But so … as the wind of thought, emotion blow, you move. So again, just as the Zen koan says, "Not the wind, not the flag; mind is moving" (Ekai, *The Gateless Gate*, N. Senzaki (trans.), 29). So changes your experience of the candle.

This is the middle ground, the heat point, the place that the psychologist D.W. Winnicott called the "play" point, where the mind can imagine anything, assume any shape, without limit. This is where the juice is, the place I call the communion, the holy communion, the meeting of mind and world, mind and other beings, meeting in such a way that they are one.

But there is also a witness, an eye, an experiencing subject, a self. And we tend to place a lot of emphasis on this self. Both philosophers and people who live and narrate their everyday lives tell themselves a lot of stories about who this "subject" is. But really, the action happens in the "play zone," the "heat" point, where the mental changes occur, where the "fixedness" of the candle, of reality, becomes unfixed. The candle transforms to smoke, the metal of the blade becomes malleable, in the literal "heat of the moment."

The heat of the moment is where the plot twists and the story turns. The flame is in the "external" candle, but that flame is also "in your experience." The flame's light is the witnessing subject. It's what shines the light of "attention," the mind's light, the mind's eye, on the world. Reality happens in that fire.

Each one of us is the whole world. You are every "leaf of grass" to Walt Whitman, "every snowflake that falls" to Mary Oliver. When two people look into each other's eyes, their two separate worlds come together, and so it is with all. All rivers lead to the seas; the pattern of rivers is the same as human veins. All roads lead to the same place, the one destination, and yet, each road is important, each path that leads there, each moment, each conscious event.

We were all meant to be together and yet we are apart and alone. Each man dies alone, but then rejoins the whole. We were alone, and yet we were never alone, but always one whole. We are both one, an individual, and one, the one thing that is all things.

Infinity and everything must include all. Non-duality means that nothing can be excluded, including, ironically, duality:

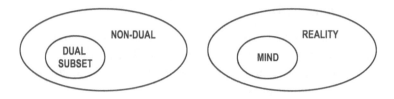

And yet in the end:

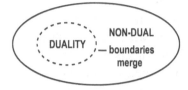

Boundaries merge. You're the singer and the song.

Wind Flag Mind Moves

Wind flag mind moves
Nothing defines you
Be whatever you imagine yourself to be.

Thought penetrates reality, then merges as one,
Your mind is in the wind,
Wu-wei—fly like the flag.

Focus always on the center.
What do you want from this life?

To know mind's nature and its "limits"—limitlessness.

Live from your *center*, all else will follow.

Awakening

You can go through your whole life asleep; many people never awaken.

Changing Your Mind

The thinking that promotes duality cannot achieve non-duality. Or, as Einstein once said, "a new type of thinking is essential if mankind is to survive and move toward higher levels." (Albert Einstein, quoted in "Atomic Education Urged by Einstein," *The New York Times*, Saturday, May 25, 1946, 11) Although such thinking can lead us the doorstep, it cannot cross the threshold. Change your mind.

I think seeing the truth or the underlying nature of reality is perhaps only one step in attaining enlightenment. Another step is integration and embodiment of these realizations, that is, learning to live with this true nature and integrate it into living daily life, embodying it.

This one's a bitch and takes constant work. We can't just float off on a cloud into the ethereal oneness of everything. We need to deal with the many things in the world while also maintaining this sense of true nature and oneness. Someone said, "Enlightenment is a great place but you can't get a decent meal there." Or for example, in Tibetan Buddhism, the highest level of enlightenment, *Mahamudra* or *dzogchen*, means attaining an enlightenment state in meditation but then learning to integrate it into daily life, such that the distinction between meditation and non-meditation blurs and disappears. This requires a lot of work for almost anyone. We all need to acknowledge that we still have a lifetime of work ahead of us, if we're being honest with ourselves.

There is another tradition of practice, the contemplative tradition, which involves contemplating certain themes, subjects, or ideas. You may visualize a full moon, a flickering candle, or raindrops, or you may imagine yourself glowing with light. There are visualizations using symbols and signs of all kinds. These all fall in the category of the contemplative tradition, rather than the meditative tradition. According to the Buddha, such practice is often merely mental gymnastics, a source of entertainment that is furthering your neurosis instead of leading to enlightenment.

Meditation is about relating with two factors. It relates you with yourself, and it also relates you with your world. Through the practice of meditation, you are able to synchronize your world and yourself. Working with the two eventually produces a spark. It is like rubbing two sticks together or striking a flint against a stone to produce a spark. The spark of light you produce is called *karuna*, or compassion.

Another way to put it is that glimpsing enlightenment and living it are very different things. There are no shortcuts to the latter in my experience. I know what it feels like to see it but struggle deeply with how to live with what you've seen. That project is pretty much my life's work.

In the West, people say, "He's in God's hands now." Or, "He was in God's hands the whole time." What does that mean?

How does this compare to the Buddhist idea of being in delusion, but also already being in enlightenment? As in: "He's free of illusion now; he's enlightened." Or "He was enlightened the whole time." Is elimination the first stage of change?

Like dreamers, we've forgotten that we're sleeping.

Suffering and Awakening

Remember that the thing that leads to awakening is suffering, the pain that arises because the world is not the way you want it to be.

To borrow from D.W. Winnicott, this fits with his observations of infants testing the reality limit in the play zone, magical thinking versus objective reality, or merging the subjective with the objective really, becoming part of the world, which is like birthing pains. It's being like a child after having gone through childhood, but there's some difference. Perhaps it is to know *samsara*—the cycle of living and dying, the world of delusion in which we all live—as well as enlightenment. See the lotus, contemplate the lotus, reflect on the meaning of lotuses, then again see them as lotuses, because again, enlightenment is a great place, but you can't get a decent meal there.

There's something inside me that has always been there, but now it's awake. It's time to face what I need to become. I've been avoiding becoming myself all my life.

Why, How, and the Purpose of Life

Knowledge is the object of our inquiry, and men do not think they know a thing till they have grasped the "why" of it (which is to grasp its primary cause). — Aristotle

Much of our interaction with the material world focuses not on "why?" but on "how?" If one has practical goals, knowing how things work is simply more important, because then phenomena can be predicted and manipulated. Knowing why would entail some sort of knowledge of the goal of nature or perhaps the goal of the artist who created nature, be it God or Nature itself or whatever. Surely, this kind of knowledge would be extremely valuable, but, on the other hand, it seems almost impossible to attain.

Of course, one could interpret the "why" and "how" more simply. How does the rain fall? Down and slightly to the left. Why does the rain fall? Because of gravity. I would still view this as an explanation of how it falls. In my view, to fully explain the why behind the falling of rain, one would have to then have to explain why gravity pulls things down, and, eventually, why there is water, force, and nature? Why does everything exist? What is the meaning of existence? If there is such a reason behind nature, then this would be the why of natural events. Why does nature make the rain fall? The causal chain will have to be traced back to some "primary" cause, as Aristotle would say. The primary cause could not be gravity because gravity is the effect of some other cause, which, in turn, is probably the effect of some other cause.

Explaining how something works only requires an account of the way it happens. Rain falls because gravity pulls it down, and gravity pulls things down because it is a force that causes objects with a small mass to gravitate towards objects with a large mass. One has still has not explained why the rain falls or why gravity is a force that works in the world. Scientific explanations stops at the natural law, the "how" of which just shows that something happens, the why of which brings into question the purposes of nature. As Aristotle writes: "It is plain then that nature is a cause, a cause that operates for a purpose." Nature is compared to a work of art—it has a meaning. Knowing the purpose behind nature's unfolding would be to know the purpose of the great artist, God. How could this kind of knowledge be anything but the most important thing one could possibly learn?

Though people may claim to know the purpose of nature, it does not seem that this is verifiable knowledge. There is no definitive, evidenced explanation of nature's purpose. This sort of knowing seems to be personal, internal, intuitive, and useful only in providing one with guidance or comfort. Objective knowledge of how things work seems to be more useful to us every day. You can tell someone with a brain tumor about the meaning of life all day long, but what they really want is a cure for cancer. Or is it? On your death bed, would you rather be given life or, finally, as you are about to die, know the purpose of the life you have lived?

I think that the "why" is all that is really important and the "how" is just a clue as to "why." But I don't think we will ever know "why." Moreover, I don't think there is a reason, so perhaps we should stick to learning "how" and wondering "why." If you ask me, this is why we are alive. It's like when you were a little kid, and you would always ask, "Why?" Then someone would explain it to you, and you'd again ask, "Why?" If you have ever tried to explain something to a child, this continues indefinitely.

Time

Dream Time

Where are we when we are dreaming? Dream time is skewed as it can dilate or speed up by uncanny amounts. In a deep dream, whole lifetimes and elaborate multidimensional experiences can be lived in a matter of hours, and then be forgotten quickly upon awakening. Something as small as the memory of playing with dragonflies as a child can live on in an eternal instant, nothing more than a flash of a memory that we can bask in for hours and which lingers on in memory for hours after waking. And each can be equally powerful. The smallest thing remembered can be like a pebble dropped in water that ripples throughout our entire psyche from deep within, then expanding as though a seed, an acorn, that has grown into an entire tree. A small flutter of wild wings can grow into the vision that drives a man, rippling throughout a lifetime. Or an entire lifetime can flash past, gone in an instant, like a man before a firing squad whose whole life, half-remembered and half-forgotten, flashes by, full of countless events that create layers of meaning.

It can be an oak grown full of leaves, so many that numberless seasons have passed and chapters of life have drifted away in the breeze, feelings and moments that each felt as deep as the sting of bee, that at that time the man swore would last forever, never forgotten. But the oak's leaves are now gone, replaced with new leaves, themselves blown away, and so on. Each leaf, brimming with the life-giving sap of the tree, is exquisitely formed from with the tree and run through with water, sunlight, and soil. Each is full of the earth itself and can carry all the heart of a man, all that he might have vested in a pivotal hand of poker or the tentative hope that this woman may say "yes" to a dance and the wonderful tumbling thereafter. Each is full, too, of the spirit of the times, brimful of the life of the times...and then all of it may be gone in a flash, in an instant.

But how can all of that be gone so quickly? A man, walking to the market to buy a basket of fruit for the woman to eat, with all that hope, all that love vested in fruit that it might nourish a child coming forth, might then see the basket shot through and the fruit tumbling over the ground, scattered for a robber's children. Or the vanishing may be the utter tragedy and dismay of two grieving parents, a lifetime's worth, whose hearts have become a hole large enough to have held food to fill the bellies of a village, but that have now come to fruition in the enthusiasm of a boy chasing after a butterfly...or was it a bee?

... All this was written upon waking from a dream, a beautiful epic, the story and contents of which I haven't the slightest recollection, but from which this rather naturally grew forth in an effort to grasp the ineffable meaning of the story as it slipped through my fingers like grains of sand, with time enough only to catch a fleeting feeling as I tried so desperately to grasp and savor every image. And so perhaps this is the meaning of a man's life and the thereafter? The feeling of timelessness, so important at the time and later just a feeling that turns out be like the butterfly, so fragile and yet powerful enough to flap its wings and with that flutter create storms that break trees, drive galaxies in their spinning and send Orion on his imaginal hunts.

"To see a World in a Grain of Sand ... And Eternity in an hour." (William Blake, "Auguries of Innocence," in *William Blake: Poems*, 37)

Helheimr!! Why does this Viking cry from Tolkien come to mind? Perhaps it is a mantra that can be used to fire up the soul for battle and yet give it the spirit to live.

Time

The wheel of time can't want anything. The wheel just calls you forward. It's not that the universe is cold and indifferent, but just neutral, without bias or want. That's just its nature. It's people who want.

On March 15, 1955, a month before his own death, Einstein's good friend, Michele Besso, died. A few days later Einstein wrote a letter of condolence to Besso's son, Vero, and his sister, Bice Rusconi, saying, "Now he has departed from this strange world a little ahead of me. That signifies nothing. For those of us who believe in physics, the distinction between past, present and future is only a stubbornly persistent illusion."

So, according to Einstein, time itself is only a "stubbornly persistent illusion," rather like the ego. Like the ego, time is also painted, constructed and dilated by the mind. A moment can seem very long, or it can seem to pass in a fraction of the actual time. The mind changes how that time feels, often by suspending measurement (like just turning off your watch for an hour). So the mind paints in time, emotions, and even our sense of self, our ego, but time is relative, rather like Einstein's metaphorical twins, one of whom travels at nearly light speed to a distant star and back, while the other twin remains on earth awaiting his sibling, only to find when the traveler returns that the traveler is now younger than he is.

Time dilation is more than a product of speed. It is mental. A moment can be eternal, and yet everything is transient. They say that time is the blink of an eye in heaven, which is what must make eternity bearable.

The Witness

Is the witness the self? The memory of the self, that is, the self that is constructed by memory and narrative, is clearly someone who is at least somewhat false, and in the end we find that really it is an illusion. We misremember things, and alter and augment them to fit the story we've told ourselves. The pieces of our story are like the parts of the Greek ship, the ship of Theseus, a thought experiment regarding a vessel that makes journey after journey, having a plank replaced here and then there as it is used, until finally over time the entirety of the ship has been replaced, and yet, it is still considered to be the same ship. We make ourselves in the same way, with just bits and pieces of the story.

But is time even really linear? Who is that "self," and is it you... really you? Because if so, you'll be a different you in a moment, and another you the moment after that, and years from now you will have misremembered so many things that you'll be a totally different person. And how you remember things is affected by your experiences and your mood, for example, whether you're riding high. You can look back on your life one day and see all its wonderful beauty and accomplishments, and the next day think, "What have I done with my life? I've been drifting through, and it's all dependent on an illusion, a story." So we can tell ourselves a different story, but the real true self is the one that's here now, the focal point where time, space, past and future, and the witnessing self collide with data from memory or dreams or imagination or fragments of books we read in childhood.

Now you need to learn to live in a way independent of that self:

> If you think that you know Spirit, or if you think you don't, Spirit is actually that which is thinking both of those thoughts. So you can doubt the objects of consciousness, but you can never believably

doubt the doubter, never really doubt the Witness of the entire display. Therefore, rest in the Witness, whether it is thinking that it knows God or not, and that witnessing, that undeniable immediacy of now-consciousness, is itself God, Spirit, Buddha-mind. The certainty lies in the pure self-felt Consciousness to which objects appear, not in the objects themselves. You will never, never, never see God, because God is the Seer, not any finite, mortal, bounded object that can be seen. (*Ken Wilber, The Simple Feeling of Being: Embracing Your True Nature*, 7)

In other words, if you're looking for the face of God, it's staring right back at you. It reflects in everything that you see in the world. Those things are mirrors, and God is you witnessing it all. Perhaps God exists in a manner relative to the way we conceive him.

The Universe

For the universe to exist, we have a long assumed there was a beginning, a creation, because everything must come from somewhere. But the beginning of the universe, it seems, may have come from nowhere. In a TED Talk, the physicist Stephen Hawking said, "Under extreme conditions, general relativity and quantum theory allow time to behave like another dimension of space. This removes the distinction between time and space, and means the laws of evolution can also determine the initial state. The universe can spontaneously create itself out of nothing." (Stephen Hawking, "Questioning the Universe," February, 2008, TED Talk)

This point of nothingness from which the universe sprang has no counterpart, because, apparently, it was nothingness teeming with everything. Similarly, we find nothing all over the universe in its dark matter and its black holes. The universe is expanding: this much we know. Where it goes from here is more of a mystery. It may expand forever into final heat death, when the stars all burn out (the "Big Freeze"), or the matter of the universe may be torn apart by its own expansion (the "Big Rip"), or, if there is enough dark matter and dark energy, it may stop expanding, start contracting, and turn into a giant black hole (the "Big Crunch"). In that case, the entire existence of the universe will be erased and probably be returned to some primordial state that predates the existence of the universe, a singularity that would contain all the energy of the universe. This seems almost like a birth as well as a death, rather than a death dragged on to infinity as in the eternal expansion scenario. Instead, it seems almost like the beginning again, because, although the universe would be annihilated, it would still exist potentially, because within the remaining singularity would be the potential for everything, for nearly infinite possibilities. Furthermore, ideologically, the idea seems to suggest some primordial unity from whence all came and will return, suggesting the possibility of an oscillating universe that re-expands after its collapse, repeating the big bang and starting the whole process over again. Personally, I like this pulsating universe idea, although what I like is hardly predictive.

Additionally, if the universe recollapsing into a singularity is the case, it begs the question: "Is everything already unified in some primordial sense by the mere fact that all time and space can be reduced to a single state?" In other words, if this final/initial singularity encompassed all the energy, mass, etc., that exists in space-time, could all the various substances actually be one thing, the universe's so-called "primordial soup"?

In their book *The Quantum and the Lotus*, Buddhist monk Matthieu Ricard and astrophysicist Trinh Xuan Thuan debate many questions such as these. (Trinh Xuan Thuan, the astrophysicist, had been raised as a Buddhist in Vietnam, while Matthieu Ricard, the Buddhist monk, also earned a doctoral degree in molecular genetics, so both men had backgrounds in Buddhism and doctoral degrees in science.) Trinh, the astrophysicist, affirms the scientific viewpoint on the Big Bang as well as the various ways the universe might end. (Matthieu Ricard and Trinh Xuan Thuan, *The Quantum and the Lotus*, 31-37)

Ricard, the monk, responds:

> In the Buddhist viewpoint, this Western obsession—in religion, philosophy, and science—with a beginning derives from a stubborn belief in the reality of phenomena: objects really "exist" as we see them, and so must have a beginning. This approach forces scientists into performing complicated juggling acts when trying to reconcile the results of quantum mechanics with a reassuring vision of the world, thus preserving us from having to put our ordinary perceptions of things into question.... Michel Bitbol has observed that the philosophical debate concerning modern physics seems dominated by the following maxim, "Whenever a realist interpretation is available in theoretical physics—whatever happens, adopt it at once." Yet if physicists drew the logical conclusions from quantum mechanics, then they could easily transform their worldview. (Matthieu Ricard and Trinh Xuan Thuan, *The Quantum and the Lotus*, 271)

In the battle of science versus reality, what science tells us about reality trumps conclusions based solely on religious faith, but religion and all philosophical views win in their sense of possibility, a realm which science cannot comment upon and still be earnest with itself. So much is untouched and unexplained by scientific truth. From science, we meticulously discover the laws of physics, but we do not even touch upon an answer as to why or from whence physics came to be.

Life

Compassion

Sometimes I'm listening to music and my heart swells and feels like it may burst. Perhaps I'll just burst into song.

Sometimes I step back from the world and see, as if in a bird's-eye view, all the happenings of the world, happening simultaneously in unison, and I want to weep for the beauty of it.

Sometimes when at work in the hospital, I pause and see all the suffering and terror, met with either so much love or so much indifference, and me still in the middle of it, and I want to shake people awake and say, "This is the time now, the only time to be alive or to love or to die."

I watch all the people watching TV, and from my vantage point this seems to be what their lives are, watching and waiting and hoping for another life when you'll only have your own.

When we go to our allies without true empathy, without truly accounting for how you are affecting another, we leave a path of damage behind us. We must develop compassion but also attention to others' positions.

Believe that conscious beings have a soul. Don't try to understand or figure it out, but just comprehend. Trying to understand it is futile.

Jesus and Buddha's Eightfold Path

Last night I watched a film about a martyr who died to save his friends, like Jesus's verse in the New Testament, "Greater love hath no man than this, that a man lay down his life for his friends."

I love this idea because it shows how actions and intentions can leave a legacy that lives on far after we die. In the New Testament, Jesus was the one brave man who literally transferred his bravery to others, who then could act bravely to save others' lives and who also transferred their bravery onto the next generation after that. It's paying it forward, like a ripple in the pond that transfers not only to the next person, but multiplies as the next person transfers that trait on, and the next person after that. It may have started with one man's actions, but then it turned into two men's actions, then four, then sixteen, then we're up to 256, and so on. This is how something like a movement or religion gets started, with Jesus or when Buddha had his realization but then taught his disciples the meaning of life, through transmission of right mind, word, and deed, and they taught their disciples. Buddha's mind-to-mind transmission was passed down this way for millennia, with each righteous person adding their own spin to the transmission through their own integrity and character, that is, their own right mind, word, and deed, yielding mind-to-mind transmission of the ultimate truth for millennia to come. It is a worthwhile goal for one's life, to write a book that influences two people, who then carry that influence on to four, and so on.

Your life is an unwritten book.

If you're afraid you've lost your dream, you haven't lost it yet.

The Fruits of Each Day

The days come and go like muffled and veiled figures sent from a distant friendly party, but they say nothing, and if we do not use the gifts they bring, they carry them as silently away. (Ralph Waldo Emerson, The Heart of Emerson's Journals, *B. Perry (ed.), 223)*

A work of art touches the timeless, but life is not a work of art, and the moment cannot last. So we must experience each thing fully for the work of art that it is, for there are moments in our lives where we touch the timeless, by witnessing beauty. Each moment has the possibility to be a work of art. If we can achieve the state of mind we attain when touching timelessness, we can appreciate anything for that kind of beauty. For beauty is in the mind's eye.

The Dark Night of the Soul

Your self deserves respect and love from you most of all. When you get an idea in your head that you're repellent, that you have a bad vibe, you may start to notice things that aren't even real. And you may manifest them. Just do you. Live for yourself.

It starts with you learning to love yourself, and I think if you try to patch the holes and put a Band-Aid on what's hurting by plugging another person into the picture, you're just going to repeat the same cycle and never get down to something that actually fixes the wound rather than just covering it with a Band-Aid. If so, you won't ever find that feeling of inherent self-worth and the inherent value of your own life. I think it's a paradox, but in order for you to feel loved, and not feel alone, you have to first be alone long enough to learn to love yourself. Then people will show up and love you, because you'll have that glow.

You know, if you're going into the depths of hell, you need a guide. I have thought that all the negative stuff that people go through might just have a purpose. Because how can we help people trapped in a cave, lost in a dark forest, or mired in a bog, if we don't know the way out ourselves?

Too often we spend our time perseverating about our problems and reinforcing them, pushing them deeper and deeper into the brain, carving ruts deeper the way a river carves a hole in the rock over millennia, making a Grand Canyon. We can create and reinforce neural pathways until we've completely rewired our brains into a high-functioning machine that will become so efficient at hating ourselves that it's like we were born to do that, like that's all our brain can do.

We can train our brains to think that way so hard that we believe it is completely real. But the truth is, if we just find a way to start thinking differently, to look at the stuff in the unconscious, show it to someone else who shows us a new perspective, it starts to throw wrenches into the wiring, chipping away at the connections and starting to break up the pattern of neural pathways in the brain, the "connectomes." And then we can begin to see we didn't have anything to be ashamed of, because we're just human beings dealing with human existence, just like everybody else.

The question isn't what you want to do with the rest of your life; the question is, what does the universe want you to do with the rest your life? If you live in the first way, you will always feel out of sync with something. If you live in the second, you'll feel in sync with everything around you.

Friendship and Saving the World

I would like to think of my friends as a single entity with its own life of mind, with many elements or members that come and go fluidly, passing through, the way thoughts, memories, dreams, and visions pass through the human consciousness, coming and going freely, of their own will and individual direction, with their own path beaten in the pursuit of answers to their own unique curiosities. For all those members, there is also a common motive: to explore, to expand, to grow, to find their place in the world, to satisfy each facet of their existence, mind, body, and soul, and find peace in and acceptance of themselves.

One could think of the human race this way, each person being a unique possibility like a thought, meant to learn what it means to be and live out that possibility. Is there meaning in heroism? Is there meaning in cowardice? Is there an answer in faith? Some find the answer there. An answer in cynicism? Some find the answer there. Will we ever find "The Answer," if there are answers in everything? Or is it not "The Answer" that we should look for? Must we embrace the infinite possibilities? By being unique individuals yet knowing each other, are we all not like a mind, one mind, scattering itself into each random possibility that surfaces from the depths of its imagination? Realizing and touching, if only for a flash, a moment, each possibility that emerges, whether in a dream, an experience, or a hallucinogenic vision quest? Or perhaps in the trenches of a world war, in the pyramids of Egypt, growing in a hole somewhere beneath the surface of a planet orbiting some faraway star.

It seems, however, that individual consciousness is a double-edged sword. It allows us to explore, to see reality from infinite perspectives, yet as a consequence it creates infinite contradictions.

The majority of us, however, don't seem to realize the importance of embracing each member of our race. People are caught in their perspective, their ego, and cannot see the poetry of our chaotic unison. With threats of nuclear war, environmental collapse, or some other catastrophic event, it would seem idealistic to say that the end of our little world is not near. Humanity can't seem to get it together.

From whence does change come?

Because we all have unique perspectives, voicing those perspectives creates conflict. Most react by choosing to remain quiet, keeping their ideas locked away even from themselves, choosing to live an oblivious existence and pass on quietly, or by choosing to participate in and perpetuate that conflict. A rare few find a peaceful balance in the tension between us, embrace it, and use it to learn and expand their minds in ways they could not expand them when limited to only their own perspective. They use communication as a forum for expression and growth, rather than as an opportunity to simply yell and scream and whine because they want things done their way. This creates a piercing ring that makes it impossible to draw any sort of sense from the jumble of voices that just sound like static. And as the voices become static, so does the progression of the world. If we do not grow, if we do not change, will we simply destroy ourselves?

Timothy Leary identified a subrace of humans. He coined the name "Futants" for this group, people who are genetically adapted to explore the future through innovative thought and experimentation. Though it is not a rule, it is likely that any innovation will come from some such intelligent people, the gifted and talented. The world is in desperate need of change. Therefore, I believe it is crucial that those who might be Futants explore new possibilities in order to bring about growth. Innovation knows no method.

Identity

Continuity is real, but so is the newness of each moment. The identity of a thing both persists and is new with each moment. It is like the Greek ship, the ship of Theseus, a thought experiment regarding a vessel that makes journey after journey, having a plank replaced here and then there as it is used, until finally over time the entirety of the ship has been replaced, and yet, it is still considered to be the same ship.

Or identity is like Descartes's wax. In his "Second Meditation," René Descartes describes his perception of the properties belonging to a certain piece of wax in a solid state. After melting the wax to a liquid state, causing its properties to change, he asks whether the wax remains the same piece of wax it was before being melted. For Descartes, it seems natural to think that it is the same piece of wax. And, if the wax remains the same piece of wax after changing, this idea suggests to Descartes that the true essence of the wax can only be grasped by the imagination.

Descartes then begins to imagine the whole range of states the wax could take, more shapes than Descartes could possibly picture: "…I would not judge correctly what the wax was if I did not believe that it takes on an even greater variety of dimensions than I could ever grasp with my imagination." (René Descartes, "Second Meditation," in *Readings in Modern Philosophy*, vol. 1, Roger Ariew, et al. (eds.), 32) Therefore, Descartes concludes that the essence of the wax cannot be perceived with the senses, or even the imagination, and is known by his mind alone. (René Descartes, "Second Meditation," in *Readings in Modern Philosophy*, vol. 1, Roger Ariew, et al. (eds.), 33) According to Descartes, the wax is only wax because he judges it to be wax, as he writes: "…what I thought I was seeing with my eyes, I actually grasped solely with the faculty of judgment, which is in my mind." (René Descartes, "Second Meditation," in *Readings in Modern Philosophy*, vol. 1, Roger Ariew, et al. (eds.), 33)

If the perception of the wax is only in Descartes's mind, then he concludes that he cannot possibly perceive corporeal substance more clearly than mental substance, because those things which seem to be corporeal or seem to come from sensory experience actually exist in a mental capacity. If Descartes's perception of the wax is most clear and distinct when he realizes that the wax exists as it does in his mind, then knowing corporeal things brings Descartes closer to an understanding of mental substances. (René Descartes, "Second Meditation," in *Readings in Modern Philosophy*, vol. 1, Roger Ariew, et al. (eds.), 33) Therefore, according to Descartes, the nature of the mind is better known than any bodily reality, if bodily reality even exists outside the mind. Its identity, it could be said, is both existent and not existent.

Mind-reality interplay is the borderline of identity, where the individual mind dissolves at its edges. This process will take you all the way to the source, the place where mind and reality are one. That reality wraps around the individual mind, but is also independent of mind. It has room for both. Also, for many minds, many pairs of eyes, perspectives are infinite, and there are ten thousand ways to see a thing, and that thing is each of those individual viewpoints, and yet also, it is what it is, no matter how we see it. It is the many beauties, but still, the one essence of a thing.

And so it is with all things: there are ten thousand of each of them, and each can be seen in ten thousand ways, and yet there is always one existence, remaining unchanged through its ten thousand changing iterations.

Love

We find fulfillment in bringing fulfillment to others.

Love is all, and yet we close ourselves off to one another. Let everything into your heart, and you will never be afraid again. How did we become lonely on a planet with so many people? Are we not all fundamentally good and wanting the same thing? And that is to connect with one another and find love, but love is all around us if we can just open our hearts, be kind to one another, and try to understand one another.

The only emotions you need are love, awe and wonder, gratitude, and compassion. These are the emotions that underlie all other emotions. Guilt occurs because you've done something that hurts someone you love, so it stems from love. Shame occurs because you've done something that makes you feel less in the eyes of the people you seek connection with, and so it stems from love. Anger occurs because you were hurt, and that hurt comes from a breaking of love.

Remember every day that we are fundamentally wanting each other to be happy. We can all wish each other well, because there is good in our hearts. Very few people wake up with the intent to spread ill will.

Real love is sticky, messy, often realistically too much to handle. But it is so much better than perfect, because it is real. Love is accepting that you're not perfect and loving you more for it.

Never say a bad word about anyone.

Two Kinds of False Love

There are two kinds of false love. The first is the kind people feel with their first young love, where are you feel intense romantic love that is based on idealizing a person and falling in love with that projection of the perfect person that you've created, rather than getting to know the real person and discovering whether you really work well together in a relationship. Often this false love involves being infatuated and head over heels in love before you've spent real time with the person and learned who they truly are, independent of your mind.

The second type of false love is codependent love. Basically it is not real love for the person, but a need to satisfy some deficiency or emotional need in your life that you believe can only be solved by being with that person. To avoid this pitfall, ideally you should have a full life before you meet them, and after you meet them as well. You should be comfortable with that person being apart from you and, more importantly, still feel good about your life and yourself.

Perhaps both of these ideas can both be applied to our love of God as well. One is a romanticized conception of God that we fall in love with but is also an ideal that we've created, instead of trying to come to God as God is.

Then, in the case of codependent love, people create a mental image of God who can forgive them and redeem their sins and solve their emotional problems. They become dependent on this God image in order to love themselves.

What is real love? Real love is altruistic and unconditional, has very little to do with self or even the specifics of the person you're in love with, especially if that is love for the whole world. It's also love without a real object, so it's not a person that you're in love with but just a feeling of love that you're willing to spread wherever you go, and not to satisfy yourself but just because you feel real love.

Given this ideal of love, what really counts as romantic love? Is romantic love always a delusion? And why do we seek this kind of love so much? We should be seeking the altruistic, unconditional, selfless love that is just love without any subject or object.

Fear and Love

Fear and love are the strongest two human emotions. And they make an interesting pair. One involves being afraid of something and hence closing ourselves against that thing. The other involves being drawn to someone or something, caring about it deeply, and wanting to open up to it. Yet they combine in strange ways. Love, for example, can involve a fear of opening up due to a fear of rejection.

Though one is positive and the other negative, love and fear can have the same object, and they can also both be based on projections, an unconscious psychological process in which one's own unconscious attributes are identified in others, rather than in oneself. You can be afraid of losing someone you're in love with and also afraid of what you think they might feel about you deep inside.

Psychologically, we know the world and one another by our projections. So real love is not influenced by fear, because real love is not a projection from you, but purely an unconditional love of the object. However, we can never truly know the object as we can never truly know one another.

God

Love and Fear of God

We must retain a sense of the universe's beauty and feelings of compassion and love, the creation of light, which is the love and wonder of God. Part of this is the concept of the world as guiding us to light, as opposed to the Buddhist concept of the clear light of the void. Are both of these true? Do your thoughts about which is reality reflect what's in your heart? Or is acceptance of both the right path? Can we reconcile these opposites, and be at peace?

As for fear of God, this is the "cold indifferent universe concept," which is the opposite of love's acceptance. It is the "hunter and prey" concept of the world and of the void. We need to retain our sense of awe, including the awesome power of the universe to crush us, to make us little, like ants, but turning away from the Western idea of "who cares if you kill a bug," and toward the Buddhist concept of protecting bugs, protecting the sanctity of all life.

Nature as the Language of God

Srinivasa Ramanujan, from the film "The Man Who Knew Infinity," said that an equation had no meaning for him unless it expressed a thought of God.

In the movie, his professor, G.H. Hardy, surmises that perhaps Ramanujan is right, since after all, "We are merely explorers of infinity... We do not invent these formulae; they already exist and lie in wait for only the very brightest of minds, like Ramanujan, ever to divine and prove." (*The Man Who Knew Infinity*, (2015) [Film]. Directed by Matt Brown, Warner Bros. (dist.))

I love this thought, that nature all around us is the language of God or, if you're an atheist like Professor Hardy, the language of the universe, speaking to us, perhaps guiding us, by means of any modality our mind is attuned to perceive, be it sound, music, language, or natural phenomena, Wordsworth's "babbling brook" (William Wordsworth, "Descriptive Sketches"), or Shakespeare's "tongues in trees, books in the running brooks, sermons in stones," (William Shakespeare, "As You Like It," Act II, Scene 1), or just in experience itself (which is communion of mind and world, ego and God).

On an interesting note, Ramanujan's ideas are now being used to explain the behavior of black holes, perhaps the most divine of all phenomena, wherein exists a singularity in which all laws, formulae, and equations, every sound or note of music, every experience and moment, as well as all of time, collapses to a single point.

Gifts of God

Your talent is God's gift to you; what you do with it is your gift back to God (which is everything, meaning all the people around you and nature and the world we are in and the reality we are in). Even if we're just a drop in the ocean, then it is also true, as the poet Jalaluddin Rumi reportedly said, "You are the entire ocean in a drop." This has significance to what you do, how that ocean ripples, because scales differ. On one scale you're just a drop in the ocean, by another scale you play a major role in the life of, for example, your child or spouse or community.

Father, Son, Holy Ghost equates to Body (the Son), Spirit/Oneness (the Father), and Mind ... the Holy Ghost. The communion of these.

As the sun passes behind the clouds, so the great eye blinks at you. It's those moments of clarity, that moment when God appears, in touch with you briefly before you return to the humdrum.

God is always talking to us; we just need to find a modality to hear him, a frequency to turn into, some way to connect to "It"—which is really a way to connect to the rest of ourselves, as we are already connected, as a tree has roots in the ground or a wave is part of the ocean. So really God is in us, speaking through us, and speaking to us—we are just another mode of God's being, the separation is an illusion, like the mind/body problem.

God is waiting for us. Because he knows will come to him eventually. But God has left us messages, calling to us silently. Waiting for us to pay attention to the events of our lives and sermons in the stones. We're being called to let go and let the path be revealed on its own, by not seeking or imposing our will or trying to control things. To let go of our ego by losing things and by death. To accept reality rather than exhibiting children's magical thinking.

Just appreciate being alive for a moment! Just be grateful to be here and experience this.

Desire

The infinite fire of desire.

Desire is insatiable by nature, by definition. If you feed a log into the fire, the fire only grows stronger. In this way desire is never-ending, because it is a fire that only gets hotter and hotter the more fuel you give it. The only way to let the fire of burning desire die down is to stop feeding it.

Consider Tolkien and the one ring and what Gandalf said of Gollum in *The Fellowship of the Ring*, that Gollum hated and loved the ring, as he hated and loved himself. Does the ring represent man's insatiable desire? Desire for anything, for pleasure in general, for anything at all, just a generic "object of desire?" In the fellowship, each person had his own intention for using the ring, but in the end, everyone (save Frodo and Sam) had a desire that could not have been resisted.

By definition, desire is never satisfied. If you step back and look at things from a macro-temporal context (i.e., on larger time scales, ultimately an infinite one), then the desire repeats itself instantaneously, even as one is experiencing the object that one craves, one is still desiring that object. Thus, if one's goal in doing so is to satisfy one's desire, there is no reason to seek the objects of one's desire. Furthermore, should one attain the object of one's desire, the unsatisfying satisfaction one experiences only accelerates the process, making life like a rampant fire.

On the other hand, if one realizes that one is burning, this facilitates coping with the pain fire inflicts. One can tell oneself that it is only a dream. Burning without all the pain of burning is a poet's way of life, as Emerson or Whitman might think of it. With proper balance, it is the bodhisattva's way of life as well, both free of samsara and participating in it.

Depression

Ships don't sink because of the water around them. They sink because the water gets inside them.

Don't let what's around you get inside you and bring you down.

Depression is like being stuck at the bottom of the hole. You're aware that the world up above is better, and you can see the sunlight of it. You can see that you could theoretically be up there, yet you see no way out because you're at the bottom of a hole.

So when people tell you to come up and play, exercise, put a smile on your face, enjoy the sunshine, just get out of there or just snap out of it, they don't get that you can't get out of there—for you there is no way out of there.

At the very least, they need to lower you a rope. But you're so weak from living in this hole, that you can't climb the rope. And they leave it there for you to climb, like "Whenever you're ready to come out, just come on out," but they don't get that you can't come out— you're not strong enough.

So they really need to come up with a plan, throw you a harness, have you tie that rope around yourself and get a group of people to pull you the hell out.

Nietzsche was right: the abyss gazes back.

Argument for the Immortality of the Soul

Sometimes something spins you so hard for so long that it changes your world down through the very core, till there's nothing left of what you used to be. It makes you wonder what you were thinking, and it makes you wonder how many lives have passed without a trace.

It doesn't just end what you are, or cut your future off, it shakes you back past time and changes who you were.... It's not that the past changes, just that you forgot. It makes me think of the life before this; it makes me think that I'm so weak that it is inevitable that I will remain without definition ... nothing and no one ... that who I am will always be shaken out of me. But then I remember the bottom, the pits of my stomach when everything goes quiet, and I remember the times I almost died, but didn't, and I think that my memory must stay with me, just completely diffused within the indefinite mass of myself, that twisted this way and that, I am inevitable, I am.

Rebirth fast rearranges you and hacks at the root that survived of past lives deep inside.

The Sage

The concept of the Sage appears throughout the history of philosophy and represents the mythical, legendary status of only the greatest masters. Examples include Lao Tzu, the Buddha, Socrates, Jesus, Bodhidharma, and others. These are teachers who have no definite written work attributable to them—a concept almost lost in the digital age.

It is almost as if they are too mythical to be real, almost as if they are metaphors, the embodiments of an ideal, "as if" fictions. One could question, for example, whether Socrates even existed, or whether he was simply the written invention of Plato and the philosopher Xenophon, who were both his students. (Socrates is also briefly mentioned in one of the plays of Aristophanes.) But chiefly he exists in Plato as a portrayal of the "ideal" philosopher, a man unimpeachable in his integrity, because little is known of his life except for the seeming martyrdom of his death. It is almost as though he appears out of the Ether to provide Plato with perfect guidance. He is unimpeachable in his integrity, ethics and lifestyle, because he does not really live, but is also unimpeachable in his thoughts, philosophy, and questions. Socrates never posits an argument. He only asks questions (although he does indirectly assert that having no view is the correct view, having a positive position is the correct position, a viewpoint similar to, for example, Bodhidharma, also on the sage list for teaching exclusively from within a cave). With the Sage, the message must just be heard and received. This is the power of the Sage.

The Sage is the perfect philosopher. He tears down our views, shows us that everything we thought we knew is wrong, turns us into philosophers, makes us start our intellectual and spiritual journey, or our epistemological and metaphysical journey, over from scratch. He makes us search for the truth, reality, man's nature, and the Self. Then he sort of dusts off his hands, stands up, and says, "My work is done, time to return to my wandering, to moseying down this path," which is presumably an aim-less wandering with no origin or destination, whose purpose is only the journey through a formless Ether where earth and sky, heaven and earth, worldly and celestial blur together and interweave such that who knows whether our Sage is man or an immortal force of the universe? Perhaps he has manifested at different times as Lao Tzu, as Socrates, as Buddha or Bodhidharma, or as Jesus.

The only thing that I am certain of about the Sage is that we should all have one, to represent our higher self, to appear in tough moments and ask us the difficult but resoundingly true question that hits at the center of us and rings true, that shocks our heart like a defibrillator and strikes our mind like a resounding gong.

Perhaps the Sage whispers that one piece of wisdom, "Let it be," that brings it all into focus, the one word we could not hear had it come from ourselves, which our tiny self could not think to say, but our higher self can.

Perhaps this is what God, or Jesus, or the prophets are to all men, though perhaps the masses are not creative enough or wise enough or in touch with themselves enough, or perhaps they fail to spend sufficient time examining their concept of God, Truth, or Self to create their own, so they just use whichever pre-fab model of Sage best clicks with them or their culture—the local church, perhaps, or even the body? Or perhaps the faithless person—one in despair or one who has been disillusioned by the bullshit of culture and for whom "God has died," but for whom the journey toward a new model has not yet begun—finds that the Void is the best sage for him at this time, although I hope he doesn't die with only a Void to comfort him.

I only know that we should create our Sage and stay in touch with him regularly, in writing, in thought, and in life's decisions.

The Mind Space and Winnicott's "Play Space"

In the case of a child's viewpoint, there is no way to clearly discern whether children are "taken in" by a book, or whether they can clearly distinguish fact from fiction, without relying on primary research. Winnicott's research suggests that children, at least during the earliest phases of development, cannot distinguish "…between fantasy and fact, between inner objects and external objects, between primary creativity and perception." (D.W. Winnicott, *Playing and Reality*, 6) According to Winnicott's analysis, based on his study of infants and children, what he terms as the "transitional object" plays a major role in the infant's growing ability to discern inner psychic reality and the external world. The transitional object serves as a medium that is both an inner object and an external one; it is an intermediary between a stage in which babies still feel they are inseparable from their mother and the stage when they can come into the first possession of object, meaning that they recognize an object as external and, in some way, claim ownership of it. The infant is given the illusion from birth, as a result of a mother's careful attention or adaptation, that objects are under his magical control, because he knows them as part of himself—they are internal mental representations, though based on the external world. According to Winnicott, the job of the mother is to slowly disillusion infants and allow them to rely on a transitional object, to let them go through the process of reality testing and reality acceptance on their own.

According to Winnicott, reality is never fully accepted, as it were, "… no human being is free from the strain of relating inner and outer reality, and … relief from this strain is provided by an intermediate area of experience…. This intermediate area is in direct continuity with the play area of the small child who is 'lost' in play." (D.W. Winnicott, *Playing and Reality*, 13) If this is true, what implications does it hold for the child's ability to be equally "lost" in a picture book? Furthermore, what does it say about the adult's ability to be similarly enveloped in fantasy?

And just as mind can imagine anything (in the "play space" or "transitional space," as Winnicott might say), so I could become anything by thought. I could be a unicorn, a star, a galaxy. My mind could fill any space and become any shape.

The mind space is the vast space that's clear light and that can produce infinite imaginations and dreams, much like Winnicott's "play space." For there is no limit to the forms we can imagine; the only limitations are the methods of transmission: language, visual art, musical space, etc. But the dream vision itself cannot be captured fully in words, art, or representations—but only by the experience itself, which can be shared when two minds are close and connected enough, just as tree roots communicate, or birds form patterns in flight, echelons and murmurations, or when human partners finish each other's sentences.

This is the middle ground—the heat point, or, to evoke D.W. Winnicott, the "play" point.

Truth

The Two Truths

Some people say the truth is singular, but in a way, it is not.

I may see things from a different angle, or with different capacities, such as perspectivism, the theory that knowledge of a subject is inevitably partial and limited by the individual perspective from which it is viewed. Another example of relative truth is the "apple in a box," which suggests that if an apple were to be left untouched in a box for billions of years, its fundamental particles would theoretically traverse every possible state, eventually leading the apple to return to its original state.

Still, some people claim that if there is an objective truth, then all subjective versions of it are falsehoods. And yet, they are true in another sense, subjectively.

So the truth has versions *and* is singular. *And* those versions are in a sense false, but in another sense true. This is the Buddhist notion of the Two Truths, the objective/ultimate truth and the many subjective truths. I dislike the word "objective," because it is not true from certain subjective perspectives. The ultimate truth must contain all subjective truths and the objective truth. It is non-dual truth, which includes all.

If non-dual truth is our ultimate truth, then we no longer need the notion of the two truths, because they are both included in the one ultimate truth.

It's just that this ultimate truth is a paradox beyond human reason, and so we must maintain a binary explanation that can only allude to...THE ONE.

Relative and Absolute Truth

Ultimate Truth, the sum truth of all things, is presently well beyond our comprehension and is probably beyond the potential for human understanding. A human being experiences life in an isolated consciousness, in a certain space and time, and therefore experiences only a small of part of the Ultimate Reality. As individuals, we cannot go beyond our own subjective reality to experience the whole Truth; the realm of the real we can accurately deal with is limited to our immediate perception. We can, however, experience truth in our world from our own relative viewpoint, make statements about our experience and our perception that are true, and relate those statements to others. We each know certain truths about the universe, because our reality is clearly real to us and is therefore a part of the Ultimate Reality, just as we are. The Truth may be absolute, but it can only exist to us or be conceived of relatively, meaning that our perception and experience of truth is relative and constantly changing, while the ideal, the Truth itself, remains the unchanging and absolute sum of all truths. Each individual's experience is one of many realities that have existed across time and space, all of which are a part of the Ultimate Reality.

A human life is a subjective experience; it is an experience only within our own mind. This isolation makes it impossible for us to go beyond our own reality, which makes it impossible to determine any truths that are not part of our experience. This also means that any truths we determine about our subjective reality are absolute for us. They cannot be disputed, because each individual's state of perception is completely unique. When one believes that there is a pen on the table because that's what one's senses perceive, then it is true that in that person's own reality, there is a pen on the table. But there is no way of knowing any truths about a reality that is not one's own.

Imagine the perspective of someone who, from birth, has been living inside a virtual reality machine capable of completely recreating a human experience electrically in the brain. Such a person would not be able to know any reality outside of their own reality; they would live and die in their own mind. All the experiences they had and all the people they met would seem completely real, and they would never know the difference between their own conception of the real and the conceptions of other people. They might say that there is a pen on the table in front of them when in fact there is neither a table nor a pen, but just a set of goggles. Does this make the life of this person less real than the life of the scientist who first put the goggles on a baby? Each person's experience is equally real and true, but it is impossible to truly know another's experience, just as it is impossible to know the reality of a person attached to a virtual reality machine.

Through language and communication, humans have learned to compare their relative realities to one other and to begin to derive a common reality that seems to make simple things basically true. Isolation makes it impossible for us to definitively know another's experience or to step out of our own experience.

What then does this mean in terms of our quest to determine truth? First of all, it means that there are a great many truths that we can determine absolutely for ourselves, but that all those truths are limited to the realm of our own perspective. Within that realm, however, we can choose to accept any truth we would like to. This means that, if we choose to accept certain assumptions as true because they seem overwhelmingly real to us, then those assumptions become working truths in our world.

It seems only reasonable that anyone who has any desire to actually participate in reality would readily accept that other human beings exist, that each human has a specific perspective, that we participate in a common reality, and that use of a common language has shown itself to be a fairly accurate way of communicating. Though none of these assumptions can be proven, they can all be adopted as common truths, and they can become functional truths within the workings of our minds and the way in which we live our lives. Since we can choose to believe anything, we can choose to make anything in our reality an absolute truth of that reality, provided that we understand that it is still within our own personal reality, whether we like it or not.

Technically, it is impossible to see from another's perspective, but nevertheless, in my subjective reality, there are people who appear to have their own subjective reality, and, regardless of whether they are figments or illusions of some kind, I find that by talking to them and trying to view the world from their perspective, I can grow and learn to see my reality in a new way, though that way is not entirely from another person's perspective, but rather is a new addition to my own perspective. Therefore, I choose to include my subjective reality in this network of realities, using my imagination to conceive of new perspectives and ideas and allowing this network to stimulate my imagination, helping my consciousness and perspective to expand. This creates an enormous amount of potential, because it essentially does allow us to redefine our own absolute experience of reality, at least relatively.

By the standards of anyone involved in a community, the development of a communal reality is a very reasonable way to determine the place of our subjective reality within the Ultimate Reality. Communal realities are based on the relation of one reality to another. To create a network of relative comparisons is to create a reality by using this network as a forum to modify our own subjective reality and allow us to grow together. We use this forum to combine each other's perspectives and learn more about Ultimate Reality by looking at it from more than one relative perspective. Clearly, we cannot know anything about our place in external reality by looking only from an internal point of view, meaning that we cannot see ourselves or our place in reality by looking through our own eyes (even if our external reality is actually inside our mind, which is a point irrelevant to our daily life). By sharing one another's perspectives in a community, we are able to use other human beings and our surroundings as a sort of mirror or relative standard of measurement, allowing us to see our place in the world and to see ourselves in a new way. Furthermore, by using the external world as a mirror and allowing the external world to use us as a mirror, we can learn to integrate our relative perspectives and develop a common understanding of reality or a communal truth. This type of truth is based on subjective truths, but it only includes truths which are agreed upon by all members of that community.

What have we made basically true? Across what domains does communal truth range, and how do communal truths have to relate to the common reality in order to be true? What's true in our minds is true regardless of whether it corresponds to reality, simply because it is still true in our minds, though generally, truths in our minds are based on reality and therefore correspond to it. If a community of people sitting around a table all sincerely believe there is no table there, then there is some real explanation for that which involves their perceptions or some other variable. Perhaps they have lost all their senses, or there is some other strange circumstance. Regardless, in that communal reality there is no table, because none of them believe there is a table there. If someone who does believe there is a table is introduced to the community, then he is not part of that communal truth. His truth is part of the community, probably the majority, which thinks there is a table. Is either more true than the other? No, but one is more widely accepted as true, and therefore will be more commonly employed in functional reality or day-to-day life, which is ultimately all that matters in communal truth since we have already moved beyond absolute subjective truths into the realm of realistic truths, meaning truths that seem to simply be true of our common accepted reality. For instance, a community may find that a certain catapult can launch a projectile q distance, where q is determined by an equation that this community has derived by studying the force of the catapult. Technically speaking, there is no way to prove that there actually is a catapult or other people, yet that would not help crush an enemy's catapult that is about to crush me. It is only reasonable to accept that our reality is real to us and therefore can be studied empirically. The formula for the catapult is a realistic truth or a practical truth based on a simple assumption about our reality, and the community which derived the formula found it to be realistically true. Realistic truths can be determined by community agreement, whether on a practical level or even an artistic level, though almost always truths of a practical nature are accepted widely, while artistic truths are generally agreed upon in smaller subsets of the larger community. Regardless, any realistic type of truth, or truth that has to do with day-to-day life, is relative to the community's perspective (or the individual's perspective if there is only one member who believes it) and can only be determined with a certain degree of common sense, faith, deliberation, discussion, and the study of our reality. The people who think there is no table may accept that there is a table by putting faith in someone they believe is more qualified to judge the question of tableness, just as we put faith in experts. Common sense is most important, however, because for a community to all come to a common agreement, everyone must choose to be reasonable in working with each other, learning to concede certain things as true that are only apparent to other people, and generally trying to use our best judgment to determine truths about our common reality as best we can, because, despite the many extreme, far-fetched philosophical examples, most of us find that our realities are fairly similar.

Is there a truth outside our own perspective? Clearly, one cannot learn anything about the external aspects of one's experience, even if they are actually inside one's mind, without having some form of relative comparison, meaning that external aspects must be verified. Such a comparison is an excellent forum for learning and discussion and is probably the most accurate way of learning.

This does not mean, however, that we are capable of changing reality. We are only capable of changing the way we *perceive* reality. Furthermore, most people are only capable of changing their perception of reality sincerely, meaning only if there is a real reason that arises which leads them to change their views.

We are all trapped inside our own subjective experience, and therefore the experience is only real and true to the one living it. Multiple subjective realities yield multiple and sometimes contradictory truths that can all be relatively true. But absolute truth is ultimate reality, *if* we can discover it.

Monologue of a Man Trapped in His Own Reality

The sky is still up.

The mainland is still there; the islands are always just mirages, and I'm still flailing. I'm caged in myself, and so are others, who are actually part of me, too.

I am very tired. I am very tired of the cell I'm in. I'm very tired of its walls, although its inside is beautiful and amazing. Its bricks are transparent, and I can see through them, but they blur the other side. I don't know *what* it is I see through them; I can't know. The walls made sure of that, for if I knew the outside ... then the walls would be traversable, too. They would not only be transparent, but completely non-existent. Instead, they are clinging to their purpose, as I would, had I been allowed to find mine.

If I stare at the bricks long enough, I can begin to make out images on the outside. It's so beautiful. I'm overwhelmed. I feel free, I know. But soon it is just brick again. And I can't remember exactly how I made that image in the bricks ... which dots to connect? Slowly, I begin to redraw it in my mind.

I live for these moments, but in the end, it's always brick, and the image always fades. Sometimes, the flowers inside are so much more beautiful; sometimes, they're too cheap.

Either way, I have been here so long that the flowers always distract me. The wall is always brick, I don't see images anymore, and then I distract the flowers.

I have been here so long that I am becoming brick myself; I am taking my place, reinforcing the wall, blocking up my hole through it, just so I can touch the outside with part of myself. Slowly, I am solidifying. I still can see the other side, but eventually, my eyes will be enveloped in stone....

I'm in love with the outside, where the others reside.

If something is not blurred it becomes futile! I'm tired of the walls, but sometimes they're more beautiful than anything I could ever see.

I'm in search of the Tabula Rasa, the clean slate where I have no preconceived ideas or predetermined goals.

There are moments of truth, and I try to understand.

If "the sky is still up," then it is the man's own beliefs that restrain him, while the wall is made of his projections and other's beliefs. The others are perhaps actually part of his projection, his voices of reason.

Why do we believe what we believe? Those moments of truth and delusion give us blurred ideals and hopeful beliefs. The wall, representing others and collective reality, gives us concrete beliefs, reality, and, at times, beliefs that turn out to be futile. The question is: Will we know the difference between the brick wall and the outside, if we do ever see the outside? Because the concrete beliefs are so intimidating that they seem stronger. It is a question of faith against temptation, where faith is good and temptation is evil.

Then, too, at times we experience an overwhelming moment of understanding that for some reason is not enough. It is not satisfying, not the real end, because it is but a cognitive truth. Actual truth is conveyed by emotion, because emotions ring true. Still, the emotional moment of truth is not enough for me, because it always goes away. I want to be aware of it consciously, so I can repeat it.

Free Will

The Illusion of Free Will

The illusion of free will is enough to satisfy me. Moreover, I do not even cling to this illusion. I find great comfort in the idea that the universe is deterministic. This would mean that we are just like flowing water, and our only responsibility is to fulfill our role in nature, which we will inevitably do. All we know is the illusion of free will, and so it seems irrelevant whether the human will is truly free. We still believe in choice and must make choices about our lives every day. I do not even know what a "truly free will" is, exactly. The question of true freedom is a slightly different question, the answer to which will be personal.

I try not to identify myself with the individual that I call myself. I would prefer to think of myself as a part of a whole. The question of our place in this whole is what I think motivates humans in the pursuits of philosophy, religion, and similar studies. I would prefer not to identify the ideal of freedom with my own will, but with some sort of cosmic order. In other words, my choice will play a role in the whole universe. As part of this whole, the choice is not "mine" (regardless of whether my choices are predetermined), because "I" am a giant universe. Walt Whitman described himself as "a kosmos." (Walt Whitman, *Song of Myself* XXIV, line 1) Freedom belongs to nature and all natural things. The "will" is that of a collective force.

I prefer to think of freedom as water flowing or a growing vine. The vine is free to grow in the way it will, but the direction the vine will grow is adaptive. The vine grows into the places that most naturally suit its growth. In this manner, the vine grows by going with the flow. It grows in accordance with its environment and its nature. I like to think of true freedom as the freedom for all things to be as they are, for the natural order to unfold.

Freedom, in my sense, is not so much about choice or will, but about a human's psychological state. Each thing has the freedom to be as it is. Humans also have self-awareness and the illusion of will, which allows them to recognize their situation and to be either comfortable or uncomfortable filling their place in the world.

In terms of the free will debate, freedom usually means the ability to exercise free will and make choices independently of any external determining force. (G. Ronald, "Freedom" in *The Encyclopaedia of Philosophy*, 222) Here are some alternative definitions that better fit my use of the word:

- the ability to speak or act without restriction, interference, or fear;
- the state of being unaffected by, or not subject to, something unpleasant or unwanted;
- the right to use or occupy a place and treat it as your own;
- openness and friendliness in speech or behavior.

I like these definitions better because they omit the "external determining force." I prefer to think of freedom as a psychological state where one can be open, naturally, and freely be oneself and "speak without restriction or fear." Whether humans have free will, as I am defining it, would not be an either/or question about whether reality functions mechanically, but a question of how the person views reality.

Free will would be the ability to align the individual will with the natural will, to free oneself of psychological fixations of the will, to see beyond mental limitations and work constructively with any element of experience that is perceived as a restriction, to free oneself of the feeling of being limited to one's place in nature and see one's role in nature as freely being oneself, to be in touch with the natural way and one's own nature, to "use a space and treat it as your own," to be as you are without feeling restricted by some dominating external force or controlling psychological phantom, to see the world in the mind as a play-pen rather than a prison.

Heisenberg and Free Will

What are the implications of Heisenberg's uncertainty principle regarding free will? In one sense, it can be said that Heisenberg's discoveries disprove determinism. While the ramifications of the uncertainty principle are the purview of science, it seems to me that it can only prove that we will never *know* that there is a deterministic universe. That is, it effectively disproves the nightmare case of *extreme* determinism, but does not decisively disprove determinism. Although determinism may be rendered moot if we could never know whether it is true, it seems to me that it still could be correct.

As I understand it, the uncertainty principle shows that we cannot know with certainty both the position of a particle and its momentum. That may be true, but how can we know that there is not a "grand plan" that knows both position and momentum simultaneously? How do we know that the randomness is not actually part of a complex design that does not follow the kinds of rules used in modern physics? It is possible that this design may not be organized by systematic laws and may even be the creator of the laws. It still seems possible to me that everything we see and think could be the arbitrary choice of some great force we do not fully understand.

Subatomic particles appear to be the epitome of free will, but those particles generally seem to act a certain way. Are we just like bright halogens, very reactive, hungering instinctively and predictably for an extra electron to make us complete ... only then to become inert, like positive and negative ions, attracting and repelling, balancing each other with our disposition, maybe just diffusing until we find a bit of equilibrium?

How can we ever know the consequence of what we do? We definitely have a will of our own, and often the only thing that seems real to us is our present perception, but it only perpetuates the chaos and confusion—our desire for fusion.

I've always struggled desperately to be on my own, to have a will of my own, to understand consequence and hold myself responsible for only that, myself.

Odds and Ends

Beauty

There's a day in the life of every young heart when we see something that suddenly strikes us, something so beautiful that it bewilders us before something greater, and from that day for the rest of our lives there is a part of us that understands the essence of living and the beauty of earth. Whether we lose touch with that, or choose to deny that it cut through our withered armor the way light shines through a shadow, is another matter.

Connection

We all float around in so many tiny bubbles, and sometimes we connect like a Venn diagram, and sometimes we merge in the water as if into a bathtub, and we merge into one. So true connection is when two people lose themselves in the shared space, the "play area," the space that permeates all, that brings two individual minds into communion.

We need to connect with this mindset over the whole of humanity, and view the world as a transcendental space.

Consciousness

Where did life first form? Humans are like waves of the ocean, emerging and evolving from fish. But consciousness was always around them. Take, for example, Japanese author Masaru Emoto, who exposed water to either positive or negative language, on the one hand, or harmonious or dissonant music on the other, then froze the water and examined the resulting ice crystals. He found that positive words and music produced ordered, symmetrical, and beautiful crystals, while discordant music and negative language led to incongruous and disordered forms, suggesting that water itself possesses some form of awareness. (Masaru Emoto, *The Hidden Messages in Water*) It's a reductionistic, obtuse view to think that only the effect of your actions on the world and not your conscious experience matters.

So, what is the inherent voice of yourself? What is that feeling, that whisper that guides you if you tune into it? Can that voice come from nowhere, or does it evolve? If it arises from other traits like memory and improvisation, is it a voice of your own, or a voice of conditioning, the environment, and evolution?

Is that whisper in your center the whisper of silence? Of the universe? In silence, your own thoughts surface and become amplified, reflecting who you really are and what you really think. But what is that silence itself? A space for things to appear? A space-time moment that is filled with you, your consciousness? Or is it the movie theater for Ken Wilber's "witness"?

> [Y]our personal mind-and-body may be in pain, or humiliation, or fear, but as long as you abide as the witness of these affairs, as if from on high, they no longer threaten you, and thus you are no longer moved to manipulate them, wrestle with them, or subdue them. Because you are willing to witness them, to look at them impartially, you are able to transcend them. (Ken Wilber, *No Boundary: Eastern and Western Approaches to Personal Growth*, 128)

A philosopher's art form is the conscious experience. You must examine all aspects of consciousness. Consider the diet of the mind, and the idea that the grass that is watered grows. Alex Grey says:

> We are all artists of consciousness creating our "pictures" of reality. Neuroscientists concur, every bit of what we experience is a figment of our imagination. Authorship of the story of our lives is in our hearts, minds and hands. So, how will we most positively and powerfully interpret the circumstances of this moment to best inform and guide the precious life we have ahead? With the raw material of past experience, in the mental factory of our thoughts, our future is sculpted with the "chisel" of our worldview. To create the most evolutionary thoughts and ideas, the Craftsman-of-our-Being accepts mentorship from the divine imagination, source of beauty, truth and goodness.
>
> (Alex Grey, https://www.facebook.com/AlexGreyCoSM/posts/we-are-all-artists-of-consciousness-creating-our-pictures-of-reality-neuroscient/10157982294756086//)

Bring yourself every day to the altar of experience.

Certainty

Certainty is the most precarious and fallible of states, while faith, developing comfort with uncertainty, is the most stable and reliable one. We need to bring back the wonder of older times, the magic of possibility. Nihilism and science killed God, magic, and spirit, but fear and the idea that we're all alone is a motivation for belief in God.

What is one minute of your life like? Being present is awesome, as in filled with awe. Just be present. The cure for fear of death is transformation. Transforming is dying, over and over, moment by moment.

See yourself in the world and the world as part of our group, one of us. What are we to the world? Perhaps to the world we're a plant, or some other growth. We're using the abilities we have to try to find a way to intimately relate to the world, to God, as we would our most intimate companions, our fellow humans.

We are all part of one thing with many facets. Everything is interrelated so intimately and inextricably that to think otherwise is simply ignorance. Yet everything is different, and this truth must also be respected but not over-emphasized. There is a world, an infinity, in anything.

The Pattern of Nature

There's this pattern of joining into one and splitting into many that repeats itself in all the world: the way that streams trickle into creeks, then into rivers, then into oceans, which evaporate mist to form rain that collects in streams again. The way that branches of a tree split from the trunk into the twigs and then to seeds and leaves, just as each leaf has veins that stem from a central vein, while the seeds fall to make the trunks of more trees. The circulatory system of the body, the feet of a snowflake, the arms of a galaxy, its stars growing sparser and sparser, fading and merging into darkness, all from a central cluster of light with a black hole at its center. The pattern splits into many from a central source and returns to that source again, in a repetition of gradual dissolution and reforming. What is the meaning of this pattern in which we exist? What are we to understand from going through this process over and over? And what should we do? Remain still at the center, rise like mist, fall and pour down like the rain, rage like the river. Wave like the ocean in a storm or remain in its darkest depths, amongst the rocks, shifting over eons? Flap our arms with life or wait with the patience of the dead? What can we do but feel the pull of the pattern, be with it, go with it calmly, with faith enough to remain peaceful, knowing exactly where we are, where we have been, and where we shall go. We must realize that these are places where we have always been and have never left, but only sometimes forgotten for a while. Marcus Aurelius said, "Everything we do now, echoes in eternity."

Negativity

Fear is in anticipation of things that have not yet happened, and hence an unnecessary form of suffering. Guilt is beating up on yourself over things that have already happened that cannot be changed, and hence a useless and unnecessary form of suffering. And shame is at its root a form of ego, an absorption in the self, which is fundamentally an illusion that we've allowed to be amplified and solidified by this negative emotion.

The Void

> Life's but a walking shadow, a poor player,
> That struts and frets his hour upon the stage,
> And then is heard no more. It is a tale
> Told by an idiot, full of sound and fury,
> Signifying nothing.
> (William Shakespeare, *Macbeth*, Act 5, Scene 5)

Yes, but "signifying nothing" is not bleak; it is perfect. It is the creative power of the void. The void provides absolute potential for anything to happen, like Winnicott's "mindspace of imagination." The void allows for the clear light to manifest in infinite ways, like Shakespeare writing plays, for example. We can make them about whatever we want and make them mean whatever we want…so they signify something, they stand for all that intense love and sound and fury, even though in time, as with all things, they pass… because all is impermanent, after all, but each moment is eternal also, because each eternal moment is part of the same continuum, like William Blake's finding "Eternity in an hour." (William Blake, "Auguries of Innocence," in *William Blake: Poems*, 37) The void is emptiness with space for everything that will ever be. Even Stephen Hawking recognized that, "The universe can spontaneously create itself out of nothing." (Stephen Hawking, "Questioning the Universe," February, 2008, TED Talk)

Ken Wilber on Emptiness

Having established that, according to Buddhism, all is emptiness, that all phenomena are non-existent and impermanent, and that the only real thing is permanent emptiness, we must ask: if all phenomena are illusions rooted in emptiness and do not exist at all, how does one explain the apparent existence of the phenomenal world?

In Buddhist thought, it is given that the phenomenal world does not actually exist; it is emptiness. However, this world, though it may be an illusion, still is visible and is very real to me. Though I may be an illusion, I am an illusion in which I believe. I still bleed when I am cut and will still die if I don't eat. In other words, while the phenomenal world may not exist, we still participate in existence according to its physical laws and material properties, which do exist, at the very least, in our minds. Regardless of true nature, we are still conscious of our own existence and our experience of a reality. Our existence, though it may ultimately be an impermanent and empty illusion, still must exist in some capacity. I know this because it exists to me.

Ken Wilber and Alex Grey have expressed their views regarding this question. According to Wilber, that which we call the universe came into existence in an event similar to the Big Bang. In his view, the existence of emptiness, of total nothingness, can only be balanced by the existence of infinite potential. His theory says that from emptiness came an explosion of infinite spiritual light, which is the life force and spirit animating all things. This light is the energy of illusion, energy of a potential nature, much like the age-old concept of the Tao. All things which apparently exist in the phenomenal world are not solid matter, but instead are a vibratory field of energy. This energy is not actually formed into objects or people but is one unified dimension of light, with infinite potential to create the illusions of many worlds and individuals across time.

This infinite potential is the balance of emptiness, but is still rooted in, comes from, and returns to emptiness. It is empty itself, but by being empty, has the potential in it for infinite possibilities.

IMMERSION

THE KETAMINE
SESSIONS

The Ketamine Sessions

Ketamine Session 1

My appointment began with the doctor asking me to pull three cards from a deck of "Soul's Journey" cards. I picked one soul's journey card from the middle of the deck, and I ended up drawing what is certainly my downfall: "Indecision—I use my intuition in all aspects of life." Then I took one card from the top, "Freedom—I possess the power and the free will to create my own happiness" and one card from the bottom, "Worry—I am learning that worry doesn't change an outcome." (James Van Praagh, *The Soul's Journey Lesson Cards: A 44-Card Deck and Guidebook*, 2014)

Then I laid on the couch in the office and treatment began. In this session, I immediately went to the clear blue light of the void place, the mind theater. But as it always does, the left hand that I injured some months ago crept in like a skeleton's claw coming up from the ground to pull me back under.

The trip was voyeuristic in that I got perspective on seeing myself bathing in the clear blue light, the fountain. Then I saw myself in the black and yellow ground, like death. My left hand took me there. I also had an "overview" effect like astronauts do, of the two ways I could go. Turn left or right, but do so decisively, no more indecision and in between. No more limbo.

It's amazing how the archetype cards in the doctor's office perfectly connected to where I was at: e.g., indecision, freedom, worry. It makes me wonder. Is synchronicity the universe sending us messages, or just our minds making meaning of the world? Again, this is a false dichotomy, like free will and determinism (which is a problem created by dualists, setting up impossible dualities and then trying to resolve them by separating two things that are one, just like outer and inner, the mind-body problem, and so on). The mind has to be tuned in to see and hear the whispers from the universe in the silence, e.g., the cards you drew. But there was another synchronicity also, the music in the car—the way I was driving and wanted Holocene to come on my playlist, so I turned on my music, and out of 350 songs, it did!! Just a reminder that your mind can manifest your reality.

Ketamine Session 2

In this session, I went to a deep place, Kairos, timeless time, time stilled, nonlinear, a single moment that has ripened into a moment for changing the course of our lives. Kairos shone the healing light deep inside, and I finally acknowledged that out loud: I have to accept what's happened; but it's okay from the perspective of Kairos time, eternal time. I need to accept it and move on, that I am wounded but can become the healer, the same way the eternal light was making me feel healed and okay in that moment. That this is my hand and I need to start using it, put it to work doing good things in this life with this frail body before it all withers like my hand, which is just a preview of frailty and death. But this stuff started to sink down deep into me, like I said: "This medicine reaches inside and changes you." It made me feel my wounds, healed them for a moment, long enough for me to feel what it is to feel healing power, and that made me want to share that healing power with the world, to wake people up, having received the gift of understanding how Chronos, chronological time, wounds matter only a little when viewed in the healing light of Kairos, and it showed me I have the power within me to see this.

You told yourself said that studying philosophy in college at Hampshire was like a peak where you could see the valley of your life that you had to walk through. Well, this is what it is to be in the valley forest, lost, unaware, unconscious of your overall situation, of the path you are on. But you will see it again when you reach the next peak. As Bodhidharma said:

The brush of thought and consciousness paints Razor Mountains and Sword Forests, and yet it is thought and the consciousnesses that fear them. (Jeff Broughton, *The Bodhidharma Anthology*, 21)

You wondered what it was like for people to be in the shadow of delusion. Well, this has been what it is like. This year has stripped "Ryan" down to nothing. Yet something remains. What is this something? Your core self.

What is your core self? The fruitful darkness. Rumi tells us to follow our pain, saying, "The cure for pain is in the pain." ("There's Nothing Ahead," *The Rumi Collection: An Anthology of Translations by Mevlâna Jalâluddin Rumi*, Kabir Helminski (ed.), 6) Recall in your mid-20s that you wanted to intentionally explore the darkness, because you wanted to know what it was like in there so you could help others out of it. Because you had your delusion cracked open at a very young age, fourteen.

Ketamine Session 3

The Mindspace

The Seed was the archetype card I drew for this trip.

It said, "Beginnings come in many forms. They are not always a beautiful seed placed intentionally in nourishing soil.... Simply stated, the end is present in the beginning; or the entire oak tree resides within the acorn." (*The Wild Unknown Archetypes Deck and Guidebook*, Kim Krans, 2019)

I growled like I needed to be strong at start of the trip.

I entered an unfathomably deep and wide expanse, like outer space. It was in darkness but glowing with a multi-colored sheen and gloss, like the light of a dream, like the sheen the world takes when you're seeing stars from a blow to the body or when you're flooded with endorphins from a runner's high, or the sheen it takes for a moment when you wake suddenly from a dream or are hypnopompic, or when you're on a hallucinogen like this one. This space was also framed by a dark blue that transitioned to a clear blue light that gently permeated the space.

There was a definite feeling of a presence there that felt like one giant creature, but also like many angelic creatures, one and many at the same time. The giant presence felt like a giant shadow, a monster, at the end of the black tunnel that ran deep, a shadow in the darkness. It was a figure that merged with its surroundings, separate and yet unified, in the black expanse before me, and it felt as though it was staring into a bottomless pit. It was above me and overshadowed me, like it was reaching out and enveloping me (but in an okay and welcoming way). The clear light blue angel presences had dark faces, with features made of the clear blue light, and their bodies lined the edges of the tunnel, again welcoming me into the space and inviting me to move further forward into it.

I said that this was the meeting room where we all gathered to make decisions about how the universe should run.

I realized that this was a meeting of the minds. We all communicated by telepathy as though our minds met and merged, so close as to be one functioning unity, as arms move in coordination with the head, as separate voices in a choir, each voice indistinguishable from the one sound they're making, separate yet one. This being an expanse of universal mind, I began to travel by thought, moving instantly and filling space as enormous as galaxies with my mind.

I began to feel that mind could travel anywhere and be anything. I felt separate from my body and could not believe that my body was on the doctor's couch, while my mind was floating free. Then I began to ask: "What am I? I'm not sure that I'm a human being. I don't know what I am." I was just a being of consciousness, floating free.

And just as mind can imagine anything (in the "play space" or "transitional space," as Winnicott might say), so I could become anything by my thoughts, by thinking it. I could be a unicorn, a star, a galaxy. My mind could fill any space and become any shape. As GZA said, "You remain stuck trying to figure the shape of space." (GZA, "Amplified Sample," *Beneath the Surface*)

Remember that identity is a metaphor, that it is like a wave in the ocean. "Empty your mind, be formless. Shapeless, like water. If you put water into a cup, it becomes the cup. You put water into a bottle, and it becomes the bottle. You put it in a teapot, it becomes the teapot. Now, water can flow or it can crash. Be water, my friend." (Bruce Lee, in *Tao Te Ching: Power for the Peaceful*, M. Mullinax (trans.), 46)

So again I asked: "What am I? If I am a presence that can be anything, a unicorn, a star, or space itself, changing instantly, traveling, or more accurately, being anywhere, what am I?" The individual self is like a wave in the ocean, arising up and appearing from all that energy, until it crashes and returns to the ocean. The wave was just another way for water to be for a while.

This is like the classic problem of identity, transitioning moment-by-moment like Descartes's mutating candle. At what point is it no longer a candle? Was it always just wax? Or the Greek ship that gets its boards replaced one by one till none of the original boards remain, yet it still has the configuration of the same ship.

But with mind this process is instantaneous; at least it was in the place I was in. It was space beyond space, infinite, and time beyond time, eternal, such that it is simultaneously all possible things at once. (Note to self: remember that, by definition, the non-dual must include all possibilities, even that of duality.)

So again, what am I? If I'm feeling eternal, can I die? So I asked the presence to show me what death was, and the space darkened for a moment and I sank deeper into it, as though lying in bed, feeling my eyes begin to get heavy, as though I'm sinking into sleep. But after I sank for a moment, I was still in the same space of darkness and clear light. I was in a place where space and time and thought aren't the separate things they appear to be in ordinary, Chronos time.

Afterward I was thinking about the power of this experience, the way I could become anything by my thoughts, by simply thinking it, and I remembered a similar idea from an old episode of *Star Trek: The Next Generation* (season 1, episode 6, "Where No One Has Gone Before"), where the crew encounters the mysterious alien, The Traveler, who has the ability to channel thought into reality. He brings the ship millions of light years away from the Milky Way to the "Outer Rim" of the universe, where the crew also experience their thoughts as reality in much the same way I did today.

I would say this experience is just the mind altered by ketamine, but these sorts of themes have arisen through my life in many circumstances. And many others have had similar experiences (e.g., Alex Grey, "Universal Mind Lattice") which certainly could have shaped my vision, but at other times when I've encountered these themes, no outside influence could have shaped them.

For example, when I was fourteen I had an experience with hallucinogens that led me to believe in four equations or ideas, that everything (e) is really nothing (n), but that nothingness is everything, as though existing in potential, like an oak tree is within a seed. So...

$$e = n$$
$$n = e$$
$$n = n$$
$$e = e$$

Years later, in college, I took a course on Buddhism and realized that this is the central idea of the "Heart Sutra," the heart of the "Heart Sutra," as it were, which is really at the heart of Buddhism itself:

emptiness is form
form is emptiness
form is form
emptiness is emptiness

This sort of universality of experience is like an account of near-death experiences, where the vision of the white light at the end of a tunnel (often lined by loving presences in your life like grandparents and friends, etc.) is an experience that happens to many people across cultures and with no reference that would influence the vision. I even saw an interview with a small child, maybe seven years old or less, who said he traveled through the center of a giant noodle to get to a star at the end.

So I feel intuitively that this is real. How much do we understand about the mind, consciousness, and where the "What is it like?" aspect of experience is located? We can't find pictures in the brain. So where is the mind?

Also, in perception, we feel the mind's presence: "Not the wind, not the flag; mind is moving." (Ekai, *The Gateless Gate*, N. Senzaki (trans.), 29)

I feel intuitively that the gargantuan presence in the mind-space is my true face. The space is like a mirror. Mind cannot see or feel itself without a mirror, just as an eye cannot see itself. The mirror here is whatever shape is imagined from the void of empty space: a unicorn, a star, a galaxy, vast darkness. To paraphrase Walt Whitman, "There once was a boy that went forth, and whatever he saw, he became." (Walt Whitman, "There Was A Child Went Forth," in *Whitman: Poetry and Prose*, 138) The mirror is whatever sound beckons from the deep silence, and the song that serenades you is your true song.

In this space the mind meets or is confronted with itself, and intention echoes back. If yours is a song of love, you will be immersed in love, and if it is of hate, you will be confronted by hate. Shame will feel shaming, ashamed.

But I ask you, if you sink deep into silence, way down to really hear your truest song, sung from the bottom of your heart and not clouded by loud noise and unstable emotion, who among us would really sing of hate? Trust your song.

In our heart of hearts, at the root of it all, in the seed, is love, deep, deep love.

This emptiness and nothingness is the oak within the acorn, the potential to become anything, an emptiness full of infinite possibility that creates space for anything to become. In such a space, who would become evil and the cause of suffering, both others' suffering and your own? Really, those people have not cut through their insecurity, their hurt. Pain is projected on others.

What am I? What are we? Perhaps we are travelers with no particular place to go, just moved by awe and wonder, just wanting to see and experience new things. Perhaps this is why humans love traveling the globe. It's in our nature, being anywhere, being anything, and right now we are passengers, beings of light and energy that for a while are passengers within this body, on this planet. And like a wave from the ocean, we are just a way for energy to be for a while.

And this energy takes a certain configuration, like the Greek ship, our parts always fluctuating, cells replacing, body transmuting or transmutating, patterns of thought and consciousness always transforming, always transient, like a traveler on a journey, always knowing we will see this sight, feel this moment. Yet, like many journeys, we are always moving forward, but moving forward in our journey, going further. It means we are getting closer to the return home.

> I embrace my desire to feel the rhythm, to feel connected enough
> to step aside and weep like a widow, to feel inspired, to fathom the
> power, to witness the beauty, to bathe in the fountain, to swing on
> the spiral of our divinity and still be a human. - Tool

Our mind is at its core a witness, like the eye, seeing whatever arises in the mind's space, whatever appears to the mind's eye. We are that eye, sometimes feeling like it's become whatever it sees…for a while. But what is present through all the transient experiences and bodily moments is the witnessing subject in the background, its lack of self-consciousness a veil that shields it from feeling a lack of self. The witnessing subject needs to be shaped by its visions in order to know what it is at a given moment, just as I need to know what I am. So I am a traveler, here to be a witness and testify about the wondrous world, its unfathomable beauty and its horror.

Ketamine Session 4

Today I recorded an audio of my ketamine session. I had realized prior to the session that when I talk out loud on ketamine, that is one way to approach the medicine experience. Talking lets me see what words come out. They just pop into my mind without thinking, like maybe they come directly from the subconscious? It's like I'm having this experience, and I don't know what words I will say until after I hear myself say them. It is speaking without thinking first.

So I literally do not know what I'm about to say; I only know what I'm thinking after the fact, when I hear myself. (As an aside, this is super interesting from a philosophy of mind perspective. Think of this in terms of a language of thought hypothesis, where speaking is thinking.) I've realized that I'm speaking without thinking, where I don't know what I'm thinking until I hear myself say it. This is similar in a way to the idea of language learning and language of thought as I approached it in my essay on Wilfrid Sellars's work, where I discuss reacting to an object behaviorally, e.g., learning to reliably respond to a blue thing by uttering the sound "blue," such as when a child speaks the sound before it knows the meaning of the word. Here I'm doing the same thing: I'm letting the utterance come out, and that utterance tells me what is going on in my mind. I'm introspecting by speaking out loud. Rather than having a thought and then speaking it, I'm speaking and then knowing I've had the thought. In this way, I'm understanding my non-conceptual ketamine experience by just letting words come out, which is rather like free association, learning what I'm experiencing as the words come out…so I'm introspecting on my experience by letting words out. This sheds light on what the experience means to me. If I weren't narrating the experience, I wouldn't know what it meant to me.

So this is one approach to working with the medicine. The other is a meditative, non-thinking, no-mind approach. But today, having decided to record, I approached the experience by hearing what came out of my mouth. The following is a transcription of the audio of my ketamine session:

> All right. Away we go. Commitments. Decisiveness. Trust the self. Trust my feet to walk. Trust my feet to walk. Go deep. Bring intention to your actions and commit to your actions. Commit. Commit. See you on the other side. Settle in here. Here we go.

> Pray. Pray for me. Pray. There it is. Prayer. Prayer. Here we go. Here we go. The journey begins. Whew.... Help me. This is the space. Ah.... I don't know where I am. I don't know where I am. Wow. There's a physical body somewhere, but I don't know about it. I want to take people with me on these trips. I just don't want to be alone. Oh, this feels like the room at the condo where I live. What is this trip? I guess it's a blank space. God, I'm healing.

God, I'm healing. I want to heal. I don't know what anything is anymore. I don't know what *anything* is anymore. Ah....

Just get to the place. No worry. You know what I mean. Yeah. That! Yeah, that! That! That! Exactly. That's what I'm talking about. That's what I'm talking about. Whew. The party's started. I feel like you just got.... We'll do the cold, silent contemplative thing. [Singing.] I'm in a different place in time. God I wish this could just be recorded so that somebody knows that somebody was here. I don't want to be alone. That's the love. Love. Love. Love. Love connects us all. Connects everything. Love. Unity. One love. God, that sounds cheesy, but it's not 'cause it's real. Boom!! Ah, man. All right.

Whew. This is *great*. To do this and record this. Wow. Got to bring some understanding back from this. Creation, right? That's the thing, the birthing. That's what it is. The center of the universe. It's the deep, dark secret spot. The black hole with infinite possibilities. But what are those infinite possibilities? There are so many. Everything must happen. If everything must happen, then that means infinity. Oh, infinity. Infinity.

This is the sweet spot. It's always been the same lady singing to me, the same voice. Maybe it's the music the doctor puts on. Ketamine is awesome. It's like my mind pervades the universe. It's in a cloud watching the universe unfold before me. And I get to be a part of it. It's glorious! I'm like a speck, a pixel in an image that is so beautiful that it cannot be imagined. You can't see it. You need to witness it yourself. Oh, my God. That's it! Because you need someone to witness it. That's why we're here, is to witness the thing. Oh, shit! That's the point, because such beauty and perfection, darkness and death and all the trauma, the massive meat-hole of whatever, it's all this cosmic spiral, this like.... Oh, it all comes together. Oh, my God, this is a sacred space. It's like the man in the scene in "Inception," where he's like seeing fourth dimensional time, infinite possibilities. Whew, this is real, right? It has to be. It absolutely has to be. There's no other explanation for any of this. Oh, my God. To taste water. Bathe in the river. Seeing as my body floats down the river. Please. That would be how I would go, with a song. And peace. And love connects it all. Holy shit. It's like the Matrix. I can't say. [Pause.]

I'm ready. Yes, indeed. Thank you. Thank you for your blessing. Be on your way now; I understand. I'll just sit here a while, remembering, trying to hold the memory. I know I shouldn't. Oh, thank you. [Pause.]

Oh the music is sane. It's back. Welcome children. The fields, the fields. I feel like an old grandpa for some reason; I don't know why. I'm not that old. Huh. It's like I'm floating over earth. Checking on you guys. Us guys. Shoo. Oh, we're all stars. All stars. I want my all-star team to include everybody. Everything and everybody. They're all stars.

What have I got for you? Hmm. [Exhales.] Let it all melt away. Like a candle. The candle flame and the mind flame. That's a moment of self-consciousness. Oh, shit.

Why aren't we giving this drug to everybody? I think I said it should be mandatory last time. Probably better to do it before shit builds up. Get 'em once while they're young. Sorry. I'm just being silly, huh? Oh, okay. What am I going to do with myself? Get better. [Buzzing lawnmower in background.] The lawnmower is calling again. Oh. All right. When the lawnmower man comes, it's time to come back to earth. [End.]

Notes after session:

Today's session was just the one. They've been kind of building up in my system as we've done them. And my brain's gotten used to like navigating the space. Today was just like...not enlightenment, because I am still too egotistical for that. But it sure felt like it. If that wasn't enlightenment, I don't know what is, because better than that would be unbelievable. Too bad I have to come down. I guess enlightenment would be if you could feel that way but not be on drugs, or something like that.

This wasn't your mind's eye calling, but the eye of the great mind calling you to it, like that night you looked upon the flame, and it would not let you look away. You would try to find distraction, and it would call you more deeply. You would fight it, try to find excuses, and it would call you past them. You would try to look away, but it pulled your eyes deeper into it like a great gravitational force. You would try to use the thoughts as interpretations of your ego, and it would call you into the flame in which ego dissolves. And finally, when you surrendered, it showed you the light, the light that is not seen, but known only by being light itself. A star, perhaps? And knowing what it is to be light, to shine, like Pink Floyd's crazy diamond, in the net of Indra. You can finally know that what you see is shown to you by the great power in which we exist, which is all accessible to us. Again see Emerson:

And this deep power in which we exist, and whose beatitude is all accessible to us, is not only self-sufficing and perfect in every hour, but the act of seeing and the thing seen, the seer and the spectacle, the subject and the object, are one. (Ralph Waldo Emerson, "The Over-soul," in *Ralph Waldo Emerson: Essays and Lectures*, 386)

If you can live in this state of unity with the mind-flame merger, mind-reality merger, this is Mahamudra, the essence of mind itself. In that state, there is no inner world of the mind nor outer world outside the mind but only the mind-world, the mind-light. There, the "individual" or ego mind does not test the reality limit, constantly being shown its limitations, but rather knows its infinite nature, without boundary or limitation. As Stephen Hawking said, "There ought to be something special about the boundary conditions of the Universe, and what can be more special than that there is no boundary? And there should be no boundary to human endeavour." (Stephen Hawking, Speech at the 2012 London Summer Paralympics opening ceremony, August 29, 2012)

The imagination holds infinite possibility and potential, born of the infinite void. And it is only when this infinite void is completely void, not carved up into two, splitting its vastness into duality, which then splits into multitudes, that the infinite nature of its potential blooms. The imagination can take infinite shapes, a unicorn or a horse, or a unicorn that is purple or perceived through entirely different senses as through the eye of a fly, which splits it into a thousand versions of itself.

Ketamine Session 5

I begin the session by stating my intention of accessing my higher self, rather than dwelling on my lowest self and feeling stuck at that low-level of existence. I then entered the mindspace, a place of infinite, eternal light, outside of time and space where everything that can be imagined can exist. Because the mind can imagine any possible thing, there are infinite possibilities, each of which has its own place in space-time, a relative point from which it exists (i.e., its zeitgeist, its particular point of view in a specific time, location, and set of circumstances).

The medicine quickly showed me the ultimate space, then gave me awareness of the relative space (the Two Truths, the absolute and conventional, came up). It allowed me to look at my situation and body from the ultimate perspective, and from that perspective, my hand injury seemed like a small deal, not something to worry about, because when you are in that ultimate space, you are aware of all of time, all of the humans that have been, all of the infinite possibilities, and so one problem seems very small.

The mindspace is an eternity, where time dilation is infinite because it is outside space-time; thus your life is just a small portion of it, and even your death does not seem like an end. We think in four dimensions, but if we got a chance to experience infinite dimensions, as must exist from the nature of potential and possibility, we would realize that time is just a small, transient part of the ultimate.

The question posed in this session was simply, "How do I bring this ultimate perspective into my relative life?" I need help with bearing my human existence and the truths of suffering, sickness, and death. I saw clearly that I want to live from this ultimate place. My work, which is the challenge of a human life, is to find a way to bring the ultimate into the world, to manifest it.

My intentions were not in question: I want to live with love and compassion, and bring this ultimate perspective to the world, to help others.

I stated my gratitude to the medicine for showing me this space, but I asked for help in bringing the light from that space into my life and sharing it with the world around me. The deal I made was that if the ultimate keeps showing itself to me (which it always will, even if just in whispers like Oprah), then I will do my part by working hard every day to connect with it, to receive it, and to learn to transmit it to the world around me. But you have to meet it halfway: you can't expect to just be given the gift over and over, when you've already been given the gift many times in your life, and you've taken it for granted, lived as though that gift was deserved without working to manifest it in your life and to bring it into your relationships. And while that gift is everyone's birthright, I've been given every possible advantage, and so far I feel I've done very little to share that with the world and those less fortunate, whether that lack of fortune is because they cannot see or because they don't have the wealth, education, or luxury of time and health to think about these things.

The doctor and I talked about neuroplasticity. I realize that this is my chance to develop new habits, to rewire and reprogram my brain and my perspective (e.g., to take the negative kick-in-the-balls sensation that I get from waking up with my injured hand every morning and that I associate with trauma, and transform it into a prompt to connect with the space, the mindspace, the clear light of the void. If I practice this every day, especially when receiving the medicine that improves neuroplasticity, I believe I can change the association with my hand from negative to a positive prompt to connect with the light, and thus make the sensation in my hand become a positive trigger, triggering me to think of the space of light, the mind space, the clear light of the void.

I was quickly shown the light. Now let's get down to it and work together to help me utilize it to change my mind, change my habits, access the light without the medicine, access flow states without the medicine, rewire my PTSD associations in my nervous system to become positive associations (like having my hand be a prompt and reminder to connect with the light, bring it into my life, manifest it with my speech, actions, vibe, thoughts, and my work, and disassociate my hand from the trauma and negativity).

The experience was super positive. It immediately got me back in touch with something I had kind of lost touch with, and I've been happier and feeling better. That being said, I'm really looking forward to reinforcing that experience multiple times to get it to stick more, along with integration work. I'm much happier in my head, but I'm still really struggling just with my hand and the state of my life. It's like no medicine can really cure that feeling. It really just brings me down, even if my spirit is soaring.

Ketamine Session 6

This session was super anxious, and my trauma loop and hand sensations were felt super intensely!!

At the start of the session, I went in with a meditative approach. In working with ketamine, I've found there are two approaches to working with the medicine.

One can try the method of hearing yourself, where you hear the words that emerge from your throat, speaking without knowing or thinking what you are going to say, and using the words that emerge as a means of recognizing what is going on in your own mind.

The other is a meditative, non-thinking, no-mind approach. "Cut the head off," as the medicine elders say.

Today we tried the meditative approach by the subcutaneous route. At first, in starting the meditation, I drifted into a deep meditation, slowly going into the medicine's more gradual onset, which brought my meditation to a no-mind state. I even asked the doctor to hit the gong and then try silence (although it turns out that while on the medicine, having the gong hit more frequently so that there is always some sound resonating makes the meditation and experience more powerful—the "gong" sound becomes like a mantra or the breath as an anchor point to come back to when a thought creeps in and you want to acknowledge the thought and dismiss it, and "return to the breath," although in this case I'm "returning to the gong" (or "returning to the resonance"). This approach was highly effective and led me to the no-mind state very powerfully at first.

But then my experience changed, and I felt like a stone skimming along the surface of the water, where I would touch the experience but then pop back into normal reality, then touch the experience again and then pop back to normal. It became very disconcerting, because I couldn't maintain a stable experiential state.

When I popped back to normal reality, the hand sensation crept into my experience, and because I was "tripping," the hand sensation became an anchor point of sorts, as if when I wanted to "return to the breath," I would "return to the hand sensation," until the hand sensation became overwhelming.

This put me into a super-triggered state where the hand sensation became hyperactive, almost like exposure therapy, where the hand sensation that triggers my trauma loop became super-intense, like the dial was turned up to eleven. It pushed me into this super-anxious state where I was having a trip that was just anchored by PTSD anxiety. I was very uncomfortable and distressed and hyper-focused on my hand sensation, like exposure therapy. Anyway, in spite of this, I realized some things:

Looking at my life and the stressors and things influencing me and pulling me in different directions is not normal. The level of what I'm being asked to deal with is not healthy at all. My living situation is not ideal, and I need to improve it.

But I really appreciate this new doctor. He took the time to actually look at my hands with me, when other doctors have just kind of looked like, "Well, you've still got a hand there. What's the problem?" But when you compare them bilaterally, you can really see how severely damaged my left hand is, and the doctor physically felt that—like he took a deep breath in and really absorbed that I had been through a lot. He got down on eye-level with me and looked at my hands with me.

I also liked that when I apologized for laughing, because I always apologize, he just said: "Ryan, you're allowed to laugh." Which was so much the right thing to say to make me feel comfortable, because I've been walking on eggshells around everyone, and just that sentence made me realize that I don't have to walk on eggshells. I'm allowed to be and feel whatever I am and whatever I'm feeling.

The Judge and The Witness

The doctor said at the beginning that we don't need "the Judge." And I cracked up laughing. This had such strong associations for me:

I have been constantly judging myself—the inner critic has been hyperactive. My over-thinking, over-analyzing mind has been hyperactive and paralyzing. It's turned itself onto the trauma loop that I'm experiencing, and my over-thinking mind has been analyzing this loop in my head over and over again (instead of say, analyzing philosophy). Overthinking and overanalyzing has literally paralyzed me. It puts me in a state of extreme distress, fixating on the negatives, whereas the witness will allow me to let these things go!!

Buddhism focuses on non-conceptual thinking, while judgment is conceptualizing the world, the opposite of no-mind. In "Parabol," Tool says, "So familiar and overwhelmingly warm, this one, this form I hold now…" That whole song, really, would be perfect for ketamine.

The Judge and The Witness: these are the opposites. When I did card therapy with a woman in the clinic, I picked the Witness as what I most identified with, and the Witness just sees what arises, acknowledges it, lets it go, and returns to the breath and the resonance. Whereas the Judge weighs things as good or bad, rather than just letting them be what they are. The Judge bangs his gavel and hammers things home. The Witness is also the one who sees the truth, and takes an oath to speak the truth. I made the joke that, with the Judge, it's like a courtroom in my head, whereas the Witness will allow me to just be, be the truth, be as I am, not determine things are good or bad. As Shakespeare said, "there is nothing either good or bad but thinking makes it so." (William Shakespeare, *Hamlet*, Act II, Scene 2) The Judge and the courtroom are constantly thinking and determining whether things are good or bad.

I'm thinking of criticism as compassion, from Buddhist teacher Rebecca Li. Instead of thinking of the inner critic as the Judge, making things good or bad, think of the inner critic as a compassionate entity. Turn it into a compassionate entity, one that cares about you and criticizes you because it cares enough to tell you if you're on the wrong path, and it wants to help you get on the right path. So it's not criticizing you to say you are bad, but saying, "Here's the right path—I will guide you."

In this sense, the inner critic is your intuition, your guide, not making you feel bad about yourself. Take its criticism as compassion and as helping you find your way to goodness.

Ketamine Session 7

My major intentions coming into this session regarding the judge and the witness: dismiss the judge; be the witness. The witness sees the truth, observes it, testifies to it, without judgment. The judge weighs the truth, deems it good or bad, and is the source of negative self-talk. Even positive self-talk, which can narrate its commentary throughout the experience, still gets in the way of non-judgmental observation, and non-judgmental observation is the heart of peace, both among fellow men, but also within the mind. The practice is to observe the thought that arises, acknowledge it, and dismiss it without attaching to it or allowing it to force a certain conceptualization of the world, i.e., that this is good or this is bad. Even when a thing is judged to be good, it encourages the ego to attach to it and desire it, which leads to suffering.

Instead, I need to try seeking "no-mind": Building meditation to a state of non-judgment and non-conceptualization. I had a moment of this last session, and it was one of the best states of consciousness I've ever experienced (if not the best). My over-analyzing, over-thinking mind can leave me paralyzed, cut off from my intuition and heart, which can guide me and be my True North, my north star. Over-analyzing can be turned inward onto myself, dissecting me. If I can come from a state of the witness, patience, ideally a state of no-mind, then I can gain the power to turn the tool of analysis to a good purpose, a project, a problem.

During this session, I experienced and told myself to remember the eternal mind, that all this pain is an illusion. And to always approach everyone with love, including yourself. Then I focused on the experience.

I floated through a space of great clarity, vastness, settled to emptiness and thoughtlessness. God, I wish that I could capture it. It was just breathe in, breathe out, let everything go. I floated through a visualization of the Godhead and the net of being, feeling that I was the eye of God, that all I have to do is bear witness to this crazy world. And maybe not stress so much. As I came down, I felt like texting friends that I love them and will always love them, of course. I don't know what to say—just another trip to the source, feeling the eternal, where all melts to just … thusness, a place without concepts. It was beautiful. I exited feeling radiant, clear, full of love.

I did still immediately hate my hand, but we talked about being open to the possibility that I will one day feel gratitude for my hand, for where it ended up leading me, a question of, "This happened to me vs. this happened for me." Be open to the possibilities here, different ways that what you lost led to new things gained.

Ketamine Session 8

In this session, I had a distinct feeling of wandering and being lost, tossed about on the waves of time and space, wondering what will happen to me, what will become of me, asking for help. I felt like all of this is happening just for me, ketamine treatments, my parents, so much of the world revolving around trying to help me, but also feeling insignificant, the cold indifferent universe, being a speck that could be cast aside on the waves of time, feeling undeserving of all the help centered on me and feeling like I need to earn help.

After some wandering, I met with "the planners," and we decided to plan the world, the big dream, and then I said: "Eff the plans. Just let it all go." (As in, "Let it run wild and go wherever it's going to go, and just accept that. Don't be afraid of it. Just watch the fire run wild and spread over the world.") Grab the energy from the energy source, carry it in your heart a while, protect it, incubate it, then give it to the world. Then repeat. Until you die. Create reality ripples, one drop at a time. The candle that lights many lights. You need do nothing else but repeat this until you die. It's the "finding a way to give it to the world" part that's the rub. As well as how to live carrying it a while, and live with grace, as someone would who is carrying a great energy in his heart.

There's a beautiful light that I've touched, an energy that I've captured in a bottle of a body-mind for a little while, and I wish I could bring it back with me and gift it to the world. I could pour it into my hands, and cup it, and let them drink. They're all so absorbed and preoccupied with the bodily world, and so I need to communicate with them in that medium, with language, sounds, mouth, touch, taste, vision. I need to paint them a picture that they can see. Write them a book that they can read. All the troubles of the world are small and have no place in the world of the divine light, and they pale in comparison beside it.

If I could just carry this feeling with me, all the time. The feeling of floating and drifting, the sense of power, the grace, the fearlessness, the ability to handle anything that comes, the feeling that everything is small and puny in comparison. The mystical realm that I experience all the time: that is real. That is huge. All the troubles of the world are small and have no place there, and pale in comparison beside it. They are trifles compared to the great mystery and the great power and the great adventure of experiencing the divine light. But yet, the real work is on the ground, even if the real spirit is in the air.

Ketamine Session 9

Pre-flight, I am feeling the difference between knowing the path and walking the path, between hearing the Oprah whispers and the brick wall falling.

The universe changed my path by force, by taking my hand and bringing me to my knees, to submission, surrender, and hence to the path, the way, the Tao, to God, to my role in the universe.

There may well come a day when you are grateful for the hand. Also, did I choose this? Are the universe and I one, so that we decided this together?

The doctor suggests I focus on connection and love, remember that this is a two-way street of giving and receiving.

Ryan, have you really focused on receiving love in a conscious, intentional, grateful way? Remember that there doesn't have to be a reason for loving someone. Ken Wilber and his wife Treya felt love at first touch, just by him putting his hand on her lower back while standing next to each other. They both went home and journaled about how they felt vibrations and energy flowing through one another. The same way that you felt when you looked into the eyes of your first love or when you saw your girlfriend's smile!

The session itself: It's weird because this was a crystal clear, golden, glowing trip, but afterwards I'm drawing a complete blank.

I definitely made some peace with my hand on this trip. This was the first time that my hand entered into a ketamine trip in a positive, healing, non-disruptive way, instead of its feeling cold and skeletal and clawlike, like a disruptive, negative force inserting itself into the experience.

Your hands were warm and glowing, and you used them together to grip, grab, and massage each other. You know: one hand washes the other. After using my left hand firmly to grip and make binding patterns, my hand felt strong, and it felt like half a pair rather than just this weird skeletal claw hanging off your body. It felt strong and capable, and I said out loud: "This hand can do things. Let's go do them!!"

Ketamine Session 10

At a Dave Matthews concert a few days before this, I notice I still can never seem to "cut loose" or "dance like nobody's watching." I'm always thinking about what people in the crowd are thinking about. I fear the vibes I send out to people who approach.

My vision: As William Blake said, "Hold Infinity in the palm of your hand. And Eternity in an hour." "What is time?" I mumbled on ketamine. Let time—space time—wash over you like a wave. You don't need to explain yourself. Hold it in the palm of your hand: healing reaches out through hands, like hands; it wants to hold you.

Helpers want to help; lovers want to love; the compassionate want to share what's been shown to them, what makes them compassionate. They've been touched by healing hands. Hold infinity in the palm of your hand. The real medicine is the knowledge of infinity, if you hold it in the palm of your hand.

This ketamine trip had a jungle experience vibe. And somehow my friend, the one who was there when I hurt my hand, was relaxed in a cabana in there. Like maybe he has medicine that I need and I have medicine that he needs? I had this thought that the damage to my hand was him unknowingly reaching out with his pain and sharing it with me, but not to hurt, but with a desire to be healed.

I can carry the flame that he passed to me into my healing work with others. You have to know the pain and understand the pain to truly help others with it. You can help without understanding, but it's not the same. And it's also true that no one can know another person's pain, which is why we must listen.

I got burnt, which is no surprise, really, but I received the pain that thousands, billions of people have known. I now know pain, loss, grief, trauma, heartbreak, and all the inner criticism that goes with it.

So my hand's healing power has actually been multiplied by like ten thousand fold, because through this hand I've learned about a whole array of pain and suffering.

I can begin with the end of my mind. How do I want to feel when this is finished?

NAYA

Naya's Heart Chakra Dream

NAYA

This dream was powerful and really beyond comprehension. It was also surreal, but it was among the most powerful dreams I've ever had, and I'm going to try to just recount more the feeling than the events, because it almost existed as energy and not as a series of events. I'm not sure how it began, wandering maybe, daydreaming, perhaps in the office of a teacher or therapist. But I was human, I think, at the beginning, and then I kind of drifted in my mind through this bright, glowing pulsating circle of energy. It looked sort of like a wormhole, a green, maybe slightly blue-tinged pulsating circle that I walked through in space. It was in like outer space, but not really *outer* space, just space, vast blackness. And I walked through that pulsating circle, and then I transformed into this being, a tall, slender woman named Naya, with her hair kind of up, not pinned up but actually growing upwards, not like natural human hair would, and with sort of a flat top. As Naya my hair was naturally flat but more jaggedy than a flat-top, and I had these long, slender hands that had long fingers, which felt nice because my left hand always sucks now, and just a long body, but I was just walking through with my arms kind of spread out openly in a welcoming posture but low to my hips, just kind of a natural position but with my hands turned palm first, so I was like welcoming walking into this.

And I became this being, Naya, and a lot of things happened that I can't remember. I did lots of things, but what was important was that it was like mind, mental energy that I could walk through and wade through and make things happen in. I could exist in different dimensions, like I could just step into fifth dimensional space. I can't explain the fifth dimensional aspect, but what I mean is that it felt beyond the normal four dimensions, so time was not stopping me, like it would in other situations. I could move as though it were a single moment in a dream, and yet events were happening, and not necessarily in a linear order, but I could just move through things, like through time and also through events, like spatial, three-dimensional events. And I interacted with people on earth, and I'm not sure exactly how, but I think sometimes I would kind of masquerade as human, and talk with them, but even when I took a human form, there was always this kind of glowing energy, like vibrations coming off me that were just really emanating. It was almost like that feeling you get when you meet like a bodhisattva-type character, like a very advanced monk, where they just have that inner glow that you can feel. And so I could talk to people with that glow and help them sort out whatever their issue was, and I think that's mostly what I did. But I was also under scrutiny a lot. I'll come to that in a second.

So I could also help people by being in my Naya energy form, and I could just meet people inside, I guess I'd say, inside their experience? Like just step into their inner space and their mind and speak with them directly, almost like telepathically or trans-spatially, transcendentally, so I would be like an inner voice for them, but in dialogue with them, almost like a conscience, but not in a scolding way, but more in a listening way, not telling them what's right or wrong but with a listening, compassionate method, where I could bring them clarity and revive luminosity in them, like relight the spark, the glow in their chest which I've felt was missing at times since my injury, where I was just blank and there was nothing left. At those times I learned that there's still something left, and it's this little light in your heart, kind of in the chest area, that's this little glow, that's like hope and love and hope for connection—not a will to live exactly, but just a hope to be connected to something bigger and to be a part of it. And so as Naya I could touch that spot in people, almost as if I put my hand on their chest and could just kind of reignite some needed energy that would help them with whatever scenario they were dealing with, and bring them grace, I guess, grace and a feeling of being welcome in their existence.

And so I would go through these scenarios, but unfortunately, I can't seem to remember many of them. One, I think, was a school nurse where I saw something really upsetting happening with a child, and I was able to touch the nurse in that way and have her suddenly know the grace and words she needed to use with the child and the way to touch the child in such a way that the child's suffering was alleviated. That was just one of the examples I remember. I would go from scenario to scenario just walking, but I was also doing my own thing. I wasn't just helping people. I was in a state of wonder and awe and just exploring the universe, but not exploring like a trip to Thailand, because I was beyond time, so it was just watching this ever-expanding moment, and just being in it, and seeing how its subtle energy changed, how the vibrating, pulsating circle of the moment changed, so I was always in that green inner loop of space. I was in something like a circle, as if my mind couldn't comprehend something bigger. It just made this circle around me, but you could feel that the circle extended outward across infinity, basically. And it just radiated from around me all the way in waves, in energy waves, all the way throughout the universe. And there were also waves coming in, so I was sending and receiving. As I said, I would help people, but I would also encounter scrutiny.

I think some people were resistant to me, whether I met them in my human form or met them in my Naya form. When in my human form there was almost this subtle anger at me. I was just picking up on that emotion you get where people are sort of giving you the evil eye, and you're feeling unwelcome by them. But it didn't bother me. It's just that I felt it as this negative energy being directed at me, and I think people at various points did say things to me, but I also felt the resistance, as I could essentially touch their minds the same way I did with the school nurse's. I could feel my attempt to touch their minds gently, not in an invasive way, but just as a part of my natural being. It was just a function of my being, almost like a sense that I had, like seeing or hearing or touch. I was empathically and telepathically in tune, attuned with people's minds all around me. And from some people, as I walked by them or whatever, I could get that sensation that I was being resisted, that they didn't want to let in that natural burst of energy that I would give off, whatever my energy was. I think Naya thought of her energy as an energy of love and compassion, and connection and acceptance, and kinship, really, like brotherhood, sisterhood, unity. Blood relatives, but not by blood, more related by energy, like one shared energy. And some people were actively blocking it out, like they didn't want to know that energy, they didn't want see it, they didn't want to feel it. They wanted to stay to themselves. And I remember feeling especially sad for them, because I felt like it was really important to at least be open, rather than shut down, rather than shutting out a helpful energy.

But in some cases, if I'm remembering right, I found different reasons for why people were like that. And sometimes it was because they were like a white supremacist or somebody really closed off in that kind of way. Because Naya appeared as an African American woman who was tall with kind of red, flat-top hair in her human form. She was long and slender and just a very perfectly formed human, almost like the original woman would be, like Eve with plush lips and radiant skin in the way that certain women have, and then that form also took that green energy kind of glow to it, so it was also that she was literally glowing. And so I got that resistance from those kinds of closed-minded people. But I'd also get resistance from people who were suffering, like people in pain, especially people in chronic pain, as I would walk by them. And I'd want to help, but they weren't ready to receive my signal. But I could receive theirs, and it was, "Stay the eff away from me." And so I had to respect that.

I just wish I could remember more. But I just ventured through so much stuff, just feeling and sensing and just being. I would go through what felt like thousands of moments, but since my brain can't process the totality of it, it appeared as specific examples of moments, like specific encounters, but it felt larger than that somehow. It was a feeling that I was not just having one moment with one person but thousands of moments that my brain represented by just using token segments, like metaphors for an experience that was beyond understanding or communicating. And it was really a crazy feeling. I feel so warm coming out of it.

At the beginning, I think I left the teacher's office as a human, and then somehow got up and walked through that green circle, and I think at the end I ended up sitting in the office as Naya, as my Naya, my green form. I think the teacher almost stopped trying to work with me and started to just sit with me. We could just be together in empathy. I was telling the teacher a story of what I had just been through, and they were just appreciating it without the need for commentary. It felt as if I had reached a state of something like conscious purity, where there was just nothing left to say. And I think that sense of there being nothing left to say kind of rubbed off on the teacher. I felt the teacher to be a wise person, and not because they were like a monk or anything like that, but just because they were capable of listening in compassion and empathy. And since that was mutual, it felt like a very comfortable place for me, because I could just be there. It's like with those people you can just be in silence with, especially people you're really close to where you be can be in silence together and maybe even know what the other is thinking about, like enjoying a sunset with someone, where you're in love and you both know without words that what you're feeling is the beauty of the sunset washing over you, and the love of the person you're with, and it was such a refreshing way to be, so I guess it was therapeutic for me in that I'd encountered points of resistance through my day, as well as rewarding healing moments where I could help somebody, and those filled me up, too.

It wasn't as if it was just a selfless endeavor, the times where people let me in to do my thing, not healing them or fixing them, but just to meet them, really meet them where they are, as they are, in their mind as they are, the real person, like real person to real person. That connection is what is healing, and it reverberates. It's a signal in, signal out, sending and receiving, and it just lit me up, and it lit them up, and it just made our days better. And so I had a lot of those good moments, but I had the rejecting moments where I'd try to send and there would be no signal back, and so then my teacher knew me very well, so I could come back to that space, and at the end of the day of my work and of either being welcomed or rejected, I could come back and have a space of total comfort and relaxation without having to question it or test it or, you know, gently with my energetic power. It was a weird feeling, but with other people I'd have to approach gently to say, "Hi, will you accept meeting me in this way?" But with the teacher I was comfortable in a way where I knew they were accepting meeting in this way, and they knew that of me, too, so our talk was, I think, just sitting together and maybe saying a few words about how our day went and maybe kind of smiling at each other and making eye contact and just relaxing and basking in the mutual mission of trying to reach people and meet people where they're at.

I don't know; it was just such a beautiful dream. For one, the feeling of being beyond time and being this being of energy was just so welcome, because I felt pure and unweighted by my problems, like worrying about my hand and all my thoughts of past and future that are bogging me down. And just all the worries that I normally have, I was just free of them, I could just glide through the world gracefully trying to welcome people into me, and ask if I could be welcomed into them, and not be offended if they didn't accept, but just feel like, "I'm sorry that you can't feel this connection, because this is what uplifts us all."

It comes back to, I think, the thing I was just talking about, because I've been coming through this horrible couple years of pain and isolation. At points in these past two years I have been reduced to this state of total nothingness where I was just suffering in bed from the pain, the physical pain from my hand injury and the emotional pain, you know, from all the ways it was impacting my life. I was so wrapped up in just negative stuff from the traumatic events that I was reduced to just … jello. You know, not sleeping often for long periods of time, my brain just felt dead, like I was effectively brain dead, just jello, and my body had no energy, and all I could do was shiver and suffer. I just had no shred of heart or spirit, or anything, energy, bodily energy, just none of it. And at those times, I really didn't want to go on, but I did go on, and there were two reasons that I did. One was the kind of pain my loved ones would have suffered if they lost me, my mother and father or the people who have been my long-term friends. It wasn't worth it. I would rather bear the suffering I was going through than to put them through losing me, because I love them, and I realize that my life is not my own, it's shared. And that brings me to the second reason that I went on, which is that I found that when you're in a state where you're reduced to nothing, there's still *something*, and it's that little glow, that subtle glow that's just hanging on, like a candle in the wind almost at that point, but it's there, steadily glowing nonetheless, even though it's a low glow, maybe like embers from a fire. It's just whatever is left that can glow. It's not lit up; it's not happy; it's feeding on the littlest bit of energy, positive energy, that it can, but it's nonetheless steadily glowing in your chest, this subtle, pure light, and that light again is just so many feelings in one. It's hope, for sure, and desire for connection to the universe, to nature, to fellow humans especially, but to anything, just to be a part of something, and to love and feel loved. And it made me think how hard it must be for someone who's not had such a wonderful childhood like I had and had so many loving friends like I have... but at any rate, I found that glow, and with that glow, with those factors in mind, with the love, my love of other people and how losing me would have hurt them, I found I could go on.

So my sending of love, and then knowing that there's still hope and hope of connection and still love in the world for me, of my receiving love, and in that pulsating flux of signal in, signal out, almost like a heartbeat, was the glow, and I think, now that I think of it, I think it felt like the glowing rings that Naya had around her, whereas when I was in my state of nothing, of nothingness, that glow was subtle and tucked in my chest, but Naya had developed it so highly that it formed this ring rippling outwards, like a pebble dropped into a pond that ripples through infinity, because you know that energy is never destroyed—the law of conservation of energy, right? The energy is continuous. So it's just that Naya had developed that glow into this ripple that rippled through the whole universe. Damn, I did a good job of describing this dream! I can't believe I did. I didn't realize that's what was happening, but that's it. That was the dream.

And there were a lot of events, like I said, encounters with specific people and maybe even something like entities, I don't quite remember, but that was the essence of the dream. I didn't think I could find a way to put it into words, because it was just being, beyond time, feeling the sending and receiving of love as a continuous flux, and just existing in that state without worry of past or future, you know, without worry of death, without worry of any of those things that come with Father Time, and also without any of those restrictions of space that can be so fuddlesome and troubling and hard to get around. I could just sit in this pulsating energy and just travel and move and be at peace and in grace. Well, I realize that's just what I need to learn to do. I need to spend some time on the meditation cushion and become that. I mean obviously I won't transcend time, but you know, I do wonder. I do think moments are eternal, and I think time is, as Einstein said, a "stubbornly persistent illusion" where we from our human comprehension can't describe it, just like I couldn't describe it in Naya's dream. I had to use the visual image of the circle to represent the infinite radiation in my conception of the dream, but in reality, there is the universe, and the universe is not confined by time. Time is within the universe, and therefore at some level, I think all moments are eternal. The eternal moment is a theme that's come up for me in lots of writing and in philosophy, and I think I can learn to capture that sense of the eternal moment. Because you know how you can kind of slow time down or speed it up, depending on what you're doing? And meditating is the prime example of slowing time down, because ten minutes can feel like forever, whereas playing high speed sports—well, actually time can slow down then, too, because of concentration, but often you are so focused that you have no idea of time. Sitting and staring at the clock in classrooms, time moves slowly, in watching the kettle boil time moves slowly, but when you're doing something that you're involved in time seems to fly by. And when you're really absorbed, time seems to stop existing, in a way. It's a subjective perception, so perhaps you can learn to capture that sense of the eternal moment.

But wow, what a dream, and what a lesson from that dream. I'll call it the Heart Chakra Dream.

NAYA

Reflection

Ryan, you know this, but here's the real trip: it's not about having these breakthrough experiences, which you've had so many of by now. But the bottom line is the mind.... If you want to test the limits of the mind, you're going to have to do it through discipline and building it up slowly. Enlightenment is something you creep into over time, ease into, like settling into a bath. Like a comfortable seat on the couch, you sort of ease into enlightenment. Of course, with tons and tons of rigorous discipline, meditation, and work, countless hours of work. But in the end it's not going to be some breakthrough, like you just say, "Ah ha! I attained enlightenment!" It's going to be something you build your way into slowly, by working harder every day and layering practice on top of practice on top of what you can do with your mind, your sustained training level, like basic focus. Start there, and then we're going to layer on slowly to being able to hold your attention for longer and longer. I think you put in that work, a lot of it, but in the end, we need to get out to the precipice where you let go of the conceptual.

Remember that "liberation occurs when the mind stops trying to grasp its own tail. At that instant, it is not the case that bonds are broken: rather, one realizes that there never were any bonds to be broken ... that from the liberated point of view there is not even such a thing as liberation." (David R. Loy, *Nonduality*, 255) Searching for something that doesn't exist when you get there is going to be like Tommy Caldwell trying to stick that pitch 15 traverse of the Dawn Wall on El Capitan, just like these tiny razor blades that you've rehearsed a thousand times, just clinging to that fine edge to where you can really start to glimpse beyond this reality. Like I said, it's like conscious experience is the ultimate art form, creating your own experience of this world, curating it by what you feed the diet of the mind, and eventually you start to live in that place you've created, but you've got to build it first. You don't just get to hop in there.

And you must remember how you felt reduced to nothing, mind, body, will, soul—all reduced to nothing. Yet something remained: what remained was this subtle light in your heart chakra, which was not even a will to live. This subtle light was hope, a hope to be reconnected to the source, the network of light. Like Emily Dickenson said, "'Hope' is the thing with feathers - That perches in the soul." It was a hope for connection, and ultimately, it was love.

Remember that what kept you alive was love for others, and the hope to be loved, and again feel connected by the love given to you by your brothers and your parents. "To love and be loved," this is at the very center of a person's being, and all that we ultimately need, more so even than food, water, subsistence, life.

And all this just has to make me feel the faith that love and light persist beyond death—for connection certainly does, as we return to the earth, grow into the trees and grass (as Whitman said), flow back into the ocean (as Zen says), come from star-stuff and return to it, even returning to the void of a black hole (powered by the connection of gravity, by the way), only to be released again from the singularity as heat, radiation, energy emanating in whatever form Hawking radiation takes.

But I believe, ultimately, it is all form from the void of mind returned back to that void, mind to mind. As Dogen Zenji said, "Enlightenment is intimacy with all things."

After My Death

Days after my death
there will be ripples.
Two hundred years after my death
there will be ripples
from a butterfly effect.
When one first returns
an individual drop of water
to the pond
its ripples are visible.
What begins as a localized effect,
gets lost in a vast cosmic web
of cause and effect.
We might say
those huge ripples are
from that tiny drop.
Eventually that rippling energy
continues, entwined endlessly
in a network of causes and effects.
Who could say
what caused what
or what has become of the tiny drop?

WE'RE ONLY SLEEPING.

EVERYTHING IS AWAKE,

SO DON'T WORRY

LOVE FOREVER.

PART II

STUDIES

PHILOSOPHY
AND
BUDDHIST
THOUGHT

Buddhism

Candrakirti and Sunyata: The Nature of Emptiness

The development of Madhyamaka philosophy marks an evolution in Buddhist thought, and the monk and philosopher Nāgārjuna, who was active in the 2nd century C.E., is considered its founder. In a commentary on Nāgārjuna's teachings called *Lucid Exposition of the Middle Way*, the early 7th century scholar and monk Candrakirti portrays a new vision of *sunyata*, which can be translated as "emptiness." This form of Mahayana Buddhist philosophy teaches that the cessation of conceptualization is the attainment of Buddhahood, which is the goal of practice.

The claim that conceptualization is illusion places many restrictions on the Madhyamaka's philosophy. A Madhyamaka philosopher can posit no thesis, for, if it is beyond concepts (such as those delineated in language), *sunyata* cannot be described in words. The cessation of conceptualization entails the absence of philosophical views. This paradox is implicit to Mahayana teaching, which is based on the view that no view is correct.

The nature of emptiness must still be discussed philosophically (for those who have not let go of views) in order to distinguish it from, for example, the spatial notion of emptiness, as in an empty cup. If Candrakirti were to say that the cup is empty, he would be referring to the absence of any conceptual entity called "cup" whatsoever. In other words, the cup lacks self-existence. This is called the absence of being in things, which is *sunyata*. Candrakirti's claims regarding the absence of being in things and their lack of self-existence imply that ultimate reality is both a self-existent, independent singularity (i.e., an essential nature without a basis in things) and utter nothingness (i.e., the absence of self-existence or inherent nature). This duality is resolved in the singularity of *sunyata*, which is both existent and non-existent (i.e., *sunyata* is *simultaneously* nothingness and a self-existent nature).

Candrakirti is advocating the destruction of all views, or *sunyata*. In arguing on behalf of viewlessness, Candrakirti posits many views in order to prove that no view is correct. The arguments he considers are intended to deconstruct his opponents' views and to lead people toward the realization of viewlessness. In the end, Candrakirti must abandon even his own position and refer to the experience of *sunyata*, which cannot itself be regarded as a philosophical view because it is the suspension of all fixed views. Though the experience of enlightenment is beyond logical explanation, Candrakirti still uses logic to examine views and wields logic as a weapon for destroying his opponent's positions.

The first of these arguments concerns the absence of being in things or the inherent inability of things to have self-existence. In this section of the text, Candrakirti posits that "all things pretend to be what they are not because they lack self-existence and because they are unreal.... The true, however, is what does not pretend to be what it is not; *nirvana* is the sole instance of this" (Mervyn Sprung, *Lucid Exposition of the Middle Way: The Essential Chapters From The Prasannapada of Candrakirti*, 145). This means that all things lack an essential nature because they themselves are not real and therefore have no attributes. Thus *sunyata* is the only real. He then imagines possible questions about how unreal things seem to be real:

> When we say, 'What pretends is unreal', and 'What in this case pretends?' we mean, How, then, can the non-existent exist? If any object whatsoever existed then the denial of it and the theory of non-existence would constitute a Buddhist heresy. So long, however, as we discern no actual object whatsoever, then what can do the pretending? No non-existent object can exist. So your accusation is not appropriate....'The illustrious one said this in elucidating sunyata, the absence of being in things.' What the illustrious one uttered was not the elucidation of the non-existence of things, but rather the absence of being in things: that self-existent things do not arise. (Mervyn Sprung, *Lucid Exposition of the Middle Way: The Essential Chapters From The Prasannapada of Candrakirti*, 145)

It is important to clarify what is meant by self-existent. "Self-existence" and "essential nature" are synonymous terms, generally referring to the invariable property of an object that defines the inherent nature of its being. Candrakirti argues that the apparent self-existence of things is, in reality, the absence of being in things. When Candrakirti speaks of being unable to discern an actual object, he is claiming that the object is indistinguishable from "the realm of the compounded," a phrase which indicates that the world of things is a place where no thing can exist independently of the whole context in which it is known to exist. The cup has the identity of being a "cup" only because it rests on a table in a room at a certain point in time in the perspective of a particular individual's worldview. In other words, the existence of a specific, identifiable object depends on and arises from conditions; therefore, the object is not born in ultimate reality and has no existence that is independent of *sunyata* (Mervyn Sprung, *Lucid Exposition of the Middle Way: The Essential Chapters From The Prasannapada of Candrakirti*, 145). There is no essential nature in things because no "things" can be differentiated from *sunyata*, and thus, they cannot have the property or attribute that is said to be its essential nature. If Candrakirti were to posit a philosophical argument that he regarded as true, this would be his claim, because it is the most effective argument to posit against Abhidharma philosophy.

Candrakirti then imagines how an Abhidharmika, who believes that things alter over time and also have the invariable attribute of essential nature, might respond. This opponent might say that Nāgārjuna is not claiming that things lack self-existence because self-existent things do not arise, but because the essential nature of a thing changes. According to the Abhidharmika, all things change and lack an invariable nature—they are devoid of a true mode of being. Being devoid of a constant nature, however, is an invariable quality of all things. Therefore, things actually do have an essential nature, which is thought of as the attribute of lacking an inherent nature. This opponent would claim that:

> Alteration in things means that their transformation is directly observed. That is to say, if there were no essential nature in things, that is, if things were not self-existent, their alteration could not be perceived. But transformation is directly observed and so it should be recognized that the sutra is speaking of the changeableness of the essential nature of things. (Mervyn Sprung, *Lucid Exposition of the Middle Way: The Essential Chapters From The Prasannapada of Candrakirti*, 146)

Thus, this imagined opponent concludes that all things have the essential nature of lacking permanence and so alteration can be observed, as Candrakirti further describes:

> 'No thing is without an essential nature as all things are without being.' A thing lacking an essential nature does not exist, as the

absence of being is conceived of as an attribute of all things. But
it is not logically possible that an attribute could be based in a
non-existent subject.... There is therefore an essential nature in
things. (Mervyn Sprung, *Lucid Exposition of the Middle Way: The
Essential Chapters From The Prasannapada of Candrakirti*, 146)

According to this opponent's interpretation of Nāgārjuna's doctrine,
"absence of being" is a property of all things, the property of lacking an
invariable mode of being. It is the basis for the reality of their existence,
or rather, the basis for their lack a true existence in that they can be seen
to alter. In the Abhidharmika's view, there must be an essential nature because all things have the fundamental attribute of lacking self-constancy.
Things have no essential nature in and of themselves because they have no
permanent mode of being, which is the essential nature of everything. According to this interpretation, Candrakirti would be mistaking the doctrine
of essential nature to mean that things themselves have self-existence, not
that things have the self-existent property of lacking inherent nature. The
Abhidharmika would believe that he is correcting Candrakirti, claiming
that things have an essential nature, not a constancy of being, and that their
inconstancy of being is called essential nature.

Candrakirti maintains that the Abhidharmika is not only presenting a
faulty argument by positing alteration and by distorting the definition of
essential nature, but by suggesting that Nāgārjuna's doctrine even posits
the existence of an essential nature that is the basis for the absence of being in things, which the opponent interprets as the lack of inherent characteristics. In other words, the opponent misconstrues Nāgārjuna's doctrine
to mean that things undergo alteration and therefore exist only because
they have the attribute of being absent of being, which is an inconstancy
of being, their essential nature, and the source of their alteration. While
Candrakirti holds that the doctrine of absence of being in things means
that there is no essential nature in things. According to Candrakirti, no
things truly exist and so neither does their attribute of essential nature. The
"absence" of essential nature in things is *sunyata*, which, paradoxically,
is like essential nature itself, that is, it is "self-existent" in some sense, a
point that will resurface later. Thus Candrakirti proceeds to dismantle each
component of his opponent's position.

He begins by discussing the imagined Abhidharmika's misconception
of essential nature. Candrakirti writes that "[a] characteristic which is invariable in a thing is commonly said to be its essential nature; that is, it is
not conjoined with any other thing" (Mervyn Sprung, *Lucid Exposition of
the Middle Way: The Essential Chapters From The Prasannapada of Candrakirti*, 147). Essential nature is the property of a thing that is invariable.

Therefore, it is, by definition, impossible for it to vary or alter. He continues:

> But if this invariable essential nature is something real, then be-
> cause of its invariableness it could not become other. After all
> coldness cannot become a property of fire. Thus, if we accept an
> essential nature in things, alteration is not possible. But alteration
> *is* directly perceived in things so there can be no essential nature.
> (Mervyn Sprung, *Lucid Exposition of the Middle Way: The Essen-
> tial Chapters From The Prasannapada of Candrakirti*, 147)

If a thing's only real aspect is invariable, then nothing that is real
changes. Using only claims that this imagined Abhidharmika has made,
Candrakirti pins his opponent into a corner. In light of this argument, the
Abhidharmika cannot hold both that there is an essential nature in things
and that things really undergo alteration. Things cannot have the property
of "having a varying mode of being" and the property of "invariably lacking any real mode of being" because the latter property explicitly excludes
the possibility that the former exists. Both of these views are foundational to Abhidharma philosophy. Candrakirti senses that it is time to attack,
going on to prove that alteration is not real and that, ultimately, not even
essential nature can be said to be truly real.

Candrakirti claims that alteration is logically impossible because identifiable states of existence are mutually exclusive. He argues this point
using Nāgārjuna's example of youth and old age. If a young man is said
to "change" into an old man, then he is no longer the same young man,
because being a young man involves youthfulness, the essential characteristic of being young. Nāgārjuna writes that "[i]f one and the same
thing becomes other, then milk itself would be curd" (Mervyn Sprung,
*Lucid Exposition of the Middle Way: The Essential Chapters From The
Prasannapada of Candrakirti*, 148). State *a* and state *b* of the object are
mutually exclusive, therefore, the object in state *b* is not the same object
that exists in state *a*. Thus, there is no single, identifiable object that could
have undergone alteration. In other words, state *a* and state *b* define different objects, which are identifiable only by their state of existence. Since
an object is defined by its state of existence, objects in differing states of
existence cannot be seen as identical objects. Therefore, the alteration of
an identifiable object cannot occur or be directly perceived.

Candrakirti has already shown that an object's essential nature could
not possibly change, because essential nature is defined as the invariable
properties of an object (e.g., heat is an essential property of fire, which cannot be fire without heat). He has further shown that a specific object's state
of existence cannot undergo change because the object would no longer

be the same object (e.g., wood is not ash or smoke). Thus he concludes that "...alteration is impossible, how can it be established that things have an essential nature from the observation of change? That would be absurd" (Mervyn Sprung, *Lucid Exposition of the Middle Way: The Essential Chapters From The Prasannapada of Candrakirti*, 148). The imagined Abhidharmika claimed that "...there is an essential nature in things which is the base for the absence of being in them" (Mervyn Sprung, *Lucid Exposition of the Middle Way: The Essential Chapters From The Prasannapada of Candrakirti*, 149) and argued for this conclusion with the premise that the alteration of objects can be directly observed.

Candrakirti has revealed that the Abhidharmika's argument is faulty because his account of alteration is false and because it is logically incoherent to derive conclusions about the invariable nature of things from postulates about variation. Candrakirti will now argue that there is, in fact, no essential nature serving as a basis for the absence of being in things, and that this is what is meant by Nāgārjuna's doctrine of the absence of being in things.

Candrakirti argues that, if all things are devoid of being, then there is no essential nature as defined. Thus far, essential nature has been defined as the invariable properties of an object. The metaphor of heat as the essential nature of fire is not to be taken literally; it is an illustration of how essential nature is thought of as a property. This conception of essential nature is based on the claim that all things have the property of a universal nature, which is the only reality of their existence. If essential nature is defined as "the invariable properties of a thing," then, in Candrakirti's view, there is no essential nature because there are no things. There is no non-devoid in existence that can have the property of devoidness; therefore, there is no property of devoidness or essential nature. Though Candrakirti concludes that there is no essential nature, this point raises complicated questions that get to the heart of Madhyamaka philosophy.

These complications stem from one kind of question that I will now address. Is *sunyata* self-existent? If so, in what sense is *sunyata* self-existent? To phrase this another way, one could ask: If no elements of existence are real, and no non-existence remains when existence is seen to be unreal, what does remain? Is Buddhism nihilistic? Basically, the question is: What is the ontological status of *sunyata*?

There is nothing separate from *sunyata*, therefore, nothing has the property of "appearing as some existing variable that is not real and is actually non-existent." All things simply are empty and have no properties, which is to say they are absent of being. *Sunyata* has no properties because there is nothing separate from *sunyata* that could be characterized as a property belonging to *sunyata*. Candrakirti writes:

If there were something called devoidness of being there would be an essential nature in each thing as its basis. But it is not so. The reasoning here is that, if we suppose devoidness of being to be the universal characteristic of all elements of existence, there can be no non-devoidness because there is no element which is not devoid.... If there is no non-devoidness...there will certainly not be any devoidness either.... If there is no devoidness of being no entities will exist as basis for it. (Mervyn Sprung, *Lucid Exposition of the Middle Way: The Essential Chapters From The Prasannapada of Candrakirti*, 149)

This means that *sunyata* is not devoidness or non-devoidness. It is the thusness that remains when the concepts of non-devoidness and devoidness are both seen to be unreal; it is viewlessness. In other words, the only "property" of *sunyata* is *sunyata* itself. *Sunyata* is all that is and it is thus. It has neither existence nor non-existence as a characteristic property. *Sunyata* is what remains when the categories of devoidness and non-devoidness blur into thusness.

The categories of existence and non-existence (i.e., devoidness and non-devoidness) have plasticity in this context because *sunyata* is the suspension of conceptual and categorical schematics. Nāgārjuna teaches that: "If existence is not accepted, non-existence cannot be established. [This is true b]ecause people say that non-existence is being other than existence" (Mervyn Sprung, *Lucid Exposition of the Middle Way: The Essential Chapters From The Prasannapada of Candrakirti*, 157). This begins to hint at the idea that the reason why *sunyata* is not consistently regarded as existent or non-existent is because standard views of these two categories are flawed and inappropriate. If the reader believes that existence and non-existence are two separate kinds of reality, then there is no way to describe the singularity of *sunyata* in terms of these two categories because *sunyata* is not divided into different kinds of reality, nor can it be encompassed by a delimiting term. Conceptualizing this whole reality in neatly delineated categories is to divide the indivisible and is the root of delusion.

How *sunyata* is represented in ontological terms, like being and non-being, depends upon what view a deluded person has become attached to and must let go. Nāgārjuna's graduated teaching for enlightened Buddhas, who have already surpassed the limitations of fixed views and whose goal is now to save the deluded, states that: "Everything in this world can be taken as real or not real; or both real and not real; or neither real nor not real" (Mervyn Sprung, *Lucid Exposition of the Middle Way: The Essential Chapters From The Prasannapada of Candrakirti*, 181). This is taught because *sunyata* is the point when real and unreal cease to be differentiated, and it no longer matters which terms one uses to point towards the reality of *sunyata*. All such terminology is relevant only insomuch as it can help people comprehend viewlessness. For example, *sunyata* is often described as devoidness of being, but this characterization only helps portray reality to certain unenlightened people. This description might be used when a person is clinging to existence and must realize that existence is not fixed. In a similar manner, Candrakirti's claim that there is no such thing as essential nature is used to help those who cling to the non-existence of things and become attached to devoidness as a delimited object, as he describes: "The one for whom the absence of being itself becomes a fixed belief, I call incurable" (Mervyn Sprung, *Lucid Exposition of the Middle Way: The Essential Chapters From The Prasannapada of Candrakirti*, 151). Thus Candrakirti teaches:

> Of what nature is the illustrious one exactly? He comprehends existence and non-existence. One whose nature it is to comprehend existence and non-existence is a comprehender of existence and non-existence. From his ultimate grasp of self-existence in the true sense as related to existence and non-existence, as we have explained it, only the illustrious one is said to be a comprehender of existence and non-existence. Therefore he rejects both views: that things are in being or that things are not in being. It follows that it does not make sense to insist that the true way of things can be seen in terms of existence or non-existence. (Mervyn Sprung, *Lucid Exposition of the Middle Way: The Essential Chapters From The Prasannapada of Candrakirti*, 159)

The point to be taken from this is that all views of existence and non-existence are false except those that stem from comprehension of the nature of ultimate reality, which is free from fixed views of existence and non-existence. This having been said, the next point that should be clarified is the point of what actually does exist and why Candrakirti's ontology is not nihilistic.

Buddhist discourse generally agrees that the elements of existence are not ultimately real, but there is some controversy as to whether devoidness is ultimately real. The elements of existence are regarded as dependently existent, which seems to imply that they are real in some sense of the word. The status of the illusion of existence can be explained by the Abhidharmika's view that illusion is actually emptiness that sometimes appears as various forms, which only exist because their inherent emptiness is real. As I have shown, Candrakirti holds that there is no inherent nature in things because there are no things. On this account, it may seem that the elements of existence are not real in any sense of the word because the basis for their existence is unreal. Nevertheless, Candrakirti's language often betrays what appears, at first glance, to be a nihilistic philosophy. One passage reads:

> All things are devoid of self-existence, and for this reason…there is an absence of being in all elements as such…. You may object that if…all things are unreal because they are not what they pretend to be, then, if this is so, all things must be non-existent. But the denial of reality of things would be a Buddhist heresy. (Mervyn Sprung, *Lucid Exposition of the Middle Way: The Essential Chapters From The Prasannapada of Candrakirti*, 145)

If denying existence is heresy, it may initially seem that Candrakirti is a heretic, because his argument is based on the claim that there are no particular things. Passages like this, however, seem to clearly imply that things exist in some capacity. This also indicates that the realm of the compounded is ultimately empty precisely because all things are absent of being. This description seems to portray absence of being as a property that is invariably found in all things within the realm of the compounded. One could easily interpret the phrase, "all things are absent of being," as saying that "all things have the property of lacking self-existence." Such a reading is consistent with the Abhidharmika's claim that essential nature is the invariable property of lacking an essential nature. Candrakirti rejects this interpretation of the absence of being in things. When addressing Candrakirti's account, the question of how the realm of the compounded can be shown to be empty is reversed. We might ask Candrakirti the opposite question: "If nothing can be differentiated from *sunyata*, how do you explain the apparent existence of the realm of the compounded and the soteriological motive of salvation from the realm of illusions?"

According to Candrakirti, this is not a philosophical question and should not be answered with a logical argument. Instead, the "answer" is found in the epistemic condition of viewlessness. I previously discussed self-existence and Candrakirti's response to the question of what does the pretending if all that pretends is unreal. Candrakirti says that this question is misguided and inappropriate. If delimited objects could be discerned, then it would be necessary for Candrakirti to deny the existence of things in order to preserve his argument; he would have to explain what does the pretending. But no particular objects can be differentiated from the realm of the compounded. Candrakirti claims that, since he discerns no particular objects, it is not necessary to explain their existence or non-existence. Thus he holds that the illustrious one does not teach the non-existence of things but rather the absence of being in things, which means that self-existent things do not arise. The important difference between these two teachings is that the doctrine of absence of being allows for the existence of things provided that no thing is identified as a delimited object. The existence of uncreated, unformed things need not be explained. Particular things are not self-existent and are identified with the unborn.

One point here requires further attention. Though Candrakirti clearly demonstrates that specific things are not independent of the realm of the compounded, it is unclear why the whole realm of the compounded—all of existence—cannot be differentiated from *sunyata*.

Saying that particular things do not exist is not the same as claiming that there is no existence whatsoever. If no particular things are discerned, then neither are the delimited things called "existence" and "non-existence." There is no self-existence of particular things; true self-existence is being without differentiation of any kind, of not giving rise to constructions of thought, of having the potential for existence and non-existence without limiting oneself to either option. This *is what remains:* the potential for existence or non-existence without anything actually being created...self-existence is the unborn that is pregnant with potential new sense of self. Existence is that which is.

> Whatever it is in fire and other things that does not come into existence at any point in time because it is not dependent on anything other than itself and because it is not created, that is said to be its self-existent nature. (Mervyn Sprung, *Lucid Exposition of the Middle Way: The Essential Chapters From The Prasannapada of Candrakirti*, 156)

What remains? What is viewlessness or absence of being or *sunyata* according to the text?

> The exhaustion, the ceasing to function of all ways of holding to fixed concepts stemming from theories or views of any kind whatsoever, is the absence of being in things. (Mervyn Sprung, *Lucid Exposition of the Middle Way: The Essential Chapters From The Prasannapada of Candrakirti*, 150)

Viewlessness is decisively not a "view of nothingness"—this is the point of Candrakirti's argument. Viewlessness is not devoidness. Viewlessness is being without the conception of emptiness and without the conception of form. This is true emptiness.

Sunyata is when all such categorical conceptions are suspended. This is what is meant by the absence of being in things. Thus, the truth remains encoded in a paradox that is resolved through awareness of viewlessness, the ability to resolve two options, nihilism and self-existent nature. Thus duality is absorbed and engulfed in other, or rather was never there to begin with:

> Buddha, you declare all the elements of existence devoid of self; you liberate men from belief in individual being. Free from any path you have attained liberation; you have reached the other shore without leaving this one. Having crossed the ocean of existence you have reached the other shore. But there is no individual as such who has gone beyond. There is neither a shore here nor there; it is simply a manner of speaking to say you have crossed over. (Mervyn Sprung, *Lucid Exposition of the Middle Way: The Essential Chapters From The Prasannapada of Candrakirti*, 148)

This total absence of anything is not nihilism; it is reality. If nothing is self-existent, even the *Tathagata*, what remains is *sunyata*.

Bodhidharma: Discrimination and No-View

Mental discriminations define all aspects of subjective experience. They distinguish various objects from the background and separate the background of objective reality from the self. They demarcate the concepts that construct each individual's identity and worldview. Ken Wilber calls original discrimination "the original act of severance" (Ken Wilber, *The Spectrum of Consciousness*, 96) whereby a knower is distinguished from the known. This split between subject and object creates the reality known from the perspective of a self, thus enabling further bifurcation and elaboration of this reality. In Buddhist philosophy, however, phenomenal reality and the self are thought to be *maya*, meaning "illusion."

Bodhidharma, a mythical master of Chan Buddhism, presents a view of Buddhist thought based upon having no-view and no-thought, claiming that true nature is the non-discriminative state of mind. He teaches that all discriminations are illusory creations of the mind, and that the various illusions are real, but are not the ultimate nature of mind itself. Therefore, Bodhidharma stared at the wall in order to quiet his mind and settle into the fundamental quiescence in which all concepts are void.

How does discrimination function as a mode of thought responsible for forming illusions, and what does Bodhidharma's principle of non-discrimination imply about his practice of wall-examining? I propose that wall-examining is aimed at knowing mind itself, by freeing the mind of thought, thus understanding not only the wall, but also the mind of the observer and all other mental discriminations that are thoughts in the mind focused on an illusory ego-reality that is ultimately void and inseparable from mind's void-quiescent nature, which is a mode of knowing not limited by conceptualizations (i.e., non-discriminative knowing).

It is inherently problematic to make statements about true nature because it is beyond characteristics. According to Bodhidharma, "The insight of all the Buddhas cannot be shown to people through speech" (Jeffrey Broughton, *The Bodhidharma Anthology*, 33). Words are rooted in false thought and can only point toward truth. In other words, I could describe a tree, but I could never convey my actual experience of the tree using language. D.T. Suzuki says that when a word is detached from real experience, it is "no longer what masters call 'the one word'" (D.T. Suzuki, *Zen and Culture*, 8). The meaning of the one word is an experience that can only be referred to with empty abstractions like 'true nature." Symbolic communications can inspire or accompany true realization, but cannot express realization itself. Ideas about mind can be expressed with descriptions, but to describe is to discriminate. Characterizing mind as void, omnipresent, above, or beyond imposes illusory limits and features on that which cannot be characterized.

In response to this problem, Bodhidharma often poses contradictions and negates previous claims about the nature of truth, indicating that true nature is beyond the reach of dualistic language. Bodhidharma's answers depend on what he is trying to teach about the practice of the path and are meant to inspire subjective realization; they are not intended to construct a logically sequenced philosophical argument about the nature of reality, but to help sentient beings abandon dualistic logic so that they may comprehend mind's true nature. Masters like Bodhidharma have found amazingly innovative ways around issues of Zen verbalism, but the problem is unavoidable. True nature is beyond explanation. When considering Bodhidharma's writing or the descriptions of true nature, meaning must be sensed intuitively, not taken directly from the literal sense, because the language often makes little sense by ordinary standards of logic. Any statements about Bodhidharma's philosophy are creative interpretations that will inevitably impart false claims about true nature, the truth of which can only be understood experientially.

Bodhidharma claims that "existence is not existent in and of itself. The calculations of your own mind have created that existence" (Jeffrey Broughton, *The Bodhidharma Anthology*, 38). In other words, mind dreams the existence of a self as well as the reality that is perceived and distinguished in relation to the self. Thus, in teaching the path to awakening, Bodhidharma says: "If there were a who, then it would be necessary to cultivate the path" (Jeffrey Broughton, *The Bodhidharma Anthology*, 27). Discriminative thought is the cause of such illusions; "It is merely that whatever involves mental discrimination, calculation, and [the realm of objects] manifested by one's mind is a dream" (Jeffrey Broughton, *The Bodhidharma Anthology*, 78). "These are false conceptualizations of thought, mind, and the consciousnesses" (Jeffrey Broughton, *The Bodhidharma Anthology*, 18).

Discrimination, calculation, and false thought are all terms that essentially describe a mental process of objectification through conceptualization. A thought, for example, the idea of an ego, is conceived and fixed as an object in awareness, meaning that the mind becomes attached to a conception and limited by its characteristics. Mental distinctions are self-imposed boundaries on the vast liberation of mind's nature. Therefore, Bodhidharma teaches that "Dharma can cross over the ego [into nirvana]. How can this be known? By seizing characteristics, one falls into a hell. By examining Dharma, one is liberated" (Jeffrey Broughton, *The Bodhidharma Anthology*, 34). False thought is self-perpetuating and could be represented as a karmic cycle, that is to say, fixing an object in the mind results in further constructions around that object. For instance, if I were convinced that a given object makes me happy, I may think about it or pursue some course of calculated action in order to satisfy myself, perhaps a scheme devised to acquire the object or to abandon my desire. Both uphold false thought. Bodhidharma describes in detail the mind's production of karma and suffering resulting from attachment to illusion:

> The brush of thought and consciousness paints Razor Mountains and Sword Forests, and yet it is thought and the consciousnesses that fear them. If you are fearless in mind, then false thoughts will be eliminated. The brush of mind and the consciousnesses discriminates and draws forms, sounds, smells, tastes, and touchables, and, upon looking at them in turn, produces greed, anger, and stupidity. Sometimes it is fascinated and sometimes repelled. Due to the discriminations of thought, mind, and the consciousnesses, various sorts of karma are in turn produced.... These things are discriminated by their own minds, but they are then controlled by these things, and so they undergo various sufferings. Realize that whatever mind discriminates is merely forms. If you awaken to the fact that mind from the outset has been void-quiescent and know that mind is not itself a form, then mind is unconnected....

you will attain liberation. (Jeff Broughton, *The Bodhidharma Anthology*, 21)

If all discriminations result in false thought, yet mind itself has always been void-quiescent, three questions follow: what is discrimination, what is the root or cause of discriminative thought, and what does it mean to cut off discrimination at the root?

I suggest that discrimination can be understood to mean division into two, that the "that construct is and is-not" (Jeffrey Broughton, *The Bodhidharma Anthology*, 22). False thought refers to anything that is distinguished from the original oneness of mind and all conceptualizations formed from a dualistic mode of knowing. Discriminative thought creates two things from one, separates one from voidness, and distinguishes a myriad of things from one another. Bodhidharma claims that these are fabrications, that the mind sees duality when there is oneness. This is most clearly illustrated by a basic example of a discrimination provided by Ken Wilber. If one draws a filled-in, black circle on a page, the plane can appear to be divided into two sections—the figure of the disk and the white background. The perception of separation is an illusory, dualistic construction of the mind. The viewer does not actually see the disk as separate from the page but, in fact, sees the entire visual field of disk, page, and some surrounding area (Ken Wilber, *The Spectrum of Consciousness*, 106). I argue that, in the same manner, all discriminations are a function of the mind and real only because the mind perceives them to be. Mind itself neither has characteristics nor is without characteristics. It transcends this paradox and is beyond all conditions of dualistic interdependency.

Various discriminations determine the construction of personal identity and reality, but they are all fundamentally the same. All dualisms stem from what Ken Wilber calls the primary dualism, the primordial division of subject and object caused by original discrimination (Ken Wilber, *The Spectrum of Consciousness*, 97). This is the point at which a sense of self is distinguished from true nature, a dichotomy drawn in the mind just as marks are differentiated from the page or stars from the sky. If mind is fundamentally non-discriminative, any discriminations must be made by a discriminator; this is the root of discrimination. The existence of such a thing appears to be an impossible paradox, but is not, because it is not considered existent or inexistent. This is non-discrimination. In Mahayana Buddhist discourse, the arbitrary cause of dualism is attributed to the *manas*, as discussed in the Lankavatara Sutra:

the one Mind is seen as a duality by the ignorant when it is reflected in a mirror constructed by their memory....The function of the Manas is to reflect upon [Mind] and to create and to discriminate subject and object from the pure oneness of the [Mind]. The memory constructed in the latter is now divided into dualities of all forms and all kinds. (D.T. Suzuki, *Studies in the Lankavatara Sutra*, 133, 190)

The perspective of the self limits mind to a dualistic mode of knowing. Once the idea of a self is formed in the mind, reality will be experienced in relation to the self. Thus Bodhidharma teaches that "When human beings fall into a hell, from mind they calculate an ego.... From the outset no such things have existed, but they arbitrarily remember and discriminate, saying that they exist. This is the evil karma" (Jeffrey Broughton, *The Bodhidharma Anthology*, 34). The ego-mind is attached to fixed characteristics attributed to the subjective or objective reality, like two sections of a page distinguished from one, continuous experience and inseparably integrated during this same experience. Mind becomes localized in an egocentric perspective, though "Mind has no boundaries. It is unlocalized. Because mind is without characteristics, it does not have limits. It does not have limits nor is it limitless, and therefore it is called the mind of the Reality Limit" (Jeffrey Broughton, *The Bodhidharma Anthology*, 37). Since it is beyond all dualistic views and distinctions, "Buddha Mind cannot be known from the point of view of existence" (Jeffrey Broughton, *The Bodhidharma Anthology*, 33). Therefore, Bodhidharma teaches that "If there were no ego, then, no matter what might come, you would not produce is and is-not" (Jeffrey Broughton, *The Bodhidharma Anthology*, 27). To truly see beyond any discrimination, the act of seeing must be detached from the viewpoint and memory of the discriminator. To be beyond the ego is to be beyond duality.

If true nature is always already non-dual thusness, there can be no cause for original discrimination. True nature, inclusive of all things it appears to be, has no origin. "Mind has neither arising nor extinguishing" (Jeffrey Broughton, *The Bodhidharma Anthology*, 38). Discrimination has no arising; "There is nothing that arises" (Jeffrey Broughton, *The Bodhidharma Anthology*, 34). The discriminator is void-quiescent, so detaching from its perspective means realizing that the perception of a perceiver, along with any object of awareness, is an empty illusion, indistinguishable from the voidness of mind. Bodhidharma says that "Discrimination is a void dharma, but common men are broiled by it" (Jeffrey Broughton, *The Bodhidharma Anthology*, 15). Non-dual insight reveals that illusions are only mind, that, "Things have always been in a state of quiescence and there has never existed a perceiving subject" (Jeffrey Broughton, *The Bodhidharma Anthology*, 14). No reason can be given for the arising of discrimination because true nature is beyond reason, beyond cause and effect, neither dependent nor independent, beyond conditions of non-arising or existence, beyond having or not-having characteristics, and beyond all limitations, even that of being limitless. "Mind has neither variation nor variationlessness….Mind's lack of transformation is called variation. Its transformation according to things is called variationlessness. And so it is also called the mind of True Thusness" (Jeffrey Broughton, *The Bodhidharma Anthology*, 37). No cause can be attributed to the origination of discrimination because it is neither existent nor non-existent. There is no thought of arising or non-arising and no reason to distinguish such notions from the thusness of mind. Nothing is distinguished and nothing is not distinguished. When awakened to a non-discriminative state of mind, "There is neither an awakener nor something to awaken to. If one awakens according to Dharma, when one truly awakens there is no self-awakening at all. Ultimately, no awakening exists" (Jeffrey Broughton, *The Bodhidharma Anthology*, 18). There is no awakening because there is neither a self nor discriminations made on its behalf. Nothing wavers from mind's nature, remaining liberated thusness. Therefore, the path is no-path because there is no path to here.

Discrimination does not truly arise and so it may seem unnecessary to consider what is achieved by extinguishing discriminative thought. However, when Bodhidharma claims that judgment does not arise, he is only trying to prompt the realization that mind is fundamentally liberated. He is not claiming that illusions are utterly non-existent, nor is he claiming that they are truly existent, for they do not exist independently and cannot be separated from the whole. Though dualistic language fails to clearly explain the inherent non-existence of personal existence, one point can be easily inferred. Illusions still appear real to those who do not yet realize they are the awakened Buddha, identical to true nature, otherwise there would be no need for teachings. And so we ask what it means to cut-off discrimination and how this can be done. According to Bodhidharma, "one examines delusion and realizes that from the outset delusion has no place to arise from, and by this device is able to cut off doubt and delusion" (Jeffrey Broughton, *The Bodhidharma Anthology*, 18). Thus he teaches that "When mind arises, rely on Dharma to gaze at the place it arises from. If mind discriminates, rely on Dharma to gaze at the place of discrimination" (Jeffrey Broughton, *The Bodhidharma Anthology*, 20). Discriminative thought is transcended by directly comprehending mind's quiescent nature. This is the goal of Bodhidharma's practice of wall-examining.

Physically speaking, wall-examining is sitting on the ground in a meditative posture and staring at the wall. However, it is also an exercise of the mind. Bodhidharma claims that "If one rejects the false and reverts to the real and in a coagulated state abides in wall-examining, then self and other, common man and sage, are identical....this is mysteriously tallying with principle. It is non-discriminative, quiescent, inactive" (Jeffrey Broughton, *The Bodhidharma Anthology*, 9). The non-discriminative state of mind is entered by focusing the mind into its own void nature. Bodhidharma says: "One sees a pillar and makes the interpretation pillar. This is to see the pillar characteristic and make the interpretation pillar. Observe that mind is the pillar dharma and that no pillar characteristic exists. Therefore, when one sees a pillar, it is the apprehension of a pillar dharma. The seeing of all forms is like this" (Jeffrey Broughton, *The Bodhidharma Anthology*, 15). This suggests that one can see mind by looking at an object, though this looking is clearly more than just visual perception—it is the vision of the mind's eye. True seeing comes from the practice of observing mind, through passively watching all thoughts and mental objects pass through awareness without discriminating, thereby settling into quiescence. Thus Bodhidharma teaches:

> By seizing characteristics, one falls into a hell. By examining Dharma, one is liberated....If you see that the Dharma-Realm nature is the nirvana nature and you are without memory and discrimination, then it is the substance of the Dharma Realm.... The mind substance is the substance of the Dharma Realm. This Dharma is insubstantive. It is without boundaries, as expansive as space, invisible. (Jeffrey Broughton, *The Bodhidharma Anthology*, 34)

To know mind is to be liberated from discriminations and boundaries. Mind can be comprehended by quieting thought and settling into utter voidness. "If the consciousnesses and thought are calmed, so that there is not a single pulse of thought, it is to be called perfect awakening" (Jeffrey Broughton, *The Bodhidharma Anthology*, 18). Without attachment to forms (i.e., objects of awareness), no responses or discriminative thoughts are produced, meaning that there is no thought at all. Mind is completely freed from the dualistic mode of awareness and the vast liberation of mind is revealed. "Thus quieting mind is wall-examining" (Jeffrey Broughton, *The Bodhidharma Anthology*, 9).

If comprehending mind is the goal of practice, what is mind and what does it mean to know mind? Bodhidharma tells us that "Seeing the mind of things is [seeing that] the nature of things is not characterized by thingness, that things are thingless. This is called seeing the nature of things" (Jeffrey Broughton, *The Bodhidharma Anthology*, 30). This can be understood as non-discriminative knowing, when all conceptions are void. If the fundamental nature of all mental objects is void-quiescence, the knowing of true nature is a voidness of knowing, and comprehending mind means producing no mind at all.

Bodhidharma's philosophy of mind is definitively not a position of subjective idealism, but describes a state of total non-discrimination. Subjective and objective realities are not considered existent or non-existent, being identified with the all-inclusive oneness of mind. With regard to mind, "Dhyana Master Wen says: 'Because of the existence of the truth of suffering, it is not voidness. Because of the nonexistence inherent in the truth [that all dharmas] are devoid [of essence], it is not existence. Because the two truths are dual, it is not oneness. The sage illumines non-duality *in voidness*'" (Jeffrey Broughton, *The Bodhidharma Anthology*, 51). Non-discrimination entails understanding that, "The mind nature is neither existent nor non-existent" (Jeffrey Broughton, *The Bodhidharma Anthology*, 37). Such distinctions are false; "you must not have such views as good/bad, like/dislike, cause/effect, is/is-not" (Jeffrey Broughton, *The Bodhidharma Anthology*, 22). "Having no mental discrimination is called correct, and having the mind interpret dharmas is called false. When you come to the point of being unaware of both false and correct, that for the first time can be called correct" (Jeffrey Broughton, *The Bodhidharma Anthology*, 25). The bodhisattva mind makes no judgments or conceptual discriminations, produces no thoughts in response to forms, and is not limited by dualistic views. "Because he relies on Dharma to gaze at the lack of difference between the false and correct" (Jeffrey Broughton, *The Bodhidharma Anthology*, 29), his mind remains unwavering with no attachments to be moved by, as Bodhidharma describes:

> When in the midst of things you do not give rise to views, it is called comprehension. Comprehension means not engendering thought in relation to things ... and not engendering defilements in connection with things. When forms are formless, it is called comprehending forms.... When Dharma is dharmaless, it is called comprehending Dharma. No matter what he meets, he directly comprehends.... No matter what may come, he is incapable of seeing differences or sameness in characteristics.... Because false views are the same as correct views, the bodhisattva is immobile.... Immobility means not being apart from the correct and not being apart from the false. Just at the time of correct understanding, there is no false and correct, and it is unnecessary to reject the false to seek the correct. (Jeffrey Broughton, *The Bodhidharma Anthology*, 28)

At the root of all judgments is the discriminative viewpoint of an ego. "The reason why the sage meets suffering without being sad and encounters pleasure without being happy is that he does not see a self" (Jeffrey Broughton, *The Bodhidharma Anthology*, 26). One can realize that ego is egoless through practice. When the illusory nature of self is revealed, all views become transparent. The distinctions between existence and non-existence dissolve:

> As to the bodhisattva's being fixed to immobility, being fixed to the unfixed is fixedness. Because outsiders take pleasure in the various views, the bodhisattva teaches that views are viewless and that one does not toil over getting rid of views, only afterward to have viewlessness....[the bodhisattva] wishes to make [sentient beings] awaken to the fact that birth is birthless and that one does not have to wait for the rejection of birth in order to enter birthlessness. (Jeffrey Broughton, *The Bodhidharma Anthology*, 29)

Viewlessness describes the fundamental voidness of all views and conceptions, not a view of voidness. It does not abide in the non-abiding quiescence of mind, but is no-mind, neither abiding nor non-abiding.

Bodhidharma describes the difference between the Hinayana and Mahayana notions of enlightenment in this way: "If you care for a Buddha's enlightenment, then you will reject disturbance and seize quietude, reject stupidity and seize wisdom, reject the conditioned and seize the unconditioned. You will not be able to cut off duality and be unimpeded" (Jeffrey Broughton, *The Bodhidharma Anthology*, 25). In this instance, the phrase "a Buddha's enlightenment" refers to the Hinayana notion of an exclusive, undisturbed *nirvana* that is separate from the cycle of rebirth. This is not the same as Chan's mind of non-discrimination, which is all-inclusive, rejecting neither forms nor formlessness. Having no view means not rejecting views and not being attached to views. This is immobility or true fixedness (i.e., being fixed to the unfixed). Bodhidharma's emphasis on this point makes sense in the overall context of Buddhist philosophy's historical development because the choice to abide in the non-existence of the Hinayana *nirvana* is based on a discriminative view and personal preference. In the opening of his first record, Bodhidharma says that "Buddhas speak of void dharmas in order to destroy views, but if you are in turn attached to voidness [as a view], you are one whom the Buddhas cannot transform" (Jeffrey Broughton, *The Bodhidharma Anthology*, 14). Seeing without a view means that even the knowing of voidness is void. This is what is meant by the voidness of voidness or nonduality in voidness. Mind is no-mind; all views are viewlessness in voidness, and therefore it is unnecessary to discriminate between views and viewlessness. Existence is existenceless, "Therefore, the bodhisattva does not reject birth-and-death to enter nirvana, because birth-and-death is identical to nirvana" (Jeffrey

Broughton, *The Bodhidharma Anthology*, 29). Thus seeing without a view is true non-discrimination.

Non-discriminative knowing is not to be understood as knowing in the typical sense of the word. The term cannot be used as a verb or in a context with subject and object—it is just another abstract designation for true nature. Any definition of knowing that suggests one has a knowledge of something or nothingness is misleading. There is no recognition of knowing when knowing no-mind, and so it is not known as knowing. Viewlessness describes a state in which there is no knower, nothing known, and all is fundamentally void. "If you know that all dharmas are ultimately void, then knower and known are also void; the knowing of the knower is also void; and the dharmas that are known are also void" (Jeffrey Broughton, *The Bodhidharma Anthology*, 45). Therefore, Bodhidharma teaches:

> If mind does not know and does not see, this is called seeing Dharma....Not knowing is unimpeded knowing, not seeing is unimpeded seeing....No awakening is awakening, and awakening in a state of identity with Dharma is Buddha awakening. If you are diligent in the practice of gazing at the characteristics of mind, you will see dharma characteristics. If you are diligent in the practice of gazing at the locus of mind, [then you will realize that] it is the locus of quiescence, that it is the locus of non-arising, the locus of liberation, the locus of voidness, the locus of enlightenment.
> (Jeffrey Broughton, *The Bodhidharma Anthology*, 35)

The very idea that not-knowing is knowing of any form presents a paradox. This passage implies that after all knowing is suspended and no knowing remains, there is still some sort of unimpeded knowing that remains. Through this kind of knowing, it is understood that there is no paradox, that no-knowing is the same as knowing, and vice versa. Whether knowing mind or knowing no-mind, all is thusness and cannot be distinguished in any way, shape, or form.

The awakened state of mind cannot be characterized by any discriminative symbolic expression because doing so excludes some possibility from the all-inclusive void. The claim that true insight is not-knowing implies that it is without knowing. Therefore, Bodhidharma teaches that "Not knowing knowing and not knowing no-knowing is called knowing Dharma. An understanding such as this is also called false thought. Mind is no-mind....Today's practitioners understand this as the destruction of all delusions" (Jeffrey Broughton, *The Bodhidharma Anthology*, 37). When all views are viewless, no-mind remains. Mind has nothing to know and nothing by which to know, yet it knows. Bodhidharma teaches that:

Dharma is soundless. Therefore, one hears it by no-hearing. Insight does not have knowing. Therefore, one knows by no-knowing....[Insight] is incapable of knowing itself, and so it is not something that has knowing, and yet, because it knows vis-à-vis things, it is not something that lacks knowing. (Jeffrey Broughton, *The Bodhidharma Anthology*, 15)

An eye cannot see itself without a mirror. Similarly, mind cannot know of itself if all the mirrors or *manas* are the translucent void of mind, yet the unwavering light of insight remains, indistinguishable from voidness. In Tibetan traditions, this is known as the clear light of the void.

True nature is enlightened mind. This is the heart of Bodhidharma's teaching. Awakening does not mean having insight *about* the true nature of reality. If one claims to see no-mind, Bodhidharma replies: "Do you see mind? Whether there is no-mind in mind or mind in no-mind, there is **still your mind**" (Jeffrey Broughton, *The Bodhidharma Anthology*, 15). When there is no-mind, there is still mind. When there is no knower, nothing known, and no knowing, there is still knowing. This is no-knowing or enlightened knowing. Thus the bodhisattva hears by no-hearing or "hears of the path without producing the mind of the hearer" (Jeffrey Broughton, *The Bodhidharma Anthology*, 26). Knowing no-mind is not a knowledge of mind's void-quiescence; it *is* mind's quiescence. The "hearing" itself is mind's true nature, not the mind of the hearer or the sound. To know without discrimination is to be identified with and identical to true nature. This is the state of no-mind or no-thought, which is essentially awareness without conceptualization.

Through this mode of awareness, mind is comprehended—the only content of mind's knowing is the void of mind itself, of non-discriminative knowing itself, of no-knowing. It is an absolute singularity that can only be known reflexively, meaning that it can only be comprehended through the experience of being itself, of enlightened knowing. One does not have insight into mind, nor does insight realize itself. Insight simply is, always remaining thusness. Mind's knowing is known without the intellectual work of knowing, without knowing, because it is itself. This is similar to the way in which our own consciousness is only a subtle sense of presence. We cannot know of our awareness per se. The observer, awareness itself, cannot be observed because anything that can be observed is an object within awareness and, therefore, not awareness itself. Any awareness of awareness or recognition of awareness by a subjective knower is merely an illusory conceptualization. Not knowing of awareness or anything else is to be pure awareness. Being awareness (i.e., knowing it directly, not via conceptualizations) is to be without awareness of anything because you are the all-inclusive void of awareness and have no object separate from yourself to be aware of. Without any concept of a subjective mind to view as an object of knowledge, no mind can be known to exist and, therefore, no discriminations are produced from the viewlessness of this unknown knowing. Thus mind's pure nature is non-discriminative, quiescent, and inactive. Being this nature is called comprehending mind.

This exegesis of *The Bodhidharma Anthology* has hopefully provided a clear explanation of Bodhidharma's method for knowing mind as well as textual evidence that the goal of his practice is to clear the mind of thought, thereby returning to the liberated singularity of non-discriminative knowing. Implicit to my thesis is the claim that liberation means being freed from the dualistic viewpoint of the ego, which I have argued is the root of discrimination, a point I will now clarify further.

Terms like ego-mind and subjective mind describe when mind has a recognition of knowing, a sense that I know I am knowing or a sense of a knower in the act of knowing. This indicates a shift to a dualistic mode of knowing based upon a false conceptualization of knowing, which limits knowing to the localized perspective of a knower and appears to be removed from the direct experience of unimpeded knowing. Objective reality is known only as it is perceived in relation to this knower, through the filter of a subjective worldview, just as the self is only known in the context of experience, through interaction with objects. When examining this relationship between subject and object in light of non-discrimination, it is immediately evident that the two interdependent realities perceived as internal and external are actually one mutually inclusive ego-reality, which is the location of subjective experience. This ego-consciousness is itself void and indistinguishable from the whole of mind's nature, its ultimate identity. In wall-examining, when all thoughts and conceptions about one's own mind and being are suspended and one can simply be, whatever was known as "mind" is suspended, and mind's void-quiescent presence is directly experienced. "In summary, mind is no-mind, and this is called comprehending the mind path" (Jeffrey Broughton, *The Bodhidharma Anthology*, 28).

Buddhist Mysticism and Pure Consciousness

Literature on the subject of mystical experience has suggested the possibility of an altered state of consciousness referred to as pure consciousness, a mental state that is utterly contentless and lacks phenomenal properties of any kind. In an article titled "Pure Consciousness and Indian Buddhism," the Buddhist scholar Paul Griffiths (*The Problem of Pure Consciousness*, R.K.C. Forman (ed.)) provides a Buddhist perspective on the debate surrounding the notion of pure consciousness. He examines the nondualistic consciousness thesis, an alternative thesis, and argues that this thesis more accurately describes certain Buddhist accounts of mystical experience. In particular, he gives an account of "cessation" and "unconstructed awareness," two kinds of mystical experience that are described by a vast corpus of Buddhist texts. How do these categories of mystical experience fit into the debate about the nature of mystical experiences? Which is the most satisfying and plausible account of "veridical awareness," that is, some state of awareness from which one realizes "ultimate truth" of some kind? What is the most satisfying account of Buddhism's ultimate soteriological goal and why? I believe a certain interpretation of the nondualistic consciousness thesis offers the best way to reconcile Buddhist accounts of mystical experience with an intentional model of consciousness.

I. Two Theses

The distinction between nondualistic consciousness and pure consciousness provides a helpful framework for understanding the variety of mystical experiences in Indian Buddhist tradition. Griffiths states the pure consciousness thesis as such: "It is logically possible that there occur a mental event with no phenomenological attributes and no content" (Paul Griffiths, "Pure Consciousness and Indian Buddhism," in *The Problem of Pure Consciousness*, R.K.C. Forman (ed.), 75). The claim that pure consciousness is empty of mental content is not the same as the claim that pure consciousness has content with the phenomenal character of "being empty of content" or "nothingness." The former of these is problematic because there is no way to phenomenologically differentiate such a state from unconscious mental states. It is not clear that such a form of consciousness would be a form of consciousness at all.

The nondualistic consciousness thesis is a more minimalistic thesis than that entailed by the pure consciousness thesis. The nondualistic consciousness thesis claims that, "For any experience (E) it is possible that E's phenomenological attributes and content not include any structural opposition between subject and object, apprehender and apprehended" (Paul Griffiths, "Pure Consciousness and Indian Buddhism" in *The Problem of Pure Consciousness*, R.K.C. Forman (ed.), 77). Such a state could have other phenomenal properties; nevertheless, the notion of a nondualistic form of consciousness is not without its problems. What exactly are the implications of the claim that it is possible for there to be a form of consciousness that is without a sense of self?

These claims require clarification and provide room for a wide range of interpretations. Specific accounts of mystical experience will fit somewhere in the spectrum between pure consciousness and nondualistic consciousness, each providing its own set of details and variations on the two more general theses. The view of Buddhism discussed is generally consistent with the school of Buddhist thought commonly referred to as Yogacara Buddhism.

II. The Buddhist Model of Consciousness

Before discussing Buddhist accounts of mystical experience, it is helpful to have an idea of how Buddhist philosophers conceive of consciousness. *Vijnapti* is a technical term meaning "representation." For Buddhists, consciousness can generally be defined as all mental events which have an intentional object, that is, any state that has something represented or communicated to the experiencer (Paul Griffiths, *On Being Mindless: Buddhist Meditation and the Mind-Body Problem*, 80). In other words, to be conscious is to be conscious of something, to be conscious of *vijnapti*. Consciousness is composed of mind (*citta*) and representation (*vijnapti*), which can be understood as awareness and objects of awareness.

Almost all schools of Buddhist thought use an intentional model of consciousness not unlike certain modern conceptions of consciousness. A standard definition of intentionality is "the ability of the mind to represent objects and states of affairs in the world" (J. Searle & M. Boden, *The Great Debate on AI and Mind*). In the case of Buddhist philosophy, it may only be necessary to omit "the world" from this definition. In Buddhist ontology, representations have "dependent" existence in the mind while the world does not exist in any sense. Mind is all that exists and representations are part of the mind—they are "mind stuff."

Representations are regarded as illusions primarily because they are taken by the experiencer to represent something about his or her life in the world. In other words, the representation of self is an illusion only when it is attached to belief that "*I* exist in the world as represented in *my* mind." Some schools of Buddhist thought, however, hold that any representation is false because it indicates that some species of belief is present. In other words, all representations are false because they are, by definition, attached to a certain conception of one's place in the world. This led to the idea that all thinking must cease in order to be freed from illusions.

III. Cessation as Pure Consciousness

Cessation refers to a state in which there occurs no mental event of any kind. This state is analogous to pure consciousness. As I mentioned above, there are two ways to interpret the notion of pure or contentless consciousness. The first is to say that "contentless" means that the content of the state is nothingness; the second is to say that this state is truly without any kind of mental content. Both interpretations of pure consciousness are found in Buddhist systems of meditation that aim to attain cessation.

One standard system of meditation describes the practitioner's ascension through a series of eight spheres, the sixth of which is called the sphere of "infinite nothingness" (Paul Griffiths, "Pure Consciousness and Indian Buddhism," in *The Problem of Pure Consciousness*, R.K.C. Forman (ed.), 81). Upon reaching this state, the subject's only mental content is a representation of nothingness. This state is consistent with the Buddhist's intentional model of consciousness. Awareness remains present and attention is directed upon a specific object, the representation of "infinite nothingness." This is not the attainment of cessation, however. According to Buddhist doctrine, the sixth sphere of consciousness has no soteriological significance in and of itself—its only virtue is to prepare the mind for cessation.

Cessation is contentless in the more extreme sense, that is, it is utterly empty of content. According to the Buddhist model of consciousness, consciousness must have an object—being conscious means being conscious of *something*. Therefore, the Buddhists do not view cessation as form of consciousness but rather as the temporary termination of consciousness. Cessation can only be differentiated from death by the preservation of vital signs (e.g., breath, pulse, etc.) and the subject's ability to wake from the state (Paul Griffiths, "Pure Consciousness and Indian Buddhism," in *The Problem of Pure Consciousness*, R.K.C. Forman (ed.), 79). The practitioner is unconscious, and there is no mental activity of any kind (although the brain is still functioning). Early Buddhists regard this state as salvific, which it is to say that cessation was regarded as enlightenment, the ultimate soteriological goal of Buddhism.

It should be clear that Buddhist doctrines of cessation do not advocate either version of the pure consciousness thesis discussed here. Buddhist accounts regard the weaker version of the pure consciousness thesis (which holds that it is possible for there to be a mental state that has the representative content of nothingness) as true but relatively unimportant in comparison with ultimate goals. Meditating on nothingness is a useful practice that helps train the mind to attain a mystical state. The stronger version of the pure consciousness thesis, which holds that it is possible for there to be a mental event without any kind of content, is explicitly denied by Buddhist accounts. The Buddhists claim that such a state is not a mental state (i.e., it is unconscious). If the Buddhist's intentional model of consciousness is to be maintained, contentless consciousness is a logical impossibility.

IV. Two Types of Unconstructed Awareness

Around the 4th century C.E., Buddhist monks began writing extensively about the notion of Buddhahood, a different account of the ultimate goal that is emphatically distinguished from cessation (Paul Griffiths, *On Being Buddha: The Classical Doctrine of Buddhahood,* 156). Essentially, the goal was to create a picture of Buddha's awareness that can be clearly differentiated from vegetative or comatose states. Such an account ought to enable Buddhas to participate in the world as individual people, while preserving the view that the self and the world perceived by the self are illusions. Descriptions of unconstructed awareness suggest that enlightenment states have phenomenal attributes, although it is still unclear whether such a state can be considered conscious. Accounts of Buddhahood differ greatly from text to text, but almost all agree that Buddha's awareness is nondualistic and without *vikalpa*, which means "conceptual construction."

The term "unconstructed awareness" indicates that *vikalpa* is absent. *Vikalpa* is defined in various ways, yielding different accounts of unconstructed awareness. This concept is usually explained in terms of different kinds of conceptual construction. These can be grouped into three categories: (1) conceptual discrimination of material objects, (2) conceptual designation of "I" and construction of personal identity, and (3) conceptions that have the potential for causing negative and positive affective responses (Paul Griffiths, "Pure Consciousness and Indian Buddhism," in *The Problem of Pure Consciousness*, R.K.C. Forman (ed.), 86). In short, unconstructed awareness is a state in which there is no sense of self, no identifiable object of awareness, and no variation in emotion. It is not immediately clear how this is different from cessation. If there is no object of awareness, what kind of mental content could remain?

In order to answer this question, it may be helpful to consider two versions of unconstructed awareness. The first can be placed closer to pure consciousness on the spectrum between pure and nondual consciousness. The second is strictly nondual, which is to say that it only requires that phenomenal content not include a representation with the property of "subject in relation to object." The primary distinction between these forms of unconstructed awareness is that of whether they are said to possess *akara* or a "mode of appearance."

The first version is that unconstructed awareness is *nirakara* or "free from modes of appearance." On this account, Buddha's awareness has no recognizable phenomenal content. "Mirror-awareness becomes empty, pure, contentless: the mirror reflects nothing but its own inherent radiance" (Paul Griffiths, "Omniscience in the Mahayanasutralamkara." *Indo-Iranian Journal*, vol. 33, no. 2, 105). This seems to be exactly like cessation or pure consciousness, which is to say that it does not seem to be a form of consciousness. Many Buddhist texts, however, insist that there is still some form of awareness present.

According to Griffiths, this view implies that, in order for an object to have a mode of appearance, attention must be directed upon the object like a searchlight (Paul Griffiths, *On Being Buddha: The Classical Doctrine of Buddhahood*, 167). Buddha's attention is not directed toward specific objects, therefore, it is nirakara. In the absence of directed attention, the objects are still said to have some fuzzy presence in the background of awareness, but they are not regarded as "having a mode of appearance" because Buddha does not conceptually identify their phenomenal characteristics as "green" or whatever else. For example, one text states:

> [The mirror-awareness] does not function in accordance with the division of objects into things such as form/color, nor in accordance with the division of modes of appearance into such things as blue. This is because it is a construction-free awareness in which what takes a mental object and what is taken as a mental object are identical; also, its mental object is actuality. (Paul Griffiths, *On Being Buddha: The Classical Doctrine of Buddhahood*, 167)

The second version is that unconstructed awareness has *akara* or mode of appearance. According to Griffiths, this view requires that objects can have *akara* without any volitional turning of attention on the part of Buddha (Paul Griffiths, *On Being Buddha: The Classical Doctrine of Buddhahood*, 168). Buddha's awareness is compared to a mirror, reflecting its objects perfectly without doing any work. Even though Buddha's awareness is said to have phenomenal content, the status of this content is not clear. Whatever kind of content there remains must be without *vikalpa*, without conceptual construction. On this account, mirror-awareness is still *nirvi-kalpa* (a non-conceptual state of awareness of reality) but not *nirakara* (free from modes of appearance) (Paul Griffiths, "Omniscience in the Mahayanasutralamkara." *Indo-Iranian Journal*, vol. 33, no. 2, 105).

Overall, these views are not dissimilar; there is only a small discrepancy about what should be regarded as "having a mode of appearance." Both accounts seem to hold that some kind of content and awareness remains, whether or not they regard this content as having akara, or a mode of appearance. As Griffiths suggests, "the best reading of what the digests say about this awareness is not to deny that it has content, but rather to deny that it has the kind of content capable of engaging the attention of the possessor of the awareness in question" (Paul Griffiths, *On Being Buddha: The Classical Doctrine of Buddhahood*, 166). The point of interest is that Buddhist doctrines do not seem to regard these views as incompatible. Another passage says:

> In a mirror-mandala, there are many and varied modes of appearance, and yet there are no modes of appearance therein. Also, in a mirror-mandala there is neither effort nor volitional activity. In just the same way, the reflected images in the mirror awareness belonging to the Tathagatas have many and varied modes of appearance, and yet there are no reflected images at all in this mirror-awareness. Also, the reflected images belonging to the mirror-awareness are free from effort and volitional mental activity. (Paul Griffiths, *On Being Buddha: The Classical Doctrine of Buddhahood*, 167)

This passage seems to suggest a paradox, if not an explicit contradiction. Buddha's awareness has *akara* and is *nirakara*, that is, it both has and is free from a mode of appearance. Buddhas can be free from modes of appearance while still perceiving modes of appearance. What is to be made of this tension? Buddha must simultaneously have two modes of knowing. I will call these modes of unconstructed awareness "empty vision" and "formed vision."

V. Phenomenology of Unconstructed Awareness

Unconstructed awareness is said to be "contentless" or "objectless" in a different sense than cessation or pure consciousness. It has phenomenal content and is still somehow contentless in that its content is "unconstructed." It has representational content, and yet its only content is "the indescribability of things" or the "thusness of absence of self." So what is unconstructed awareness like? In *On Being Buddha*, Griffiths argues that there is nothing that it is like to be Buddha (Paul Griffiths, *On Being Buddha: The Classical Doctrine of Buddhahood*, 190). Being Buddha is like being a rock; it has no subjective character, no "what-it-is-like." Claiming that Buddhahood has no subjective character is to say that Buddhahood is not a conscious mental state.

In Griffiths' view, Buddha's awareness must lack various properties in order for Buddha to have empty-vision, that is, for Buddha's awareness to be both *nirakara* and *nirvikalpa*, that is, having a non-conceptual state of awareness that is also free from modes of appearance. According to Griffiths (*On Being Buddha: The Classical Doctrine of Buddhahood*, 194), these properties can be summarized as follows:

1) Buddha has no memorial experiences and no sense of personal history.
2) Buddha has no affective responses.
3) Buddha has no beliefs.
4) Buddha has no sense of time.
5) Buddha is not involved in conscious decision-making.
6) Buddha does not form verbal representations.
7) Buddha's awareness has no phenomenal content with the property of "subject in relation to object."

Griffiths claims that this list of properties clearly indicates that Buddha is unconscious (Paul Griffiths, *On Being Buddha: The Classical Doctrine of Buddhahood*, 196). If Buddha has empty-vision, he does not have formed vision. Furthermore, Griffiths argues that the seventh property alone is reason to claim that Buddha is unconscious as described by the Buddhist model of consciousness. If Buddha has no recognition of being aware, is he really aware at all?

Self-awareness may be essential to consciousness. Griffiths concludes that nondualistic states, whose content does not have the property of "subject in relation to object," are unconscious states (Paul Griffiths, *On Being Buddha: The Classical Doctrine of Buddhahood*, 193). Both modes of unconstructed awareness are simply unconscious and not phenomenologically different from cessation. If Buddhas are unconscious, they cannot fulfill the worldly roles that, according to doctrine, Buddhas must fulfill.

Formed vision (i.e., unconstructed awareness that has *akara* but not *vikalpa*, or mode of appearance without conceptual construction) does not have any of these properties except the lack of division between subject and object and lack of affective responses in order to remain free from *vikalpa* (Paul Griffiths, "Omniscience in the Mahayanasutralamkara," *Indo-Iranian Journal*, vol. 33, no. 2, 105). It can have temporal context, verbal representation, and even beliefs, provided that there is no knowledge of the fact that these beliefs belong to the concept "me," who is the owner and experiencer of beliefs and such. As Griffiths claims, the lack of this central belief may mean that being Buddha is like being a rock. In my opinion, formed vision provides a much more plausible account of Buddhahood.

It is possible to provide an interpretation of the tensions found in Buddhist doctrine that allows unconstructed awareness to be a form of consciousness that is implicated with language and the various other phenomenal properties listed above, while still being without *vikalpa* and nondualistic. In other words, there is an interpretation of Buddhist doctrine that allows Buddhas to be conscious and to have the "dual-vision" of both seeing a self and seeing beyond a self.

VI. The Status of "Unconstructed" Mental Content

This can be achieved by not identifying with the self-representation, by lacking the belief that the representation is that of your awareness. In Fred Dretske's terms, one has an experience of the self-representation, not the belief that "this is me." This mere representation is not who Buddha is. Buddha is mind (*citta*), which includes representations (*vijnapti*) such as the self-representation. Thus, Buddha is beyond self, yet Buddha can see a representation of an individual man who was born in India and whose name is Siddhartha Gautama, the Buddha.

Fred Dretske argues for a distinction between state consciousness and creature consciousness (Fred Dretske, *Perception, Knowledge, and Belief*, 127). State-consciousness means that one is conscious of some *thing*, some kind of mental state. Creature consciousness means that one is conscious of the *fact* that one is conscious of a mental state. Dretske argues that state-consciousness does not require creature consciousness. Consciousness does not require one to be aware of the fact that one is aware, it only requires state-consciousness (Fred Dretske, *Perception, Knowledge, and Belief*, 136). In Dretske's view, the implication of this is that consciousness does not require self-awareness or creature consciousness.

The distinction between being thing-conscious and fact-conscious is crucial here. One can see a thing scurry across the road without being conscious of the fact that it is called an "armadillo," or that it is an animal (Fred Dretske, *Perception, Knowledge, and Belief*, 117). From a Buddhist perspective, it is interesting to notice that facts can often be assumptions.

Who is to say that the armadillo running across the road is not actually a mechanical robot? A Buddhist would hold that the armadillo is an illusion. Buddha has empty vision; his awareness is *nirakara*, free from modes of appearance. He can separate the fact-consciousness from the thing-consciousness. At the same time, however, Buddha sees the armadillo. He can point to the armadillo and teach that the armadillo is an illusion. His awareness has *akara*, or mode of appearance.

I argue that Buddha can have all forms of thing-consciousness and can also have almost all forms of fact-consciousness. The only fact that Buddha must not be aware of is the fact that "I am the one experiencing these experiences." He can know that the representation referred to as "Siddhartha Gautama, the Buddha" is having these experiences as long as he does not know that he is Siddhartha Gautama. He must only remain unaware of one simple fact, the fact that I am me. This may be the most central fact in our conception of the world and the most difficult fact to disregard in living one's life.

The nondualistic consciousness thesis can be interpreted to mean that there is simply no knowledge of the fact that a certain representation is that of a "subject." In other words, Buddha can have any conscious mental state in which there is a relationship between two objects. Buddha can know any facts about these objects as long as he does not know the fact that one of the representational objects is a "subject." This is the interpretation of the nondualistic consciousness thesis that I believe is most plausible and is most easily reconciled with an intentional model of mind. This version does not require Buddhists to either abandon their model of consciousness or to hold that Buddha is necessarily unconscious (providing that Dretske's argument holds up).

The nondualistic consciousness thesis states that: "For any experience (E) it is possible that E's phenomenological attributes and content not include any structural opposition between subject and object, apprehender and apprehended" (Paul Griffiths, "Pure Consciousness and Indian Buddhism," in *The Problem of Pure Consciousness*, R.K.C. Forman (ed.), 77). I'd like to explain this in terms of being aware of the fact that there is actually a subject. The self-representation is not gone; it is just not labeled as "self-representation" or "subject." It is like seeing the armadillo and being unaware of the fact that it is called an "armadillo." You can still see the armadillo and a representation of self seeing the armadillo, providing that these are not labeled "subject in relation to object." If one does not have the belief that one is identified with the self-representation, then seeing an angry, charging bear does not produce affective response, because it is not *you* that is about to be eaten, just some generic representation eating another generic representation. Thus Buddha's awareness can be *vikalpa,* or without conceptual construction, and still be a form of consciousness.

Flow

Flow is a state of heightened focus, often involving a decrease in self-awareness, so it is difficult for the person experiencing flow to realize what they are thinking without being distracted by their own thought processes.

It is a flow of states of consciousness. Since there is no destination, there is no direction. Like a dream, one minute they are in the real word, one minute drifting, a dream sequence.

In the behavioral model, behavioral responses build up and develop into conditioned repetitive behavioral responses, which leads to the development of expertise, which is, perhaps, the source of intuition, that automatic knowing versus reasoned knowing, knowing *how* versus knowing *that*.

But compared to the behavioral model, think about the spiritual model, like centering prayer perhaps. Or the illusion of self in meditation, versus the actual eternal self (which is not exactly a self at all, as it is unfixed with no permanent basis). Then what part of it is eternal exactly?

Flow and Expertise

What drives a skilled performer? In order to understand the process of learning and skill development, one must first examine performance. This could be assessed through subjective accounts or the objective factors involved in skilled performance, particularly the cognitive processes of the performer. Performance can be assessed in terms of two theories: a model of skill acquisition developed by Stuart and Hubert Dreyfus, and the theory of "optimal experience" proposed by Mihaly Csikszentmihalyi.

In Dreyfus and Dreyfus's view, experts perform in a manner that seems instinctive, executing complicated and difficult tasks during which many decisions occur simultaneously without a break in performance and without conscious processing. According to their model, decision making gradually becomes intuitive rather than rational and rule-based. They use the term "flow" to describe performances in which skill execution seems to be completely intuitive, natural, and effortless, such that the performer need not pay any attention to task execution. This occurs only at the highest levels of experience, after the performer has internalized the skill and can perform it automatically. According to Dreyfus and Dreyfus, this type of ability is based on intuition or "know-how," which they use synonymously. Alternatively, the converse of intuitive decision making is conscious skill execution based on rule-following, described as "deliberative rationality" by Stewart and Hubert Dreyfus in their book *Mind Over Machine*.

In his book, *Flow: The Psychology of Optimal Experience*, Mihaly Csikszentmihalyi sets forth a different, very specific definition and set of criteria to define the flow experience. According to Csikszentmihalyi, flow or optimal experience is a very common phenomenon. His research involves compiling introspective reports from a wide cross-section of subjects. He then analyzes these accounts from a psychological perspective, distinguishing various types of experiences which he has, for the purposes of his theory, grouped into two broad categories: optimal experience and psychic entropy. According to Csikszentmihalyi, the goal of any activity for any individual should be to make the progression from psychic entropy toward psychic harmony (i.e., flow).

Dreyfus and Dreyfus describe a five-stage model of skill acquisition, which can be compared to Csikszentmihalyi's theory of optimal experience.

The five-stage model of skill acquisition is supported by scientific research, but it is ultimately based upon the authors' stance in an unresolved, philosophical debate. Dreyfus and Dreyfus hold that the experience-based, intuitive decision-making process of the expert cannot be simulated by computer programs using complex systems of rules. In support of this claim, they cite a wide cross-section of perceptual testing and other experimental evidence dealing with the way humans process information and make decisions. They compare this data with research in the field of artificial intelligence, emphasizing the contrast between the manner in which humans make decisions and the way computers process complicated sets of situational data. Drawing upon these sources along with their personal observations, Dreyfus and Dreyfus identify several different modes of decision making that humans use when approaching a task. They arrange these in a progression through five stages, representing differing levels of task-related abilities and experience.

Dreyfus and Dreyfus's Five-Stage Model of Skill Acquisition

The five-stage model of skill acquisition describes an individual's learning of any specific skill domain through instruction, imitation, and practice. Each stage describes a specific mode of information processing, that is, how the performer perceives and processes salient information. In order to achieve expertise, an individual will go through five qualitatively different ways of perceiving the task, determined by the individual's mental approach to a problem in the skill domain (i.e., his method of decision making). At first, the performer uses learned rules to identify relevant features of a situation and process them. As the level of experience in the skill domain increases, the performer builds up "know-how," which can be substituted for "knowing-that." This marks a transition from detached, deliberative rationality to involved, intuitive decision making.

It is important to be clear about what Dreyfus and Dreyfus mean when referring to intuition. In terms of this model, know-how is comprised of two elements: task-specific procedural memory and what Dreyfus and Dreyfus call holistic similarity recognition (Hubert L. Dreyfus and Stuart E. Dreyfus, *Mind Over Machine: The Power of Human Intuition and Expertise in the Era of the Computer*). The first refers to proceduralized knowledge of various tasks in the skill domain. The ability to work a clutch, for example, is a learned skill in itself that must be practiced to drive at higher levels of proficiency. The second, holistic similarity recognition, is the ability to recognize domain-related situational patterns without decomposing them into component features. The elements of a situation toward which a performer will direct his attention, the features he will perceive as salient, are determined by associated memories of skill-related experiences and the performer's ability to recognize whole constellations of situational elements.

Dreyfus and Dreyfus point out that pattern recognition is a basic human ability and must be used to recognize even basic component features in a skill domain, such as the road signs seen while driving (Hubert L. Dreyfus and Stuart E. Dreyfus, *Mind Over Machine: The Power of Human Intuition and Expertise in the Era of the Computer*). The ability to recognize whole situational patterns, that is, to recognize the overall context composed by all salient features without decomposing them into isolated, component features, allows the performer to recall and execute memorized courses of action based on proceduralized knowledge. In Dreyfus and Dreyfus's view, intuition based on holistic situational recognition and task-specific procedural memory is what makes fluid, expert performance possible, enabling the expert to make difficult decisions without conscious processing.

Expert decision making is not based on calculative rationality and is irreducible to rules, yet intuition and analysis both play important roles in skill development. Though intuitive performance is the goal of skill development, analysis is beneficial for beginners and even for those who perform at higher levels of expertise, where it can help to refine intuitive judgments. It may be useful to think of the overall progression of this model as a transition from relying on explicit knowledge toward the ability to substitute implicit knowledge.

Implicit knowledge is not entirely accessible to consciousness. One cannot recall every skill-related memory, but these experiences still inform know-how. The performer may also know how to perform complex tasks within the skill domain but may not be able to explain how they are performed. During expert performance, sudden focus of conscious attention on proceduralized skills or how one is performing the skill, i.e., a shift from "knowing how" to "knowing that," results in a severe degradation in performance.

An individual can perform at any level depending on the circumstances. An expert may encounter a situation that he approaches as a merely competent performer. Similarly, a beginner could have a stroke of luck and quickly begin to function as an expert would. The model only indicates that individuals will perform best overall by functioning at the level most fitting to their abilities and are most likely to function at this level when given a problem in the skill domain. The stages are ordered as they are because individuals who employ the kind of thinking characteristic of the higher stages are more likely to perform better than those in the lower stages, given equal individual talent and circumstances. This will be evident after the five stages are made clear.

Stage 1: Novice. The inexperienced novice learns by instruction and observation to identify certain features and elements of a situation as important and acquires precise rules for determining a course of action based upon these features. Elements that the novice will perceive as salient are so clearly defined by objective instructions that the novice recognizes them without considering the overall context. Dreyfus and Dreyfus call these "context-free" elements. The novice chess player, for example, is taught a point system to help identify the value of the pieces on the board, and he will apply the context-free rules regardless of how the pieces are positioned. The novice driver may learn to stay a certain distance away from the car in front of him, but will probably maintain this distance without considering the speed at which he is traveling or the traffic density.

Calculation and manipulation of context-free elements by clearly-defined rules is called calculative rationality. The novice does not yet have sufficient experience to use holistic similarity recognition. Since he lacks an overall sense of the skill domain, his performance will be determined by how well he follows learned rules, but learning rules will help guide him during the early accumulation of experience. These memorized rules help the novice direct his attention toward relevant features of a situation and gives him an idea of how to process these features. For the novice, attention must be focused on making a rule-based decision about each specific feature. The novice is not free to view these features in their overall context.

Stage 2: Advanced Beginner. The mindset of the advanced beginner can only be employed after gaining some experience performing the skill in real-world situations. By this point, the performer has become capable of recognizing more context-free features and using more sophisticated rules to process them. More importantly, the advanced beginner has learned to understand the skill on his own. Through practical experience with real elements, which could not be defined in context-free features, the performer learns to recognize recurring "situational elements." These can be recalled without deliberation through associated, implicit memories of skill-related experiences (i.e., holistic similarity recognition). A driver at this stage probably knows what a stop sign is and does not need to think about it. The performer has learned to identify recurring component elements, but is not yet able to recognize constellations of these elements.

At this stage, experience and practice are more important learning tools than verbal instruction, but the performer is still reliant on context-free rules and still makes decisions deliberatively using context-free features and situational elements. Attention must be directed toward processing the elements perceived as salient and placing them in the overall context of the situation. When experiential knowledge fails, the advanced beginner finds analytic thinking immensely useful and may shortly find himself reverting to the totally rule-based thought processes of the novice.

Stage 3: Competence. With more experience, the performer is capable of identifying so many context-free and situational facets and has learned so many different rules for processing them that the task of evaluating them all becomes overwhelming and detracts from performance. Therefore, a hierarchical procedure for decision-making is adopted in order to identify the most important features of the situation and to act upon them with a specific goal in mind.

The competent performer sees the situation as a set of facts and features. Approaching the situation with an organizing plan allows the performer to place these features in their overall context. The performer determines which features are most important through a systematic, analytic mode of decision-making. The competent driver, for example, no longer focuses his attention on using memorized rules that allow him to operate the vehicle, but recognizes important aspects and focuses attention on ordering these in terms of their importance for achieving a goal. For example, if the driver's goal is to get somewhere as quickly as possible, he will focus his attention on elements like distance, speed limits, and traffic lights when choosing a route.

Choosing an organizing plan is required in order to approach a problem at the level of competency. This choice not only helps to put the situation into perspective, but also represents a personal investment on behalf of the performer. The competent performer makes decisions in a detached, deliberative manner often referred to as "problem-solving" by cognitive scientists. Unlike the beginner, however, the competent performer is not merely following rules but is using his judgment in order to decide how to make a decision or what rules to follow. He has a personalized approach to the problem and adopts an attitude of nonobjectivity. Though he decides in a detached manner, he is emotionally involved in the outcome. Positive and negative feedback are more deeply felt and registered, producing deeper situational recognition in the future. Dreyfus and Dreyfus suggest that problem-solving is sufficient to produce certain intelligent behaviors but is not necessary to produce intelligence, as is shown by the proficient or expert performer.

The organizing plan allows the performer to perceive the situation as an ordered whole by systematically attending to the elements of the situation, one by one placing them in the overall context determined by the organizing plan. Holistic pattern recognition develops from practice using organizing plans. The performer learns to develop coherent plans to organize a whole constellation of elements. As these plans are practiced and applied to various situations, they eventually become implicit, proceduralized plans of action triggered by memorable constellations of elements.

Stage 4: Proficiency. This stage marks an important progression in the performer's mode of decision-making as he learns to make full use of an ability which has been developing gradually. Until this stage, the performer has made conscious decisions about the goals, organizing plan, and course of action and often has been merely following rules that make the choice clear. The proficient performer is able to use intuition rather than deliberation to determine a course of action. Using intuition means that there is no need for a detached decision-making process to occur. He is intensely involved in the activity and is perceiving it from a very personal perspective constructed from past experiences in the skill domain, especially the outcomes of more recent events. This organizing perspective could be thought of as an internalized and intuitively applied repertoire of adaptable organizing plans for various types of situations, a repertoire built up over time by devising and observing various organizing plans that can be recalled holistically, that is, as a whole, memorized pattern. These organizing plans are developed during earlier stages and are built on all learned rules, features, and skill-related experiences. The performer's organizing perspective causes certain features to stand out and others to remain in the background.

Since the level of advanced beginner, the performer has been cataloging situational elements in his memory. He learned to identify certain elements without having to use rules; now he can do the same with whole situational patterns. This type of holistic situational recognition allows the performer to make choices without conscious processing because an appropriate course of action can be triggered automatically in response to a familiar situation in the skill domain. A proficient driver knows what route to take not by combining rules, but when the whole situation triggers a sense of similarity to successful experiences in the past. The decision happens like a learned reflex, in the same manner as one might quickly grasp for a drink that is knocked over. This is not a purely physical reflex like being tapped on the knee but an implicit, learned ability. He has "know-how." This means that he is capable of drawing upon pattern recognition and procedural memory to produce automatic responses.

The performer is capable of automatic responses based on task-specific procedural memory, but this does not mean he is not paying attention to the situation. Attentional involvement in the situation is necessary for recognition of whole, situational patterns. Therefore, the performer must be involved to produce automatic responses to these patterns with any level of success. The performer does not have to attend to these responses, think about them analytically, or process them consciously.

Though intuitively understanding and organizing the task, the proficient performer has not abandoned conscious decision-making and will from time to time experience lapses in the flow of intuitive response. He may find himself thinking consciously about what to do or stopping to question his intuitions before acting on them. Dreyfus and Dreyfus call this "attentional monitoring." A proficient driver, drawing upon a repertoire of many known situations, can get a sense of the situation without conscious processing. At this level, the driver knows intuitively what he must do but may still choose to think about it analytically in order to check his intuitions and refine his exact course of action based on his intuitive sense of the situation. For example, the driver may realize intuitively that he is driving too fast around a corner and must slow down, but then consciously decide how to reduce his speed. The proficient performer is still not fully confident in intuitive decision making but has a highly developed intuitive sense of situations in the skill domain.

Stage 5: Expertise. The thought processes characteristic of the expert facilitate the highest level of performance in an individual. In most skill-related situations, the expert knows how to act based on a highly developed, practiced understanding. Just as we do not make conscious, deliberative choices when we walk or talk, the expert does not think about the situation as a problem to be solved, nor does he devise plans. Knowledge of goals, possible methods, and features involved in skill-related situations is implicit and is accessed without conscious processing. Experts don't need to think about what to do. Under normal circumstances, experts simply do what normally works and do not need to deliberate.

This does not mean that experts never deliberate or that they always make the correct intuitive judgment. Experts are not infallible. They can find themselves in situations they could not have foreseen, and they cannot respond intuitively to every situation. An expert American driver, for example, can drive in the right-hand lane without conscious attention. If he were driving in England, however, he would have to concentrate on remaining in the left-hand lane and may drive at the level of a proficient performer. Experts are, however, more equipped than the less proficient to process these new situations.

The expert's perspective or basis of experience is more than a mere collection of situational patterns; it can be adapted to new situations and represents a profound grasp of the skill domain. This library of experiences is far more detailed and extensive than an individual's vocabulary and therefore defies verbal description. The situational understanding of an expert cannot be explained rationally nor taught through instruction. Experts act arationally, in a manner that is not dependent on conscious deliberation and can only be fully understood through experiential knowledge.

Expertise enables the most precise and fluid performances that often seem effortless, almost second nature. Dreyfus and Dreyfus state that, "An expert's skill has become so much a part of him that he need be no more aware of it than he is of his own body" (Hubert L. Dreyfus and Stuart E. Dreyfus, *Mind Over Machine: The Power of Human Intuition and Expertise in the Era of the Computer*, 30). By this point, not only has an understanding of many situations in the skill domain been internalized, but the appropriate responses are triggered automatically. This does not mean the expert must follow his intuitions. He can stop and deliberate, but when the expert does not monitor his responses, he is capable of automatic, intuitive response. Dreyfus and Dreyfus quote a Japanese Zen master and martial artist named Taisen Deshimaru, who remarks: "There is no choosing. It happens unconsciously, automatically, naturally. There can be no thought, because if there is thought, there is a time of thought and that means a flaw.... If you take the time to think 'I must use this or that technique,' you will be struck while you are thinking" (Hubert L. Dreyfus and Stuart E. Dreyfus, *Mind Over Machine: The Power of Human Intuition and Expertise in the Era of the Computer*, 32). Such a stream of unconscious, automatic responses characterizes what Dreyfus and Dreyfus call "flow."

Before discussing what they view as flow, it is important to understand Dreyfus and Dreyfus's thoughts about the expert's use of rationality. Conscious use of calculative rationality is to forsake know-how and results in regression to the level of competency or lower. However, experts can employ another sort of rationality that involves critically reflecting on their intuitions. Because no two experiences can be exactly the same, experts look at the differences. The master chess player, for example, will look at the things that seem out of place and decide whether specific aspects of the position seem threatening based on his implicit knowledge of the situation. He might also examine a sequence of moves leading to new positions that he evaluates intuitively to determine his response. It is as if he is playing intuitively in his head. This is a faster form of processing than calculative rationality, but still involves attentional monitoring and can still cause a break in performance, especially in activities that are more fast-paced than chess.

In the case of the proficient or expert performer, when a certain perspective is adopted, tunnel vision can occur. Tunnel vision results from a failure to recognize and adapt to new situations, thus missing altogether a potential new perspective. Attention is so involved in responding to the changing situational patterns that unimportant, irrelevant elements may be ignored. Experts deliberate to check their intuitions so they do not get stuck in the tunnel vision of their perspective. This can be beneficial to performance by allowing the expert to recognize new importance in otherwise overlooked features, but can also result in a degradation of performance resulting from a failure to make automatic, proceduralized responses.

Monitoring is the ability to remain detached from one's perspective, to attend to how well one is performing rather than simply performing and keeping attention focused on the changing situation. According to Dreyfus and Dreyfus, if learning is to occur, progress must be attended to by a monitoring mind that will catalog actions and results for the improvement of future behavior. Monitoring, however, can result in second-guessing one's intuitions, especially if the monitoring relies on conscious deliberation rather than implicit knowledge. Dreyfus and Dreyfus note that there are moments when all attentional monitoring is suspended. From their point of view, this is "flow," which usually represents a peak of performance levels.

The Theory of Optimal Experience

This experience of flow or peak performance is a fairly common one, but scientific accounts of this phenomenon are much less clear. Mihaly Csikszentmihalyi is a prominent author on the subject, but his account of flow differs from that of Dreyfus and Dreyfus.

Csikszentmihalyi's approach is primarily phenomenological, meaning that it deals with the subjective experience of flow. Csikszentmihalyi's theory is derived from subjective accounts of flow experiences. He began a world-wide research project called the Experience Sampling Method. Many individuals from many different walks of life were given pagers that went off randomly several times a day. Participants were told to write down what they doing and how they felt each time they were paged. Through this method, Csikszentmihalyi and his colleagues were able to get an overview of how people structured their conscious attention during various types of activities.

Csikszentmihalyi views consciousness as intentionally ordered information. His theory operates under the assumption that only attention determines what information will enter consciousness. The information that enters conscious experience ultimately makes up memories and determines how one thinks of the self.

The self is an internalized concept which structures an individual's goals and approach to experience (Mihaly Csikszentmihalyi, *Flow: The Psychology of Optimal Experience*). This is surprisingly similar to Dreyfus and Dreyfus's notion of a perspective, the major difference being that a perspective is only an individual's approach to a skill-related experience, whereas the self determines an individual's approach to all experiences.

Csikszentmihalyi's theory is very simple despite its far-reaching applications to the psychological study of experience. However, it is a difficult concept to define objectively because Csikszentmihalyi's definition of flow is quite subjective in nature. Csikszentmihalyi calls flow a feeling, which is the cognition of an emotional state.

According to Csikszentmihalyi, flow is essentially "order in consciousness" (Mihaly Csikszentmihalyi, *Flow: The Psychology of Optimal Experience*, 6). It occurs when all information entering consciousness is consistent with the goals and parameters of the activity in which one is involved.

In short, it is total involvement in activity, and in this aspect it is very similar to Dreyfus and Dreyfus's explanation of flow.

In order for flow to occur, attention must be focused. According to Csikszentmihalyi, the individual's attention is structured by means of his "intentions," i.e., his instincts, needs, goals, drives, and desires (Mihaly Csikszentmihalyi, *Flow: The Psychology of Optimal Experience*). He compares intentions to magnetic fields which move attention toward some features and away from others. Attention determines what information will be considered relevant. In other words, the structure of attention determines the contents of consciousness and can produce either flow or its opposite, which Csikszentmihalyi labels as "psychic entropy" (Mihaly Csikszentmihalyi, *Flow: The Psychology of Optimal Experience*, 36). The experience of psychic entropy is also subjective and can be experienced by the individual as fear, anxiety, anger, guilt, jealousy, pain, and similar emotional states (Mihaly Csikszentmihalyi, *Flow: The Psychology of Optimal Experience*).

Csikszentmihalyi sets up eight criteria for an experience to be considered an optimal experience:

1) The activity must be structured in such a way that there are clear goals for the activity.
2) There must be immediate feedback on how well one is doing, e.g., a rock climber must find that he has progressed and has not fallen.
3) The challenges must match the skill level of the performer so that the performer does not become frustrated or bored.
4) There is intense concentration resulting in a merger of action and awareness—what Csikszentmihalyi called "one-pointedness of mind."
5) Distractions must be excluded from consciousness.
6) As a result of the performer's deep involvement, there is no worry of failure.
7) The performer's self-consciousness disappears into the background.
8) The individual's sense of time becomes distorted. The performer may become engrossed and forget that time is passing, or, in fast-paced activities, time may seem to slow down and things appear to move in slow motion.

(Mihaly Csikszentmihalyi, *Creativity: Flow and the Psychology of Discovery and Invention*, 111)

The initial criteria deal with situational aspects that enable flow to occur, while the final criteria deal with the side effects of experiencing flow.

The most relevant of these in terms of what enables achievement of a flow experience are the merger of action and awareness and the exclusion of distractions from consciousness. This essentially describes what Csikszentmihalyi calls the focus of "psychic energy," which is really another name for attention (Mihaly Csikszentmihalyi, *Flow: The Psychology of Optimal Experience*, 30). The attentional processes of the performer determine whether or not he will have a flow experience. He claims that the control of consciousness is itself a complex form of expertise that cannot be routinely applied. The development of control over consciousness often parallels progress in an activity or the development of expertise in a skill, suggesting that the ability to control attention can be, to a certain extent, skill-specific.

Comparing the Two Theories

To what extent the ability to control consciousness can be developed in terms of a specific skill or how such an ability can be applied to unrelated situations is uncertain. There is no way to draw direct correlations between optimal experience and the development of expertise using these models. Within Dreyfus and Dreyfus's model, flow can only be attained through expertise, or at least proficiency, in a skill, but their model does not address a performer's abilities outside the skill domain. Conversely, Csikszentmihalyi's theory does not assess performance in terms of a skill, but in terms of the self and its experiences. Furthermore, the authors define flow and the mental aspect of performance in very different terms.

There are, however, a few major points of convergence between these two theories. Both Dreyfus and Dreyfus and Csikszentmihalyi are dealing with mental aspects of performance, and both are interested in progression from a low-level mental approach to performance to a high-level mental approach to performance. The goal of both models is the development of fluid, intuitive, and nearly automatic performance of individuals who learn to become deeply involved in an activity, a process which Dreyfus characterizes as the development of expertise and Csikszentmihalyi characterizes as the progression from psychic entropy to psychic order. Also, both theories hold that an individual performs best when adopting a personal perspective on the situation which allows him to clarify goals, relevant information, and methods. This perspective or idea of a self is developed experientially. Furthermore, both claim that in a state of flow, the internalized perspective dissolves into the background as the performer becomes deeply involved in the situation.

Despite the congruence of subject matter, differences between the theories outweigh similarities. The emphasis of their respective approaches is very different. Csikszentmihalyi approaches the idea of performance from the perspective of an individual's subjective experience. His primary emphasis is on the feeling and emotional state of the individual and on his achieving a state of optimal experience. Conversely, Dreyfus and Dreyfus are concerned with the level of performance (i.e., the type of mental functioning the performer exhibits) and with the cognitive processes involved in skill acquisition. Dreyfus and Dreyfus are dealing with two basic types of information processing: calculative rationality characteristic of the first three stages of skill development, which is based on rule-following that is accessible to conscious thought; and intuition, which is the automatic know-how characteristic of the advanced stages of skill development.

Dreyfus and Dreyfus objectify the development of expertise to such a great extent that creativity itself is ignored and has no place in their model. They claim that most of what is taken to be creativity is simply new, unorthodox, intuitively chosen courses of action that may seem irrational to an individual utilizing deliberation rather than holistic recognition. Conversely, creativity is central to Csikszentmihalyi's theory in that it is a natural outgrowth of the flow experience which contributes to the growth of the self and makes learning possible.

Their theories are framed differently and are speaking about two very different processes. Dreyfus and Dreyfus's model is skill- or domain-specific, i.e., they are focused on achievement of expertise and development of skilled performance within the narrow framework of a specific skill, although their discussion applies broadly to anyone developing any skill of any kind. Csikszentmihalyi's theory addresses a specific phenomenon by evaluating subjective accounts of a broad range of related experiences which he is investigating independently of other factors that may be involved.

Most importantly, Dreyfus and Dreyfus and Csikszentmihalyi define flow differently. Csikszentmihalyi defines flow as order in consciousness that can be distinguished by its eight defining characteristics, while Dreyfus and Dreyfus define flow as the deepest level of involvement in the situation resulting from the cessation of monitoring activity that occurs at higher levels of expertise. For Dreyfus and Dreyfus, flow is when know-how takes over and makes skill processes automatic, thereby freeing attention to be totally involved in the performance situation with no need to monitor skill-related processes and procedures.

Dreyfus and Dreyfus and Csikszentmihalyi not only define flow differently; they set different prerequisites for attaining it. According to Dreyfus and Dreyfus, performers must be skilled to experience flow because their skill level must have progressed to such an extent that basic skill processes have become automated and can be performed intuitively. In their five-stage model of expertise, individuals performing at levels from beginner through competent generally focus their attention on skill procedures, e.g., a beginning soccer player must concentrate on how to kick or dribble the ball. For proficient and expert performers, however, knowledge and skills have become proceduralized and automated, so the performer no longer has to attend to skill execution. At these stages, consciousness is free to become immersed in a situation. In Dreyfus and Dreyfus's view, involvement is essential for holistic pattern recognition. They claim that flow can only be produced by total attentional involvement in the situation, such that attention to performance ceases. This can only be achieved at higher levels of expertise.

For Csikszentmihalyi, expertise is irrelevant. All that is required to achieve flow in Csikszentmihalyi's view is that the individual be investing attention in a manner congruent with his goals. From this perspective, involvement can occur at what Dreyfus and Dreyfus would call beginner levels of skill development and does not require experience in the skill. It does, however, require that the individual have an internalized set of goals and an intuitive knowledge of how attention should be directed in order to best facilitate the goals of the self.

Whether or not flow can be achieved by beginners is a major point of divergence between the two theories. For Csikszentmihalyi, flow only refers to the ability to focus and control attention, not to the degree of proficiency in a skill. As a matter of circumstance, the achievement of flow may often be skill-related in that those who are competent are also likely to be more practiced at controlling their consciousness in domain-related situations, but flow can exist independent of skill level and can be transferred to other skill domains. For example, an experienced yogi who is an expert at controlling consciousness could, in theory, experience flow in a wide variety of activities in varied situations. For Csikszentmihalyi, flow is more person-specific than skill-specific in that it is determined largely by the individual's proficiency at controlling his consciousness, an ability which may or may not be skill-specific, depending on the individual. Within Dreyfus and Dreyfus's model, flow is experienced only in the performance of a specific skill in which expertise has been attained.

Many questions about how these two theories are related remain unanswered and may be prime questions for future inquiry. To what extent do higher levels of skill make the performer more likely to attain optimal experience? Are there levels or degrees of optimal experience, and, if there are, do higher skill levels intensify optimal experience? Is there any relationship between what Dreyfus and Dreyfus call flow and Csikszent-mihalyi's idea of optimal experience?

Though there is not enough evidence to call this more than mere speculation, it is probable that experts would have more intense optimal experiences more frequently because they are accustomed to directing their attention in specific patterns and are accustomed to the parameters, goals, and courses of action in the skill domain. It seems correct to say that an individual progressing from novice to expert would almost certainly feel an overall progression from a tendency to experience psychic entropy toward a tendency to experience psychic harmony in skill-related situations. In this very general sense, Csikszentmihalyi's model may provide a rough overview of the subjective side of the skill acquisition process that Dreyfus and Dreyfus describe. It cannot be said for certain, however, that all individuals would experience such a progression, since it is relative to the individual's ability to have optimal experiences. In general, it still is reasonable to say that the development of skill can only enhance the ability to achieve optimal experience.

Overall, it is difficult to say how these theories are related because each addresses the notion of performance in very different terms. Though both theories seem to be referring to the same general phenomenon when they speak of flow, there is no way fit the idea of optimal experience into the framework of Dreyfus and Dreyfus's model, or vice versa. Perhaps the only definite conclusion that can be made about how optimal experience fits into Dreyfus and Dreyfus's model of expertise is that controlling consciousness is a skill, a skill that must be developed like any other skill in the five-stage model. Like any skill, it can be developed in relation with other skills. In order to play soccer well, for instance, one must first learn to dribble a soccer ball, and to do that, one must first learn to run. In the same manner, the control of consciousness can be developed in conjunction with another skill and can serve as a component of any set of skills. In terms of Dreyfus and Dreyfus's model of the development of expertise, the theory of optimal experience can only be seen as a set of rules for a skill domain in which the goal is to order conscious attention into specific patterns, just as playing football orders attention around specific goals and parameters once the performer has learned to play. Viewing optimal experience in this way may be the only way to synthesize two very different theories or to place Csikszentmihalyi's concept of optimal experience into Dreyfus and Dreyfus's model of the development of expertise.

Philosophy

What Is Philosophy?

Beliefs are dangerous. Beliefs allow the mind to stop functioning. A non-functioning mind is clinically dead. Believe in nothing....
—*Maynard James Keenan*

Several years have passed since I first realized how numerous were the false opinions that in my youth I had taken to be true, and thus how doubtful were those that I had subsequently built upon them. And thus I realized that once in my life I had to raze everything to the ground and begin again from the original foundations, if I wanted to establish anything firm and lasting in the sciences.
(René Descartes, "Meditations," Readings in Modern Philosophy, vol. 1, Roger Ariew, et al., (eds.), 27)

I. What is Philosophy?

What is philosophy? One immediate reaction is to say that philosophy is the pursuit of wisdom. When asked for more detail, one might suggest that the pursuit of wisdom is the systematic examination of reality and fundamental concepts such as truth, knowledge, being, or causality. A philosopher, however, should not be satisfied by such definitions, which conceal the meaning of philosophy in vague terms like "systematic examination." What makes a pursuit philosophical? What is this wisdom that philosophers seek? Scientific, religious, and literary thinkers also examine reality, pursue wisdom, and offer metaphysical accounts that seem quite similar to those of philosophy. What features can be used to distinguish philosophical theories and forms of discourse from those of other disciplines or modes of thought?

Other disciplines require presumptions that render their given mode of thought effective. A religious thinker will probably not stray from central doctrinal beliefs. Physical scientists assume the tenets of materialism or at least limit their investigations to phenomena they believe to be physical. It is not the scientist's job to determine whether there is a divine creator beyond space-time or whether there are mental substances outside the framework of physical reality. These kinds of questions are addressed in the philosophy of science. In philosophy, there are no boundaries. The task of the philosopher is to ask: "Are the assumptions of a given domain accurate or at least effective strategies for furthering the pursuit of knowledge? What is knowledge and do scientific methods lead to knowledge?" For example, the philosophy of mind aims to solve the mind-body problem, which is the problem of whether mental substances are physical substances that ought to be examined accordingly by scientists and neurologists.

Therefore, I propose that the best criterion for determining that an inquiry is genuinely philosophical is the absence (or at least proper use) of assumption. An assumption is a claim that is uncertain and has not been thoroughly explained or understood. Since few things are certain, it is often practical to make assumptions in order to increase the range of material that can be addressed philosophically. Philosophers ought to furnish justification for any assumption, by which I mean, provide reasons why the claim may or may not be accurate as well as practical reasons for accepting it (e.g., in order to further the development of a theory).

The philosophical ideal is to devise certain truths. When this is not possible, the philosopher ought to strive toward this ideal by developing claims that are as certain as possible. A theory will probably be incorrect if it is formed from inaccurate postulates. The purpose of philosophy is to question assumed beliefs and claims, not to find support for them wherever possible or conduct one's examination as though they are necessarily true. Philosophers ought not rely upon any belief blindly. Intuition or religious faith may inspire a philosopher to follow a certain avenue of inquiry, but the investigation itself ought to proceed as though everything this philosopher believes may be false. René Descartes, a seminal modern philosopher, summarizes this sentiment concisely:

> I will accomplish this by putting aside everything that admits of the least doubt, as if I had discovered it to be patently false. I will stay on this course until I know something certain, or, if nothing else, until I at least know for certain that nothing is certain. (René

Descartes, "Meditations," *Readings in Modern Philosophy*, vol. 1,
Roger Ariew, et al., (eds.), 30)

Being too skeptical, however, often leads nowhere. Thus, it is useful to
derive theories that will be accurate given that a certain set of postulates
are true. If a postulate is to be called philosophical, however, it must be
justified with explicit reasons.

Even in the case of a single theory, it may not be clear which claims are
truly philosophical and which claims are not. Many scientific and religious
accounts are supported by or developed upon a philosophical basis. Furthermore, many renowned philosophers (e.g., Descartes) devise theories
by combining rigorous, philosophical reasoning and religious intuitions. I
suggest that the general rule could be roughly phrased as follows: "Theories that involve fewer, more carefully explained, practical, plausible, and
minimalistic assumptions are closer to the philosophical ideal." Rather
than asking whether a theory is philosophical, it is perhaps better to ask:
"How philosophically sound are the claims and premises of this theory?"
This, I suggest, is what should be called philosophy: the questioning of
how certain one can be of claim or belief. This is analogous to the following questions: "What constitutes verification? What is knowledge or
wisdom?" Given such an account, the Socratic method and Descartes's
method of doubt are quintessential examples of philosophical practice.

II. Foundationalism and the Beginning of Philosophy

The philosophical process of René Descartes's "Meditations" served as
a prototype for modern methods. This work is a prime example of how to
proceed with philosophical inquiry as well as how to properly incorporate
uncertain intuitions into a philosophical theory. Descartes questioned everything and began his investigation with no fixed beliefs or presumptions
about the world; he writes:

> Several years have passed since I first realized how numerous
> were the false opinions that in my youth I had taken to be true, and
> thus how doubtful were those that I had subsequently built upon
> them. And thus I realized that once in my life I had to raze every-
> thing to the ground and begin again from the original foundations,
> if I wanted to establish anything firm and lasting in the sciences.
> (René Descartes, "Meditations," *Readings in Modern Philosophy*,
> vol. 1, Roger Ariew, et al., (eds.), 27)

Descartes's aim was to ascertain the most certain and fundamental truths about existence. He would then use these truths as the foundation upon which a more comprehensive metaphysical theory could be built.

Descartes would first have to determine how something could be known with certainty, what criteria ought to be used for verifying a claim, and what constitutes knowledge. He hypothesized that the faculty of reason, when used properly, enables man to think with clarity and begin to comprehend the nature of God. Thus, he used reason to reevaluate every aspect of his existence and scrutinize his every conclusion. Descartes proposed the method of doubt for eliminating potentially false beliefs:

> Reason now persuades me that I should withhold my assent no less carefully from opinions that are not completely certain and indubitable than I would from those that are patently false. For this reason, it will suffice for the rejection of all these opinions, if I find in each of them some reason for doubt.... Because undermining the foundations will cause whatever has been built upon them to crumble of its own accord, I will attack straightaway those principles which supported everything I once believed. (René Descartes, "Meditations," *Readings in Modern Philosophy*, vol. 1, Roger Ariew, et al., (eds.), 28)

Through this skeptical process, Descartes realized that many of his core beliefs were assumptions which he could not immediately verify (e.g., the belief that he had a material body). Although he was not sure that bodies are composed of "material" substance, he was at least certain that he thought of a body. Descartes had found his famous truth: "'I am, I exist' is necessarily true every time I utter it or conceive it in my mind" (René Descartes, "Meditations," *Readings in Modern Philosophy*, vol. 1, Roger Ariew, et al., (eds.), 30). In this context, the "I" is a thinking thing or a mind. Thus, Descartes proposed that one's immediate experience is a means for verifying knowledge.

The intention to derive knowledge a priori is called the principle of foundationalism. The motivation behind Descartes's foundationalism was to analyze and deconstruct his belief-system in order to rebuild his conception of existence from an indubitable basis. This principle exemplifies the philosophical ideal put forth here. All philosophical inquiry should begin by questioning and reevaluating one's most fundamental beliefs.

Descartes departed from foundationalism as his metaphysical system grew more complex. He began relying on uncertain claims that he strongly believed to be true. Although most of Descartes's conclusions are derived logically, his postulates are often beliefs or intuitions, some of which are more dubious than others. For example, two premises in Descartes's ontological argument for the existence of God are that "God has all per-fections" and that "necessary existence is a perfection." These are clearly religious beliefs, supported only by Descartes's immediate experience of faith. Such claims are hardly well-evidenced or logical inferences; they are assumptions. On my account, assumption compromises the integrity of the philosophical process, yielding a theory that is further from being ideal.

Descartes's work nearly fulfills my philosophical ideal because he properly integrated assumption into his arguments. He developed specif-ic reasons for believing his postulates. More importantly, he established that his postulates have profound implications and deserve consideration accordingly. If Descartes's premises are correct, his arguments lead to im-portant conclusions about reality (e.g., they prove the existence of God). For those with religious objectives, this is powerful motivation for accept-ing such postulates regardless of their accuracy. Descartes's assumptions are nevertheless explanatory gaps that make his theory less philosophical-ly sound.

I have offered the "Meditations" as a model for practicing philosophy, yet this work falls short of the ideals put forward here (i.e., certainty and absence of assumption). Descartes made a valiant effort to develop a cer-tain theory of reality. He is clearly an exemplary philosopher. If even Des-cartes's work does not wholly fulfill the philosophical ideal, what does? Is such an ideal even attainable or realistic? Is it practical or even possible to be a philosopher without making any assumptions? If there were such a philosopher, how might he or she practice philosophy?

III. The Wisdom of Socrates

Socrates was an accomplished philosopher who had an enormous impact on the development of Western philosophy, especially his fellow ancient Greek philosophers. Socrates wrote no known work of his own. The records of his life and work are primarily recorded in Plato's writ-ing. One could interpret Plato's portrayal of Socrates as representing the philosophical ideal. Socrates' methods and discourses yielded many im-portant contributions to philosophy without utilizing assumptions. As Pla-to would have it, Socrates rarely made decisive claims about reality and never proposed elaborate metaphysical theories. The purpose of Socrates' philosophical practice was only to ask questions. By questioning his peers ceaselessly, Socrates believed that he could help others critically examine and develop their views. This instructive tactic of ceaseless questioning became infamously known as the Socratic method. Plato writes:

The most important aspect of my skill is the ability to apply every conceivable test to see whether the young man's mental offspring is illusory and false or viable and true. But I have this feature in common with midwives—I myself am barren of wisdom. The criticism that's often made of me—that it's a lack of wisdom that makes me ask others questions, but say nothing positive myself—is perfectly true…. And they make this progress, clearly, not because they ever learn anything from me; the many fine ideas and offspring that they produce come from within themselves…. God and I are responsible for their delivery…. I myself am quite devoid of wisdom; all I know is the fact of my own ignorance. (Plato, *Theaetetus*)

Though Socrates asked insightful questions about everything, he rarely answered philosophical questions in much detail. Socrates abided by a different foundational truth; he believed that the only certainty was his uncertainty.

The pursuit of wisdom is a Socratic definition of philosophy, yet Socrates never arrived at any conclusions that he considered wise. Although Socrates never said this explicitly, a Socratic definition of wisdom is "knowing that one will (or may) never know anything certainly." If this were the case, it would seem that "knowledge" is not so rigid. Despite the ideals of defining criteria for verification and a priori truth, perhaps these notions are not so important. Perhaps knowledge is more like a toy. One can verify claims using science or mathematics or religious experience. Play with this perspective and that perspective. There is no absolute knowledge, and every perspective is worth seeing.

This kind of idea is similar to Friedrich Nietzsche's notion of perspectivism. Nietzsche held that no specific form of knowledge was supreme; therefore, examining phenomena from as many perspectives as possible was the best way to acquire knowledge. Nietzsche illustrated this with a metaphor that represents man's attempt to understand reality. There is a box with small pinholes and slits on its exterior; inside the box is an object (i.e., reality). Is the best way to learn about this object to look through only one of the slits in the box? No particular view provides "false" data, but no particular perspective provides information that is necessarily true because the data cannot be verified without opening the box. Partial data can be misleading. For example, you look inside, see a ball, and come to believe that there is a ball inside the box. There is, however, only a picture. No single perspective reveals the whole story, the complete truth. Therefore, one should not limit oneself to a single point of view.

This notion is similar to the philosophical ideal of many Buddhist philosophers, including Candrakirti and Bodhidharma. These thinkers sought to attain "viewlessness" or freedom from a fixed conception of reality. According to the bodhisattvas, no view is called true and no view is called false. This is the meaning of wisdom.

IV. The Essence of Philosophy

Explicitly defining philosophy may be impossible, since part of philosophy's purpose is to define itself. The following definitions, for example, are precisely what philosophy is not:

A particular system of thought or doctrine;

A set of basic principles or concepts underlying a particular sphere of knowledge;

A precept, or set of precepts, beliefs, principles, or aims, underlying somebody's practice or conduct.

This is what is left when philosophical questioning ceases. As mentioned, physical science is governed by a certain set of tenets. Discovering these tenets is the task of philosophy. Philosophy itself is not governed; it is the attempt to find a sense of order in the anarchy of thought. These definitions are better, but still not ideal:

The pursuit of wisdom;

An analysis of the grounds of and concepts expressing fundamental beliefs.

This, however, is where we began, and it is still not quite satisfactory. Certain philosophers hold that wisdom is knowing that one cannot entirely know wisdom. Given a perspectivist account of knowledge, the pursuit of wisdom will proceed indefinitely. Must "belief" or "knowledge" be objects of a philosopher's pursuit? I conclude that it is not the wisdom, beliefs, concepts, principles, or systems of thought that characterize philosophy as philosophical, but rather, the pursuit itself.

I suggest that questioning is the essence of philosophy; it is philosophy in its most pure and unadulterated form. This ideal is embodied by Plato's portrayal of the Socratic method. Who says that a philosopher must manufacture answers? There may not be a clear line between philosophical, religious, scientific, and literary work unless philosophy is the practice of questioning that motivates the creation of answers. I say that answers are fictions; they are philosophically motivated religious, literary, and scientific works. They are belief systems that may have been revised through philosophical questioning.

On this account, philosophy is one of the most simple and fundamental human instincts. Natural, human curiosity is the beginning of philosophy. If one begins to truly question one's conception of the world, simple questions cease to be silly and one's entire existence becomes a baffling puzzle. I have often heard adults disregard children's simplistic questions about the world. The child may ask: "Why is the sky blue?" This a profound philosophical question which the adult might answer: "This is the color called 'blue,' and it is the same color as the sky." Then, inevitably, the child will ask: "Why?" Children will sometimes ask this incessantly, responding to any explanation by asking: "Why?" On my account, such a child is the ideal philosopher.

The Quantum Mind

Many modern neurologists tend to presuppose that the brain follows the rules of classical physics. Neurology and cognitive psychology have become different branches of science, rarely considering the actual physics behind neuron firings. Though these fields have been successful in figuring out how the brain works, they have still not been able to explain how consciousness is produced from physical processes in the brain. Nobody knows where consciousness is located in the scheme of physical reality. Most scientists are materialists and rely upon the working assumption that the mind is a physical phenomenon that is produced by neural activity in the brain. There are still many scientists and philosophers, however, who are dualist-interactionists (i.e., they hold that mental and physical stuff are completely separate types of substance that somehow interact causally). The fact that, hundreds of years after Descartes, mind-body dualism is still a prevalent view says something about how little we've uncovered about a physical home for the mind. Even though we have made many advancements in brain-science, we still seem far from a clear understanding of the mind.

As new revelations in quantum mechanics have come to light, people have begun writing about the possibility of "the quantum brain." It is possible that the physical processes involved in producing consciousness cannot be fully understood in terms of classical physics. In other words, the brain may not behave in an entirely classical way. While it is fairly easy to explain most cognitive processes in terms of specific brain functions and neuronal patterns (or at least, it is easy to see how they could be explained), explanations of consciousness, the "subjective character" of experience, seem to be completely elusive. Anything that anyone says about the physical location of consciousness is purely speculative. Nobody really has a clear idea. How can some basic ideas in quantum physics help us determine what a picture of the "the quantum brain" might look like?

The physicist Werner Heisenberg showed in 1926 that, when studying things like sub-atomic particles that exist at an extremely small scale, motion is not continuous when it is observed. It seems that observation determines whether motion is continuous or discontinuous—observation determines a fixed location for a particle. This is the idea behind Niels Bohr's correspondence and complementarity principles as well as wave-particle duality. The correspondence principle suggests that the principles of quantum mechanics only apply in cases when the laws of classical physics do not, that is, at small scales where continuous motion cannot be observed. The wave-particle duality states that light behaves like a wave when propagating through space and behaves like a particle when it interacts with macroscopic objects (i.e., when an observation takes place).

Bohr's principles suggest that electrons exist as waves that collapse into a fixed location upon observation. The problem is that when waves are not observed, they do not undergo any collapse, but when they are observed, they have already collapsed, and no collapse can be observed (i.e., the interference pattern produced by light's wave-like behavior disappears when observed). Therefore, the wave state of particles cannot be observed and must be inferred—this is the point at which the probability laws of quantum mechanics apply.

Erwin Schroedinger first imagined the wave as an indeterminate stream based on a mathematical function "dancing" through space-time. Schroedinger's waves were unobservable and could only be imagined mathematically. Max Born developed the probability interpretation of Schroedinger's waves, which views these waves as fields of probability. These fields indicate where an electron is likely to appear when observation takes place. This quantum picture of reality upset the deterministic, mechanical model of the world. Physicists' attempts to study light during this period discovered cases where Newtonian laws cannot predict the behavior of particles.

The deterministic Newtonian picture of the universe based on the laws of cause and effect had dominated physical science for hundreds of years. Newton's theory was based on undisturbed observations of continuous motion at the macroscopic level of reality. Heisenberg's uncertainty principle, however, seems to prove that, at the microscopic level, undisturbed observation is impossible.

Einstein proposed a test of this theory, a thought experiment in which a particle is launched through a slit. After passing through the slit the particle could be observed, but before it passed through the slit it could not be seen. If Einstein was correct, there was a real particle with a fixed location before it passed through the slit. The particle is following "hidden" physical laws, though we do not have an account of those laws because the particle cannot yet be observed. If Bohr was correct, the particle was not there until it was observed. A later experiment by John Bell showed that the view advocated by Bohr and the discontinuists, the Copenhagen interpretation of quantum mechanics, was correct. If the Copenhagen interpretation of quantum mechanics is correct, then Einstein's theory of relativity is false at the particle level.

The Einstein, Podolsky, Rosen paradox (or EPR paradox) was another argument made against the Copenhagen interpretation of quantum mechanics. When two electrons are split, they are propelled in opposite directions and will always have opposite spins (e.g., if one electron has up-spin, the other will have down-spin). If the Copenhagen interpretation is correct, then measuring the spin of one particle will force it to take a definite property, that of up-spin or down-spin. Einstein argues that this is impossible because, in principle, the electrons could be very far away from each other. If determining the spin of one electron instantly determines the spin of the other, then the information that one particle's location has been determined would have to travel to the other particle faster than the speed of light, violating Einstein's principle that nothing can travel faster than the speed of light. The experiments proposed by John Bell again proved that Einstein was wrong.

What are the implications of quantum mechanics for a physical picture of human consciousness? One speculative picture suggests that atoms may have some kind of rudimentary "mind," that human consciousness is a macroscopic mind whose content and action is determined by many microscopic interactions. In other words, the one big mind gets its information from thousands of smaller "atomic minds" which detect information about "qwiff-possibilities." Qwiffs are basically quantum wave-functions similar to Schroedinger's waves. They are indeterminate. When a qwiff "pops," the wave-function collapses and is forced to take a definite form. A qwiff denotes a set of potential outcomes that could result from a given wave function. It is a probability-wave, which becomes determinate upon collapsing. According to this picture, atomic minds deal with information found on the level of qwiffs. These atomic minds act as quantum detectors, measuring qwiff activity and forcing qwiffs to pop. When a qwiff encounters an atomic mind, it pops and produces a definite outcome perceivable by the atomic mind. The atomic mind either opens or closes each neuron's gate; it is either on or off. Then, the macroscopic mind takes information gathered from all the atomic minds once the qwiffs have already popped and observations have taken place. The macroscopic mind takes the determinate information measured by millions of atomic minds and integrates this information into a coherent picture. In this theory, the macroscopic mind acts like a data-server for the atomic minds.

Roger Penrose in his book, *Shadows of the Mind*, illustrates a well-developed theory of the quantum mind. Penrose believes that it is ridiculous for neurologists to assume that the brain behaves in a totally classical manner. Everything is composed of atomic and subatomic stuff—why should the brain be any different?

Penrose argues that neurons act as quantum detectors. In order to understand how this might be possible, Penrose relies on biological information about the physical structure of cells. Single-cell organisms like paramecium and amoebas are capable of complex behaviors that do not require them to have any kind of nervous system. Their behavior is governed by a complex cytoskeleton. The cytoskeletal shell has cilia, whose movement is governed by the cytoskeletal shell. It also has microtubules and centrioles, which are the relevant features here. Within the cytoskeletal shell is internal fluid that remains relatively undisturbed. It is primarily affected by influences transmitted through microtubules or that otherwise disturb the cytoskeleton. The centriole then acts as an organizing center for information gathered by the microtubules and causes the shell to perform some action. The point of importance for Penrose's argument is that, even in simple organisms, microtubules can act as information processors in some very simple capacity.

The basic structure of a neuron is not completely unlike that of a single-cell organism, although its functions are more complex. Microtubules transport neurotransmitter molecules into the neuron. These microtubules form complex structures like a miniature ant colony, forming pathways that connect most parts of the neuron together. They run through the synapses, the cytoskeletal shell, and almost the entire length of the axon. They form a "communicating network" to coordinate the activity of the neuron and, ultimately, play a major role in enabling the neuron to communicate with other neurons. The biology at work here is complex, but it suffices to say that Penrose claims that microtubules can act as data transmitters, spreading information throughout the cells in the brain. At the very least, models of the brain should not only account for the overall neuronal organization of the brain, but should also consider the importance of the structures governing individual neurons (such as the cytoskeleton). Why not consider the atomic nature of neurons?

Penrose argues that microtubules act as quantum detectors and provide a protected space that can preserve a state of "quantum coherence" within an individual microtubule. This quantum coherence is attributed to a Bose-Einstein condensate. A Bose-Einstein condensate occurs when a large number of particles participate collectively in a single quantum state. The action of such a condensate can be explained with the same kind of wave-function used for explaining a single particle, only in this case, the wave function applies to a large collection of particles and is scaled to predict the behavior of a whole system of wave-functions.

Penrose concludes that when particles collide with the neuron, the microtubules act like slits in a particle detector, forcing the wave-function to collapse and take a definite location as a particle. The microtubule acts as an insulator, preserving the observation and position of the particle for a split-second. When many particles enter the microtubule and the wave-function of the Einstein-Bose condensate collapses, it creates a coherent quantum state within the microtubule. In this sense, microtubules work in a manner that is somewhat similar to the observer. The microtubule detects the overall effect of many photons. It provides a place where data about the a probability function can be gathered by taking the overall average of an Einstein-Bose condensate. To try to put it simply, the particles each take a definite "spin" and the microtubule contains information about the percentage of times that particles take an up or down spin. If this information is coherent with information gathered in other microtubules, (i.e., if there is a coherent overall quantum effect on many microtubules), the cytoskeletal shell is affected and the neuron is activated. It is at this moment that a single mental state is produced, which can then be communicated by the neuron to other neurons in a classical manner.

According to Penrose's theory, the microtubules gather data about the overall probability that an event has occurred and either affect or do not affect the neuron. This information is random (i.e., in a non-computable format) when it enters the microtubule. The cytoskeletal shell is either stimulated, causing an electrical impulse to fire across the synapse to another neuron, or is not. At this moment, the information conveyed by the neuron is computable, which means it can be translated as a series of on/off switches which correspond to microtubule stimulation. This is how Penrose argues that microscopic information is transformed into macroscopic information, producing a definite state that can be communicated to executive centers of the brain.

In Penrose's view, in order for a conscious mental event to occur, there must be a large-scale quantum coherency in more than one area of the brain. Not only must a single neuron detect quantum coherency within its microtubules, which stimulates its cytoskeletal shell and causes the neuron to transmit information that has been deemed significant, but this same coherency must be found in many neurons. If there is a large-scale quantum coherency in the brain, then consciousness is possible because many neurons will communicate with one another. In other words, if a whole pattern of neurons detects that there is some major quantum effect (i.e., the microscopic effect gets closer to forming macroscopic patterns), than these neurons start communicating and the whole brain notices. The brain "pays attention" to this more sophisticated neuronal pattern. In other words, the macroscopic mind does not notice that microscopic events have happened until the effects registered by microscopic minds are consistent with one another and produce a large-scale quantum effect. The macroscopic mind then notices that many neurons seem to be detecting something and communicating their detections to one another. This electrical pattern caused by the communication of many neurons is conscious activity in the brain.

This last statement seems like a typical theory of consciousness. In Penrose's theory, mental information is initially encoded on a microscopic, microtubule level. In this sense, mental state events are only processed by classical functions in the brain. This information is, at a fundamental level, indeterminate. Consciousness, then, is not formed solely from macroscopic phenomena. Consciousness does not result from a direct transmission of classical forces—the macroscopic phenomena are created (in part) by an interpretation of fundamentally indeterminate probabilities at the microscopic level. In other words, in Penrose's theory, consciousness results from physical processes whereby reality is (to a certain extent) reinvented. Whether or not a certain mental event will occur (for instance, seeing rays of light) is a function of probability and inherently random. The reason we see light is that enough photons have activated a sufficient number of neurons to cause a pattern of activity in the brain, which results from a corresponding large-scale quantum coherency. In this sense, mind exists on two levels, macroscopic and microscopic. The macroscopic mind is determinate—we have (relatively) definite experiences. At the microscopic level, mind is indeterminate. It is a field of quantum probability that is fundamentally indeterminate and, therefore, non-computational.

There is no clear evidence that microtubules even perform any of the basic biological functions that Penrose attributes to them, let alone the complex microscopic functions. Theories of the quantum brain (and much about quantum mechanics in general) are still in their infancy. They are the beginning of a process, but the questions raised and addressed by the theory are important and appropriate questions, even if the current answers are inadequate.

Materialism and Free Will

The philosophy of materialism holds that matter and physical processes comprise the whole of reality. One early adherent was Lucretius, a Roman philosopher of the first century BC, whose materialist viewpoint seems to exclude the possibility of free will. Since in the materialist worldview all phenomena are determined by physical processes, it would seem that consciousness is also subject to the laws of nature and determined in a similar way. At best, then, humans in this materialist world may experience the illusion of free will, when, in reality, this experience is determined by functions of the material world. Given this account, it is unlikely that there is any such thing as a "truly free" will in the materialist worldview. This, however, is dependent on one's definition of free will. There are two ways that free will could exist in a materialist universe like Lucretius's. These are based on different accounts of what free will is and how it exists.

In the first instance, it is possible that certain combinations of material aggregates could become functionally organized in such a way as to produce a mind. This mind could have some level of conscious control over the movements of this conglomeration of particles that provide the necessary functional organization. In Lucretius's account, such a cluster would have to be formed by random atomic events. Even these events, however, have order to them. Evolution, for example, is based on random processes. These random processes involve selection such that certain structures work in the world and certain structures do not. Thus, the outcome of the random process is an ordered building of physical structures that become increasingly complex and can perform "higher-level" functions. One such function may be a will of some sort. This will would only be free to a certain extent; certainly, it would not be omnipotent. As Lucretius points out, all things are subject to the decay of time, and the welfare of our crops is determined by natural forces, yet it is also a result of our natural will to harvest. Human will may be a result of nature's random processes, but perhaps it is a result intended to perpetuate the process. In other words, maybe freedom over actions is beneficial to nature's random evolution because it adds another source for generating random inputs. Ultimately, our actions and thoughts would still be based on natural processes, but perhaps, in this account, one who has the illusion of free will is genuinely free because the system has, by chance, created freedom of mind.

This leads to the second way in which free will in its ultimate sense could exist. Perhaps free will is a part of nature. Lucretius says, "nature is free and uncontrolled by proud masters and runs the universe by herself" (Lucretius, *On the Nature of the Universe*, Ronald Latham (trans.), 92). Perhaps there is a certain freedom in randomness. Just as humans could experience freedom and contribute by their choices to the random unfolding of nature, so may all the elements of nature. Perhaps free will exists at the atomic or subatomic levels as it does at the level of human experience. Perhaps particles make "choices," and these choices are the source of randomness. Freedom could be woven into the fabric of nature itself and is embedded in all of its aspects.

As Lucretius suggests, there may be many universes and many worlds. Perhaps they are all microcosms and macrocosms of nature's inherent freedom. Lucretius says that, "Nothing is ever created out of nothing," yet he also claims that no element is ever reduced to nothing, saying, "Nothing is ever annihilated" (Lucretius, *On the Nature of the Universe*, Ronald Latham (trans.), 22). Accepting these claims makes one wonder how things were first created. Lucretius seems to believe that nature herself is the "creatress and perfectress" (Lucretius, *On the Nature of the Universe*, Ronald Latham (trans.), 93). Perhaps creation itself is freedom, and the essence of nature is to create free agents that spawn more free agents. Nature is not any one universe or particle, nor a set of particles or worlds, but is rather the essence of free creation and potential that runs through all things, including human minds. Thus, identified with nature, we are free.

Still, although much of the universe resembles Lucretius's picture, part of Lucretius's picture is that of not yet knowing the picture. For example, Lucretius said that when men do not know the cause, they call it god:

> The reason why all mortals are so gripped by fear is that they see all sorts of things happening on the earth and in the sky with no discernible cause, and these they attribute to the will of a god. (Lucretius, *On the Nature of the Universe*, Ronald Latham (trans.), 13-14)

Lucretius himself is not claiming to know the original cause. He is only saying that the task of science is to pursue truth, not to fabricate easy answers to difficult questions. Thus, Lucretius does not offer a clear picture of mother nature; he only claims that our goal should be to develop a clearer picture that is not sullied with superstitions.

Descartes on Dualism

René Descartes relies on the use of doubt to call into question his most fundamental beliefs, eliminating any claim that is not absolutely certain in order to determine the foundational truths of human existence. He concludes that the only indubitable truth is that his mind exists, and he writes in his "Second Meditation":

> … I am, I exist, is necessarily true whenever it is put forward by me or conceived in my mind. But I do not yet have a sufficient understanding of what this "I" is, that now necessarily exists. So I must be on my guard against carelessly taking something else to be this "I," and so making a mistake in the very item of knowledge that I maintain is most certain and evident of all. (René Descartes, "Second Meditation," *The Philosophical Writings of Descartes*, vol. 2, John Cottingham (trans.), 17)

In his "Sixth Meditation," however, Descartes posits that the I, the mental substance which is the fundamental essence of a human being, has a physical body existing in external reality. This argument gave rise to a philosophy called substance dualism, which views mental and physical substances as two completely different types of substances that are somehow capable of causally interacting with one another. Given Descartes's claims about mental reality, Cartesian dualism's assertion that there is an external reality outside of mental experience cannot be considered a foundational truth.

It is important to give a clear exegesis of Descartes's notion of the "I" before critiquing his ideas. This, however, is more difficult than it may seem, as Descartes never states explicitly what he is except to say: "I am, then, in the strict sense only a thing that thinks; that is, I am a mind, or intelligence, or intellect, or reason—words whose meaning I have been ignorant of until now" (René Descartes, "Second Meditation," *The Philosophical Writings of Descartes*, vol. 2, John Cottingham (trans.), 18). This sort of language conveys a vague idea of what kind of a thing he is, but does not explain the meaning words like "mind" or provide a clear definition of the thing which seems to be thinking. Descartes's discussion continues to circle around the question of what it means to be a thinking thing, but, ultimately, he is unable to clearly describe a mind because, as he claims:

> It would indeed be a case of fictitious invention if I used my imag-
> ination to establish that I was something or other; for imagining is
> simply contemplating the shape or image of a corporeal thing. Yet
> I know now for certain both that I exist and at the same time that
> all such images and, in general, everything relating to the nature
> of the body, could be mere dreams....I thus realize that none of the
> things that the imagination enables me to grasp is at all relevant to
> this knowledge of myself which I possess, and that the mind must
> therefore be most carefully diverted from such things if it is to
> perceive its own nature as distinctly as possible. (René Descartes,
> "Second Meditation," *The Philosophical Writings of Descartes*,
> vol. 2, John Cottingham (trans.), 19)

In this passage, Descartes realizes that his mind cannot be accurately conceptualized in terms of what is commonly thought to be physical re-ality, which may not be real. He claims that imagined things, objects that "common sense" seems to conceive of by using sensory perception, are not useful when attempting to describe mind's nature because they are possibly fabrications of the mind that do not resemble anything real. Thus, the nature of the mind itself cannot be known, as such knowledge would merely be an imagined conceptual representation based upon other dreams of the mind. The mind is one's being, one has to be it; it is the knower, which itself cannot be an object of knowledge, but can only be directly ex-perienced as existing through the experience of being aware of thoughts.

Descartes holds, therefore, that this "...puzzling 'I' which cannot be pictured in the imagination..." can only arbitrarily be called a "thing," and he defines this thing not by discussing the nature of the thing itself, but by conceptualizing the thing in terms of its relationship to "thinking" (René Descartes, "Second Meditation," *The Philosophical Writings of Descartes*, vol. 2, John Cottingham (trans.), 20). According to Descartes, a thinking thing is something that can do things like doubt, affirm or deny, be will-ing or unwilling, imagine, and have sensory perceptions (René Descartes, "Second Meditation," *The Philosophical Writings of Descartes*, vol. 2, John Cottingham (trans.), 19). Such thoughts are also certainly real; it can-not be false that "I certainly seem to see" (René Descartes, "Second Medi-tation," *The Philosophical Writings of Descartes*, vol. 2, John Cottingham (trans.), 19). Thus, the existence of thought and the mind are the only certain truths. These two truths are inseparable, essentially amounting to one truth, as Descartes writes: "thought; this alone is inseparable from me" (René Descartes, "Second Meditation," *The Philosophical Writings of Descartes*, vol. 2, John Cottingham (trans.), 18). I interpret this as Descartes positing that the "I" is a being or "thing" which includes the world of thoughts that are attributed to this thing or experienced by this thing. Thought is a necessary aspect of this being's existence; the existence of the mind depends upon its ability to have thoughts, such as the thought that I exist (René Descartes, "Second Meditation," *The Philosophical Writings of Descartes*, vol. 2, John Cottingham (trans.), 18). This can be understood to mean that a human being's fundamental nature is the individual's sense of self-awareness, which contains all mental objects that are experienced in relation to the self.

The "I" is the whole of mental existence, including thoughts and the mind that knows them; it is the essence of a human being and the location of human experience. It is certainly what one seems to be and all that one can know oneself to be; therefore, Descartes initially claims that the "I" is all that he is. For the purposes of this explanation, Descartes's "I" could be thought of as basically similar to Martin Heidegger's idea of "being-in-the-world," though such a comparison should not entail all the specific criteria that Heidegger outlines in his ontological analysis of being-in-the-world, but rather the general idea of being-in-the-world. To borrow from Heidegger:

> Da-sein is a being which is related understandingly in its being toward that being. In saying this we are calling attention to the formal concept of existence. Da-sein exists. Furthermore, Da-sein is the being which I myself always am....These determinations of being of Da-sein, however, must now be seen and understood a priori as grounded upon that constitution of being which we call being-in-the-world.... The compound expression "being-in-the-world" indicates, in the very way we have coined it, that it stands for a unified phenomenon (Martin Heidegger, *Being and Time*, Joan Stambaugh, (trans.), 49).

In terms of my argument, Da-sein can be thought of as the "thing" or "mind" that Descartes claims is the essence of a human being. This thing's existence depends upon its being "... related understandingly in its being toward that being" (Martin Heidegger, *Being and Time*, Joan Stambaugh, (trans.), 49); that is to say, by being-in-the-world, as it necessarily is, Da-sein understands its being. This is similar to the way Descartes can know of his own being (i.e., in terms of its relationship to the world of thoughts). Thus, the "I" is necessarily "being-in-the-world," a phrase which indicates that the mental experience, the mind and thoughts of the being in question, is a singularity. This whole, singular being that is being-in-the-world is human existence; it is the only thing that can certainly be known to exist.

Descartes himself concludes in his "Second Meditation" that only this dream experience of being-in-the-world can be certainly called real. He writes of a piece of wax:

> But what is this wax which is perceived by the mind alone? It is of course the same wax which I see, which I touch, which I picture in my imagination, in short the same wax which I thought it to be from the start. And yet, and here is the point, the perception I have of it is a case not of vision or touch or imagination—nor has it ever been, despite previous appearances—but of purely mental scrutiny (René Descartes, "Second Meditation," *The Philosophical Writings of Descartes*, vol. 2, John Cottingham (trans.), 21).

Here Descartes observes that an arbitrarily chosen object that appears to be external, apparently perceived by faculties which rely on sensory perception, is actually known only in the mind (just as such faculties can be known only in the mind). All that Descartes can know of the wax's existence is his mental experience of the wax. This applies to all thoughts and, therefore, all things in his world, as he further describes:

> …I look out of the window and see men crossing the square, as I just happen to have done, I normally say that I see the men themselves, just as I say that I see the wax. Yet do I see any more than hats and coats which could conceal automatons? I judge that they are men. And so something which I thought I was seeing with my eyes is in fact grasped solely by the faculty of judgement which is in my mind. (René Descartes, "Second Meditation," *The Philosophical Writings of Descartes*, vol. 2, John Cottingham (trans.), 21).

As do many other examples of Descartes's writing, this emphasizes that only the mental experience of objects perceived as external, not the external objects themselves, can be known to exist with certainty.

This particular example, however, also brings into question the notion of what it is to be human or to be a thing that has mental experiences, specifically with regard to how mental experience could be thought of in the context of a world outside of experience. In this passage, mentality is attributed to objects within Descartes's mind that are seen as fellow humans, but their mentality, their humanity is known to be real only insofar as it is judged to be so by Descartes. In the same manner, one considers oneself to be a human being, rather than a disembodied mind or some other thing, only because one judges oneself to be a thinking person that has a body. If humans were automatons (assuming that we are not), it is interesting to wonder whether we would know the difference, just as we do not know that we are not actually brains in vats having the mental experience of being-in-the-world.

One cannot know how or from where this being-in-the-world experience is produced. The experience could be produced by an unconscious component of one's mind or a program designed to operate one's mind, or could even appear without source or cause. The origin of thought and mind cannot be known, for one can have no knowledge of how one's experience is produced except knowledge that is gained through this experience and could therefore be a dream that is real only in the mind. Thus, one can have no absolutely certain knowledge of how mind exists in a world outside experience, how such a world functions, or whether such a world even exists. As Descartes observes, there is no way to be certain that he is not dreaming all of this (René Descartes, "Second Meditation," *The Philosophical Writings of Descartes*, vol. 2, John Cottingham (trans.), 19), an accurate claim which he eventually contradicts.

In his subsequent meditations, Descartes posits the existence of an external reality which is of a completely different substance than the mind. He obviously must rely on evidence known within his mind, which is not sufficient to prove the claim that external reality necessarily exists. Yet Descartes expands his view of what is necessarily real to include the body and external reality as well as the immortal soul's direct relationship to God. In his "Sixth Meditation," Descartes argues:

> There is certainly further in me a passive quality of perception, that is, of receiving and recognizing ideas of sensible things, but this would be useless to me, if there were not either in me or in some other thing another active quality capable of forming and producing these ideas. But this active faculty cannot exist in me [inasmuch as I am a thing that thinks] seeing that it does not presuppose thought, and also that those ideas are often produced in me without my contributing in any way to the same, and often even produced against my will; it is thus necessarily the case that the faculty resides in some substance different from me in which all the reality which is objectively in the ideas that are produced by this faculty is formally and eminently contained…. And this substance is either a body, that is, a corporeal nature… or it is God Himself (René Descartes, "Meditations II, VI," *Problems in Mind: Readings in Contemporary Philosophy of Mind*, Jack S. Crumley (ed.), 29).

I object to Descartes's claim that there must be an active faculty that produces this mental experience. Furthermore, if there were such a faculty, as there may well be, one could have no certain knowledge about it and no way of knowing it certainly existed unless it existed within one's mind. One cannot know anything outside awareness because only the contents of one's awareness and one's being aware of these contents can be experienced as existent. This is my primary objection to Descartes's claims about external reality. Ultimately, Descartes concludes that corporeal reality must exist because, otherwise, God would be lying to us, whereas Descartes began his analysis with the premise that he was possibly being deceived by some such higher power (René Descartes, "Meditations II, VI," *Problems in Mind: Readings in Contemporary Philosophy of Mind*, Jack S. Crumley (ed.), 29). To posit the existence of external reality, Descartes must abandon his whole argument about the foundational truths of mental experience. Many times Descartes mentions that it is easy to slip back into old habits of thought, and I think this is exactly what he has done.

Nothing can be shown to exist outside the being-in-the-world experience. This is because, if something is known to exist, either with certainly or with the slightest suspicion, it is thus inducted into the being-in-the-world experience. This problem is the root of the mind-body problem that modern day substance dualists have yet to solve. The mind-body problem involves explaining the causal interaction between two separate types of substances. The problem is that there can be no way to relate mental experience to physical reality if mental experience is conceived of as a totally non-physical and separate realm. In this sense, dualism is equally incorrect in positing that, if there is a physical reality, that mind is a totally separate substance from it because one can have no certain knowledge about such a relationship when one is contained in a completely separate mental experience. Thus dualism disallows the empirical study of mind as well as being false to its original premise of foundationalism, the virtue of which is the proof that only mental reality can be certainly known to exist. I conclude that, in every way, it is better to posit a unified theory of experience.

Solipsism

Solipsism, which can be loosely described as the belief that nothing truly exists beyond oneself and one's own experiences, is hardly a mainstream philosophical concept. Yet it's one that we often fall back on. We have experiences like meditation or some observation of the external environment, and often we tell ourselves that our experience is true and that's that, although we know that our perceptions can be faulty. But say my experience serves as data in a rational scientific process based on the collection of all experiences, something I want to merge into the scientific model...

Frankly, my experience is already in there, and trying to artificially extract experience to find the "truly objective" is hopeless—even kind of stupid if you think about it, as mind and subjectivity are woven into literally every moment of every human's life throughout time.

But people feel the force; they hear "the whisper," and that becomes part of our scientific evidence. Perhaps we haven't found the right mind-body model, but what philosophers call physicalism or materialism is as woefully inadequate as solipsism. And frankly, both are equally unconvincing. Solipsism is the only thing we can really know for sure, and physicalism or materialism, which holds that matter is fundamental, and that mental states and consciousness are the result of the nervous system and the brain, is the only system we have that's justified by a rigorous truth-finding scientific process, except maybe combining the two.

There are compelling reasons for moving away from solipsism, but there is a profound, fundamental truth at the heart of solipsistic intuitions as well.

Arguments For and Against Solipsism

On the negative side, consider the fact that philosophy ought to be practiced for a purpose, because obviously, otherwise practicing philosophy is purposeless. One criterion for determining whether a theory, argument, or method is purposeful is its utility. The notion of philosophical utility can, of course, be construed in different ways. Utility could be measured by how helpful the theory proves to be in explaining observations, how these observations cohere, or, better yet, whether the theory enables us to predict what will be observed. In this case, we are attempting to further scientific study by philosophically reevaluating the theoretical framework according to which we formulate, determine, and set scientific precedent (such as scientific methods, verification of observational data, how we fit domain-specific data into a domain-general model, etc.). For example, some sort of overarching theory is needed to link theories, models, and data from different branches of science, for example, determining how a model of particle behavior in the field of quantum mechanics relates to a model of atomic behaviors in the field of chemistry.

This objection to solipsism stands on its own but not firmly so. The proponent of solipsism might say that, while a given theory may initially appear to be useful for explaining certain things, the theory may still prove to be wildly inaccurate overall (so hence, we should fall back on our personal experiences). To illustrate this point, imagine that we are attempting to derive the equation for a line (or graphing and plotting the best-fitting line through a certain data set). We might see a line with a given intercept and slope that fits the data perfectly in a certain specific area and so conclude, to the best of our knowledge, that the equation for that line would be the correct equation to use. However, once we zoom out a bit, it may turn out that our line only matches the data in a certain area but does not match the overall distribution of data. This fundamental truth lies at the heart of our solipsistic intuitions. In other words, although utility is a broad principle that we can invoke to refute the solipsist's view, it may not always prove the point.

Solipsism presupposes a certain framework: that we live in our minds. Once we accept this framework, solipsism is incontrovertible. However, there is no definitive reason why we should or should not accept any starting framework. The solipsist uses this to lead us to think that the default starting position should be in our own minds.

One argument that solipsists fall back upon, one that most tempts us to be solipsistic and which initially seems to be incontrovertible and beyond circumvention, is the theory of "prove it is not so." We seem to think that our minds are all that we know with certainty. Thus, if we attempt to prove anything that lies outside our minds, we find it impossible. The conjuring trick or sleight-of-hand, however, is that this conclusion presupposes that one's life is lived "inside one's mind" in a strong use of the phrase.

The solipsist's argument is that one has no grounds for making claims about the mind-external world, because one cannot be aware of anything that is external to one's mind. This argument is fine, but it presupposes that one cannot be aware of anything external to one's mind. This presupposition is the only force behind the argument.

Let us note that two of modern philosophy's most famous skeptics, René Descartes and George Berkeley, begin with a hard-core idealism in which what we know is dependent upon the activity of the mind. Then, quite quickly, they add a mind-external God. One major reason behind this addition is that we don't seem to be able to exert omnipotent control over everything in our experience. Our lives seem to be influenced by subconscious or external sources.

Most solipsists only succeed in casting doubt on the mind-external by locating human life inside the mind. In doing so, they draw a strict dichotomy between inside and outside, making the task of explaining the interaction between mind and world impossible. This also makes it impossible to understand the world we live in, which is governed in large part by factors external to that interior viewpoint. From a scientific point of view, for example, it is much easier to suppose that these causes come from the world we live in, even if some of them are not observable. (Of course, even these may, hypothetically, become observable with the advancement of instruments and methods.)

Conversely, arguments for solipsism start not in the world, but at the bottom of a hole. Solipsists trick us—or we trick ourselves somehow—into thinking that, in order to refute solipsism, one must start at the bottom of the hole (i.e., inside one's mind) and find a way out, which is, of course, impossible. There is no reason, however, why we must accept the framework according to which one is inside one's mind.

If we begin instead by positing a relational framework, hypothesizing that we live in an intermediate area of experiencing to which the "inside" and "outside" both contribute, then the distinction between inner and outer breaks down. Suddenly, we are no longer trapped inside, and can know about the outside and inside just as easily. Both the "purely outside" and the "purely inside" are theoretical, so we can only draw inferences about them from an intermediate perspective. Now, because we have stopped dichotomizing inside and outside and seeing them as in opposition to one another, the doubts of solipsism are not as irritating. Yes, it is true that we cannot certainly know anything that is mind-independent, but we cannot certainly know anything that is world-independent, either. Also, it no longer matters whether there is a real object that is causally responsible for phenomena appearing in the intermediate area. If the purely-external-world were absent, the as-far-as-we'll-ever-know-external world remains the same. We must ask ourselves whether there is any practical purpose in doing anything more than speculating and curiously wondering about the "purely outside" and the "purely inside" worlds that, by definition, humans cannot know about. While this may satisfy our spiritual questions, it has clearly become the domain of religion and not philosophy, in that it serves no philosophical utility. On the other hand, positing theoretical entities that affect the intermediate area may be useful, but we recognize that these are purely theoretical, which means that they are measured by their relation to and effect on the intermediate area, rather than by whether they "match" some unknowable, mind-external world.

No bit of knowledge is certain, and no one can prove that it is certain. How can we prove something outside our mind to be true? Therefore, it seems almost natural to assume that nothing truly exists beyond oneself and one's own experiences, which can draw us into solipsism. The problem with drawing such a conclusion is that the viewpoint that knowledge is not certain is not unique to solipsism. There are many epistemological theories which do not posit that any knowledge is certain, including perspectivism, which argues that knowledge of any subject is limited by the perspective of those viewing it (which inevitably limits our knowledge of it), and the Buddhist concept of the viewlessness of the Bodhi, argued by the Buddhist philosopher Nāgārjuna, who called for the complete abandonment of all views, including, apparently, his own.

In the words of the novelist Philip K. Dick, "Reality is that which, when you stop believing in it, doesn't go away."

Introspection and Inner States

The word "introspection" originated from the Latin words *intra* and *spicere*, which literally mean "to look within." What does this mean? Is our "looking" directed inwards when introspecting our own minds? Is it possible to observe or examine one's mental states? Let us consider what is involved in this question. As shown in its etymology, "introspection" is intended to capture the notion of "looking inwards." Thus, if we want to preserve the spirit of the word, we must determine what we mean when we say that something is "inside" a person. Historically, this has been associated with the idea that minds are like little worlds inside a person's head. Thus, we have two ways in which the notion of introspection is understood: (1) to capture the notion of looking into oneself, of trying to understand something which comes from within rather than from without; and (2) to denote the activity of trying to understand one's mind. When do these two aspects of introspection coincide?

I believe that the combination of these two dimensions of introspection may be problematic in that it may lead us to think that, in as much as minds are within a person, we have direct access to our inner states in that we can simply "look" inwards. In other words, certain interpretations of (1) and (2) can lead to the idea that full-fledged human mentality involves some form of "inner awareness," that is, a direct awareness of something within a person. But this idea has problems.

First, do we have direct access to our mental states (i.e., our thoughts or experiences)? Can we simply "look in" and witness these states? This question concerns the nature of mental states. There are two options: (a) the Cartesian idea that we directly witness mental states, which are inner, mental representations; and (b) the idea that we are never directly aware of our mental states, which are theoretical entities that are conceived in various ways according to our particular theory of mind. Option (a), the

Cartesian idea that we directly witness our mental states, is problematic. The question of whether we can directly witness our mental states depends upon whether mental states should be viewed as inner representations, that is, whether minds should be viewed as private and subjective "inner worlds."

Why is this so important? There are broadly two reasons: (1) from a scientific perspective, it is impossible to study an utterly private inner world because such a world is not publicly observable; and (2) from a sociological and interpersonal perspective, it becomes hard to accommodate the intrapersonal, that is, if we view minds as essentially private inner worlds, it becomes difficult to make sense of communication with or understanding of one another. Thus, subscribing to the notion that minds are inner worlds results in a tendency to see minds as cut-off from the world and from one another. It is important to see minds as necessarily embodied entities whose purpose is to interact. In other words, mentality is a participation in the public world and with other minds rather than a lonely and hopelessly private world. Mentality is structured by these interactions to such a great extent that, in most cases, it is appropriate to say that minds are such interactions.

The second question is as follows: How do we come to have knowledge about our mental states? Can we simply "look in" and know facts about their nature or their contents? The notion of "looking inwards" gets its foothold from the fact that we sometimes seem to "just know" our thoughts. If we reject the notion of directly witnessing our mental states by "looking inwards," as mentioned above in response to the first question, how do we explain cases in which we seem to "just know" our thoughts? But knowledge of our mental states themselves is never immediate in the sense that such knowledge presupposes the background knowledge involved in a theory of mind. Cases in which we seem to "just know" our thoughts can be explained by attaining mastery in using the psychological concepts involved in one's theory of mind. This mastery enables us to deploy these concepts in a way that does not involve conscious deliberation, that is, an automatic, rapid, and unconscious manner.

In short, the mind is never directly aware of itself or its own states. Rather, one's mental states are only known indirectly through theory-based inferences. Our "looking" (i.e., cognition's intentionality) is always directed outwards onto objects in the world, and the mind can only know or be aware of itself indirectly by looking upon a symbolic representation of itself. This is similar to the way that an eye cannot see itself without a mirror. We could characterize this conceptually mediated knowledge about one's mental states as a specific kind of self-consciousness that we might call narrative or psychological self-consciousness, used here to refer to a conceptual understanding of oneself as an intentional mental organism.

The focus here is on the epistemology of introspection, that is, how we come to acquire knowledge about our mental activities. It should be clear, however, that the view put forth necessarily involves an ontological dimension. Spatial adjectives such as "internal" and "external" are not mandatory in discussing the relationship of mind and world. Regardless of the specific terms utilized in discussing the place of mind in the world, we almost always draw some sort of distinction between "mental" and "physical" aspects of mind-in-the-world. Let us stipulate that such distinctions should be viewed as discursive tools or deliberative hand-holds rather than as metaphysically important. In other words, if we want to truly view minds as in the world, both in the context of physical science and in the context of social interaction, we must ultimately collapse this distinction or at least recognize that this distinction is only for the purposes of discussion and analysis. In short, although mind and body can be conceived of as distinct, they should not be viewed as actually distinct. Epistemology cannot be cleanly separated from ontology; similarly, mind and body cannot be cut apart as with a knife.

Regarding the epistemological dimension, let us distinguish two approaches to modeling introspection: (1) a broadly Cartesian model of introspection and (2) the philosopher Wilfrid Sellars' model of introspection, although we will slightly reformulate Sellars' views. According to the model here, introspection can be seen as adopting a third-person perspective on oneself and utilizes the same theory of mind we use in explaining the behaviors of our fellows. Roughly speaking, a theory of mind refers to the way in which we explain another person's behaviors by ascribing psychological states to the individual (e.g., beliefs, desires, perceptions, etc.). In other words, having a theory of mind means having the capacity to conceive of other organisms as intentional organisms. This capacity is also necessary for conceiving of oneself as an intentional organism or for acquiring knowledge about one's inner, mental states.

What is Introspective Knowledge?

What does it mean to have "introspective knowledge"? In this context, we'll define "introspective knowledge" as meaning conceptual, propositional knowledge about one's inner, mental states. This still leaves room for conflicting interpretations of introspection, particularly regarding what counts as an "inner, mental state." Two such viewpoints are the Cartesian view and the Sellarsian view. According to the Cartesian view, everything we think or experience (i.e., everything we directly know) is considered an inner, mental state. Hence, the category of introspective knowledge is fairly broad. For example, according to the Cartesian view, when I experience a red ball, I am experiencing an inner mental appearance of the red ball rather than the red ball itself. Hence, any conceptual, propositional knowledge about this inner, mental appearance counts as "introspective knowledge." Even a nonconceptual awareness of this red-ball-appearance would count as an "introspective awareness."

According to Sellars' view and the broadly Sellarsian view argued here, we never know our inner, mental states directly. We know physical objects directly, and we only know our mental states by analogy with such publicly available objects. In other words, having knowledge about a red ball does not count as introspective knowledge; it would instead be considered perceptual knowledge about a physical object. On this model, we might theorize about experience by saying, for example, that "Something somehow like a red ball is going on in me." Thus, the domain of introspective awareness is relatively restricted. According to this Sellarsian model, introspective awareness only refers to conceptual, propositional knowledge that involves the language of a theory of mind (i.e., knowledge about one's beliefs, desires, perceptions, and so forth). In other words, introspective knowledge necessarily involves the deployment of concepts pertaining to psychological phenomena and the language that we use for talking about intentional mental states, that is, inner states which are of or about something else. In short, introspective knowledge involves an understanding of the fact that we are thinking or that we have certain kinds of mental states.

In this broadly Sellarsian model, knowledge about what we are thinking usually does not count as introspective knowledge because what we are thinking about is always a physical object of some kind. The sole exception to this is when what we are thinking about is a physical symbol which is used to represent an inner, mental state (e.g., if what we are thinking about is a belief, desire, or the fact that "I am a thinking thing"). As we shall see, this is how we initially come to have knowledge that we are thinking, although this knowledge subsequently becomes implicit. When such knowledge becomes implicit, we can know (albeit implicitly) that we are thinking organisms without explicitly thinking about our mental states or the fact that we have minds (i.e., without requiring the fact that we are thinking to be what we are thinking about).

The Cartesian Theater

René Descartes argues that the nature of the human mind is better known than the body. Descartes employs his method of doubt in order to convince the reader that the existence of one's mind is indubitable, whereas one cannot be absolutely certain that material substance exists (René Descartes, "Second Meditation," *Readings in Modern Philosophy*, vol.1, (Roger Ariew, et al., (eds.), 31). He begins by wondering what cannot be doubted:

> Reason now persuades me that I should withhold my assent no less carefully from opinions that are not completely certain and indubitable than I would from those that are patently false. For this reason, it will suffice for the rejection of all these opinions, if I find in each of them some reason for doubt.... Because undermining the foundations will cause whatever has been built upon them to crumble of its own accord, I will attack straightaway those principles which supported everything I once believed. (René Descartes, "Second Meditation," *Readings in Modern Philosophy*, vol.1, (Roger Ariew, et al., (eds.), 28)

Through this skeptical process, Descartes realizes that many of his central beliefs were assumptions which he could possibly doubt (e.g., the belief that he had a material body). Although he is not sure that bodies are composed of "material" substance, he is at least certain that he thought of a body. Thus, Descartes proposes that one's immediate thoughts and experiences provide the most indubitable kind of knowledge. Using this premise, Descartes finds his famous, foundational truth: "'I am, I exist' is necessarily true every time I utter it or conceive it in my mind" (René Descartes, "Second Meditation," *Readings in Modern Philosophy*, vol.1, (Roger Ariew, et al., (eds.), 30). He further concludes that the "I" is a thinking thing or a mind because, as we have said, he is most sure that he has an intimate understanding of his mental life. It is this further conclusion that commits Descartes to the idea that mental states are epistemically prior to physical states, that is, that the nature of the mind is better known than the nature of the body.

Throughout his discussion, Descartes repeatedly returns to the idea that his sensory experiences of corporeal things "...are much more distinctly known than this mysterious 'I' which does not fall within the imagination" (René Descartes, "Second Meditation," *Readings in Modern Philosophy*, vol.1, (Roger Ariew, et al., (eds.), 32). Indeed, it does seem that we have a vivid impression of those things that seem to come from the senses, and it does not seem that we can perceive the mind. Descartes cannot resist this thought and temporarily suspends his doubts about the existence of corporeal things, allowing his mind to investigate its perception of a material object, a piece of wax. Using this bit of wax to illustrate his point, Descartes constructs an argument intended to show that the perception of objects occurs only in the mind and that it is through the mental faculty of judgment that objects are perceived most clearly and distinctly.

Descartes begins by describing his perception of the properties belonging to a certain piece of wax in a solid state. After melting the wax to a liquid state, causing its properties to change, he asks whether the wax remains the same piece of wax it was before being melted. Descartes accepts the assumption that it is the same body of wax as the premise of his argument. For Descartes, it seems natural to think that it is the same piece of wax and that the wax is some sort of body which appeared to have different sets of properties over time. Descartes concludes that, if the wax remains the same piece of wax after undergoing change and the properties of the wax which the senses perceive alter over time, these properties cannot be fundamental to the essence of the wax (René Descartes, "Second Meditation," *Readings in Modern Philosophy*, vol.1, (Roger Ariew, et al., (eds.), 32). This idea suggests to Descartes that the true essence of this body of wax can only be grasped by the understanding.

Descartes then begins to imagine what exactly the essence of the wax might be, asking what it is about the wax that makes it the same piece of wax in its various states. He conceives of the wax as a body that is spatially extended (i.e., occupying space), flexible, and mutable (i.e., changing shape over time). As he tries to picture the wax in terms of these properties, he realizes that he could not imagine the whole range of states implicated by the properties of mutability and extension. The wax could take more shapes than Descartes can possibly picture, as he describes: "I would not judge correctly what the wax is if I did not believe that it takes on an even greater variety of dimensions than I could ever grasp with the imagination" (René Descartes, "Second Meditation," *Readings in Modern Philosophy*, vol.1, (Roger Ariew, et al., (eds.), 32-33). Therefore, Descartes concludes that the essence of the wax cannot be perceived with the senses or the imagination and is known solely by his understanding. According to Descartes, the wax is only wax because he judges it to be wax, as he writes: "what I thought I was seeing with my eyes, I actually grasped solely with the faculty of judgment, which is in my mind" (René Descartes, "Second Meditation," *Readings in Modern Philosophy*, vol.1, (Roger Ariew, et al., (eds.), 33). The perception of the wax exists only in his mind, and knowledge about the wax comes from the mental faculty of judgment.

If the perception of the wax is only in Descartes's mind, then he cannot possibly know corporeal substances more clearly than mental substances because those things which seem to be known through one's bodily senses are actually known as thoughts in the mind. Since his knowledge of the wax is most clear and distinct when it is understood by his mental capacities, Descartes concludes that knowing corporeal things only brings him closer to an understanding of mental substances (René Descartes, "Second Meditation," *Readings in Modern Philosophy*, vol.1, (Roger Ariew, et al., (eds.), 33). Therefore, the nature of the mind is better known than whatever bodily reality might exist outside the mind, and such a bodily reality is known only through its causal effects upon Descartes's mental life. This argument introduces the idea that clear and distinct perception comes from human judgment, reason, and rationality, and the claim that mental faculties as well as an understanding of the mind provide the most certain foundation for human knowledge.

Descartes uses this argument to support a distinction between mental and physical substances. He writes:

> On the one hand I have a clear and distinct idea of myself, insofar as I am merely a thinking thing and not an extended thing, and because on the other hand I have a distinct idea of a body, insofar as it is merely an extended thing and not a thinking thing, it is certain that I am really distinct from my body, and can exist without it. (René Descartes, "Second Meditation," *Readings in Modern Philosophy*, vol.1, (Roger Ariew, et al., (eds.), 50)

A view of this sort is called "substance dualism." According to such a view, mind and body are conceived as completely different kinds of substances which somehow causally interact. A human being, then, is a composite organism, a "union," as Descartes puts it, of mental and physical substances. According to Descartes, the mind is the "I," that is, it is the human soul. As should be clear from the above passage, the mind or soul can essentially be seen as inhabiting a body and can, in an important sense, exist as a disembodied entity.

There are a number of problems with the Cartesian views, both that of substance dualism and the idea that, to the extent that mind and body are distinct, knowledge of the mind is prior to and more certain than knowledge of bodily, physical phenomena. The latter of these claims will be the focus here. Before we begin discussing a few of the specific reasons for abandoning the Cartesian view, let us take stock of the points to be gleaned from the above exegesis.

Descartes posits an indubitable truth in his famous Cogito, in which he concludes that the proposition, "I am a thinking thing," is necessarily true because he thinks it. This argument serves as the foundation upon which he rebuilds the structure of knowledge. Above all else, Descartes believes that he has clear and distinct knowledge of his thoughts. In order to know something, he must think it, and thinking a thought implies the foundational prefix, "I think that...." Thus, Descartes believes that he has certain knowledge of the fact that he is thinking and of what he is thinking.

Descartes takes it to be self-evident that the awareness of one's mental states yields knowledge with the highest degree of certainty. In his view, the mind is completely transparent to the experiencing subject, who has direct and privileged access to his or her mental states. First-person authority and introspective access are considered infallible in that one's knowledge of one's own thoughts cannot be mistaken. Thoughts are considered self-intimating in that one is necessarily aware of all occurrent thoughts. If a mental state occurs, one necessarily knows that such a state is occurring. Access to one's mental states is immediate in that knowledge of one's mental states requires no evidence, inference, or background knowledge.

The Cartesian view of introspection, privacy, and privileged access can be expressed using the metaphor of a theater in which thoughts are like a movie that can only be witnessed by the knowing subject, a Cartesian observer. The pictures displayed on the screen are not objects in the mind-external world but rather inner representations of objects outside the mind (assuming that there *are* any mind-external objects). These inner pictures constitute something like a mirror image of external reality that mediates our interaction with the outside world. Knowledge about external objects is inferred from the effects such objects have on the mind. This is similar to the way in which scientists today draw inferences about imperceptible phenomena, for example, sub-atomic particles. For Descartes, external objects seem just as imperceptible as atoms and particles in that their presence can only be inferred and indirectly known via their observable manifestations (i.e., as pictures on the screen). The metaphor of the Cartesian theater is a way of talking about the mind and the inner life of an organism. Few contemporary philosophers or scientists adhere to a full-fledged Cartesian view of introspection, but this is an important historical conception of the mind, which I believe has had significant influence on certain contemporary conceptions of introspection.

For now, we need only recognize the notions that: (1) first-personal knowledge of mental states is immediate and infallible, and the first-person subject directly witnesses his or her mental states; and (2) concepts of physical objects are secondary and inferred from knowledge of one's mental states. Physical objects are known indirectly via one's ideas of them. Thus, according to the Cartesian view, introspective knowledge occurs prior to knowledge of physical objects. "Prior" means that introspective knowledge is both epistemically and temporally prior to knowledge of physical objects. It is temporally prior in that we acquire knowledge about our thoughts before we acquire knowledge about physical objects; it is epistemically prior in that our introspective knowledge serves as the basis for deriving knowledge about physical objects, rather than the other way around.

There are many problems with the Cartesian view which have been the subject of extensive discussion in contemporary philosophy. For our purposes, the most significant of these has to do with Descartes's account of privileged access to one's mind. The doctrine of mental transparency (i.e., the joint claim that mental states are self-intimating and infallibly known) is no longer in favor for too many reasons to enumerate here, but here are a few of them.

It is commonplace in contemporary discussions of mind to speak of unconscious mental states. Sigmund Freud, for example, popularized the idea that there are motivations for a subject's behaviors which are "repressed" or otherwise unconscious, although such motivations are clearly psychological and are potentially consciously accessible (becoming conscious of such motivations is, more or less, the goal of Freudian psychotherapy). Nevertheless, the subject is not aware of these psychological states and will often adamantly deny having them in spite of evidence showing that such states influence his or her overt behaviors.

Another good reason for rejecting mental transparency are well-documented cases of "blindsight" in which a subject is clearly aware of and capable of responding to a stimulus, such as avoiding an object in his or her path, even though he or she reports otherwise. In summary, it suffices to say that first-personal knowledge of one's mind is not comprehensive and is notoriously fallible. There is a wealth of evidence justifying a rejection of, at the very least, a full-fledged Cartesian view of privileged access. When a philosophical account does not explain available evidence or gives rise to too many problems, it is time to ask whether we can do better.

Certain characteristics of the special, epistemic access to one's mental states advocated by the Cartesian view are still sometimes applied in a restricted domain. Sensations like pain, for example, are sometimes seen as self-intimating and immediately known. Can one be in pain and not know that one is in pain? If your answer is "no," then you hold that pains are self-intimating. For our purposes, the following question may be more important: How do you know that you are experiencing pain (e.g., a toothache)? It may seem that the only possible answer to such a question is that you "just know." You may take this to mean that your knowledge of the toothache is immediately known in that it does not involve any evidence, background knowledge, or process of inference. In contrast, consider the question of how you know that you have a cavity. Presumably, you acquire such knowledge by assessing evidence (e.g., by visual inspection of your tooth, having an x-ray, or by hearing the opinion of your dentist).

Is this distinction really as clear as this example portrays it to be? Consider, for example, how the dentist knows that you have a cavity. The dentist looks at your tooth and seems to "just know" that you have a cavity. It seems to require no further evidence or explicit, conscious process of inference. This knowledge, however, clearly presupposes further background knowledge concerning the nature of "cavities." And was there not a time, perhaps before the dentist first learned about the conditions of tooth decay, when the dentist did have to explicitly, consciously infer that you have a cavity when observing a black mark on your tooth? The range of facts that we seem to "just know" changes as we become accustomed to utilizing relevant background knowledge. The dentist, for example, "just knows" that you have a cavity, and he is probably able to know this in a way that seems immediate because he has become so good at identifying cavities that he can do so rapidly, automatically, and unconsciously.

Here is the important question: Is the case of the toothache any different? While it may be true that you directly experience the pain of a toothache, should this qualify as knowledge that you have a toothache? The dentist also directly witnesses your cavity, but the dentist's knowledge that you have a cavity is clearly not immediate in the fully Cartesian sense of the term. Could we not say that, just as the dentist learns to identify cavities rapidly, automatically, and unconsciously, so we learn to identify pain sensations? Here, we might draw a distinction between being in pain (e.g., experiencing a toothache) and knowing that you are in pain or from having propositional knowledge about that pain.

It seems clear that knowing that you are in pain requires a concept pertaining to "pain," which requires background knowledge about the nature of "pain." Directly experiencing pain does not necessarily have any epistemic implications. Consider the case of emotions, for example. We may directly feel our emotions, but does this mean that we can immediately, infallibly, or even readily identify those emotions? The verbal dimension of such knowledge seems to be important. For example, is it so easy to know whether one is experiencing regret, nostalgia, or sadness, perhaps with a subtle hint of anger? For our purposes, this is perhaps a more relevant objection to the Cartesian construal of direct access to one's experiences. While there are many things to which we have direct access, should we consider such access to be properly epistemic? Is any knowledge really immediate in the fully Cartesian sense of the term?

The Given

The idea of a "given," a term first coined by Wilfrid Sellars in his attack on this idea, refers to the idea that we have some sort of immediate, self-verifying factual knowledge, the positive epistemic status of which does not depend upon any further evidence, background knowledge, or process of inference. Saying that we have "factual knowledge" about a given state serves to distinguish propositional knowledge about that state from a nonconceptual awareness of that state. Before we begin discussing Sellars' views, we should be clear that Sellars uses the term "sensation" to denote non-factual experiences and uses to the term "thought" or "conceptual thinking" to refer to a propositional or factual thinking that such and such is the case. He views "perceptions" as a combination of a sensory experience with propositional thinking.

The notion of the given is essentially that a nonconceptual awareness of certain states inherently or necessarily delivers propositional knowledge of facts about that state, with these facts being self-verifying in that they are verified by a direct, nonconceptual awareness of the state in question. Proponents of the given claim that there are privileged cognitive states or mental contents of which we are incorrigibly aware as the kinds of states or contents they are. These privileged thoughts or experiences are self-intimating in the sense that one is aware of self-justifying facts about one's thoughts or experiences just by having such a thought or experience.

We should briefly distinguish two versions of the given, one rationalist and the other empiricist. The rationalist or Cartesian construal of the given holds that these privileged states are conceptual thoughts or propositional attitudes. So, for the Cartesian, thoughts are given to us as thoughts, beliefs as beliefs, doubts as doubts, and they are given to us as the kinds of thoughts they are, differentiated by their contents, about which first-person error is impossible. The empiricist view is that perceptions and sensations are given to us as the kinds of things they are, that is, that sensations are given to us as sensations. First-personal knowledge that one is in a particular sensory state is infallible and immediate. According to both versions, we develop further knowledge by using certain kinds of privileged, observable inner states as the evidence or means for drawing inductive or deductive inferences about the way things are. In any case, the general notion of the given is that there is some kind of state which is presented to consciousness and known without evidence or inference, and that these privileged facts can serve as the premises upon which we can build the structure of human knowledge.

Before we turn away from this distinction, we should briefly note that the two versions of the given are different. The rationalist version is not the same as the empiricist version. One could develop a valid argument for the claim that, in most cases, one necessarily entails the other. Sense datum theories, for example, subscribe to the notion of a given by holding that sense-data inherently or necessarily delivers perceptual facts, that is, propositional knowledge about a given sense-datum. Propositional knowledge about such sense-data would operate in a way that ensures that they serve as logical premises from which one can deduce the kind of knowledge put forth by the rationalist version of the given, that is, in a way that serves as a solid, indubitable foundation for human knowledge. For our purposes here, we will treat these two versions of the given in the same way out of a general concern regarding the claim that we directly observe any kind of mental state or inherently have any kind of factual knowledge about our mental states. This general point is developed in the discussion of Descartes, which exemplifies the notion of being in a "theater of one's mind" in which one directly observes mental phenomena and has immediate knowledge about these phenomena.

One integral tenet of Descartes's view lies in the epistemological difference between perceptual knowledge and introspective knowledge. The way we conceive and perceive the external world is based upon evidence presented in our perceptions as well as upon a theory about how our internal perceptual states are affected by external objects. However, according to Descartes, our introspective knowledge of our own internal mental states is not based upon such fallible, theory-based inferences. For Descartes, whereas objects in the external world are known indirectly and conceived in terms of their effects on one's mind, one's inner states, the objects of introspection, are directly observed in a way that delivers propositional knowledge about that state.

Sellars agrees that Descartes is correct in concluding that knowledge of the external world is not given, but incorrect in concluding that introspective knowledge of internal states is given. Sellars views introspection and perception as epistemologically similar in important respects. According to Sellars, in principle, neither is more or less fallible than the other, and our ability to make judgments without deliberation about our inner states or physical objects is not evidence that either is given to us. This point is discussed in much more detail in the following sections. First, it is important to discuss how Sellars conceives of thoughts or "inner psychological episodes."

Thoughts, Theoreticity, and Observability

Sellars denies that our knowledge of thoughts is epistemically or temporally prior to knowledge of common-sense physical objects. (By "common-sense" physical objects, I am referring to ordinary things such as trees or tables, which should stand in contrast to imperceptible objects like particles or molecules.) In some ways, this may seem counterintuitive. If we accept the idea that minds perceive objects in the world, it must be true that we experience external objects *as perceived*, that is, in a mediate and mind-dependent way. Sellars does not deny this, but he does deny that we have knowledge about our perceptions before we have knowledge about the perceived objects. In other words, Sellars holds that our knowledge about common-sense physical objects is prior to our introspective knowledge. Again, "prior" means that our knowledge of common-sense physical objects is both temporally and epistemically prior to introspective knowledge and could occur independently of introspective knowledge.

When we think carefully about our concepts pertaining to physical objects and mental states, this begins to seem quite natural. A child's first words are much more likely to be "mom" or "dad" than "thought." No child is born with certain knowledge of the fact that it is a thinking thing. Children first learn to participate in the ordinary world of physical objects and only later develop a rich inner life and the capacity for self-reflection. Thus, we have two claims, both of which seem to be correct: (1) we know about the external world via mental/cognitive processes; and (2) concepts of mental phenomena develop after concepts of physical objects.

These two intuitions can be reconciled by Sellars' claim that thought is prior to language in what Sellars calls the "order of being," which refers to the sequence of events in the world as it actually is, but subsequent in what he calls the "order of knowing," which refers to the sequence in which an ordinary human's conception of the world develops. This essentially means that thinking actually precedes and causes verbal behaviors, but we conceptualize and have knowledge about our verbal behaviors before we conceptualize and have knowledge about the thoughts that cause our verbal behaviors. This claim will take some unpacking, and we will return to it again. For now, let us start by reflecting on the place of thoughts in the world.

If we try to come up with a more tangible example of a thought, we find it difficult, for who has ever touched a thought? Who has ever seen, or tasted, or smelled one? There is perhaps a sense in which such sensations are inner perceptual states, but we usually think of the things we experience as ordinary objects, not as perceptions. Indeed, perceptions are not literally

rocks or trees. We can all accept the premise that the mind perceives physical objects. It may be true that, when we think of an object, it is the sensing of this object that makes our thinking about it possible. At the same
time, it seems equally clear that a perception is of a physical object, not
of a thought, idea, or perception. When we look at rocks, trees, and all
the furniture of the world, we do not call these things "thoughts." When
we are hungry, we do not look through the kitchen cabinets and wonder:
"Should I eat thoughts today?" Or "perhaps I should eat thoughts?" Moral-
ly-compelled vegetarians are not opposed to eating meat-thoughts because
they have ethical qualms about harming animal-thoughts! Thus, it may
not seem so strange to think of concepts of psychological phenomena as
like theoretical concepts, to suppose that we do not immediately know our
thoughts as thoughts.

So how are we to understand the nature of thoughts? Sellars believes
that it is important to have a clear understanding of theoretical entities if
we are to understand the nature of thoughts. It will be helpful, then, to understand how Sellars uses the term "theoretical." Theoretical discourse began to develop as humans began to understand that the world might not actually be the way it appears to be. We began to develop theories about what
Sellars refers to as "the order of being," the world as it actually is. It was
with the development of theoretical discourse that we first distinguished
the order of being from the order of knowing; that is, it was with the development of theoretical discourse that we began to distinguish appearance
from reality. The order of being is, of course, known only insofar as we
can conceive of it. In other words, we can only theorize about the nature of
the order of being, but this does not mean that our theories are unfounded.
Although we cannot directly observe things in the order of being, we can
infer their existence from their observable manifestations and their effects
on the things we know. As we shall see in a moment, this is how Sellars
proposes that we first come to understand the nature of thoughts.

Sellars does not view the boundary between the theoretical and the observable as inflexible—what was once theoretical can become observable.
For Sellars, a theoretical term refers to an unobserved explanatory entity,
and an observational term refers to a phenomenon that is publicly observable, even if observing that phenomenon utilizes a theory (e.g. observation
of particles in cloud chambers). Thus, the distinction between theoretical
and observational terms is, in the case of scientific investigation, a meth-
odological distinction. When scientific theories are integrated into ordinary public discourse, the distinction between theory and observation is a
matter of normative social conventions, that is, how the term is used in ordinary discourse. The role of observation in ordinary discourse is slightly
more intricate than in the context of scientific discourse. Let us consider an

example of what Sellars means when he says that a term is "observational" in the context of ordinary, public discourse.

We often use the word "force" in a way that is not dependent on the context of an articulated theory. We know about forces by observing the effects of forces and inferring that these effects are caused by a certain kind of force, but we have a great deal of experience in identifying the effects of forces such that we can identify the force without conscious deliberation. In this sense, Sellars would say that we can "observe" forces although they are, strictly speaking, imperceptible. In other words, we have become accustomed to identifying the effects of forces as being caused by a force and do so without consciously considering the tenets of a theory or drawing conscious inferences according to the laws of a theory. In such a case, we can say that the term is observational in that we deploy the term without explicitly drawing inferences that utilize the premises of an articulated theory. We have a commonsensical understanding of the term which might be thought of as a tacit or implicit folk-theory of force. This issue is discussed in more detail later.

For now, it suffices to say that the fluidity of the distinction between theory and observation can help to explain how theory-laden terms and concepts can be utilized in an observational way. In other words, the fluidity of the distinction between theoretical and observable entities explains how observational knowledge can be developed from a foundation which is fundamentally theoretical. It is important that theoretical terms can become observational. If nothing is given to us, then all observation, whether of oneself, another, or objects in the world, is in some sense theory-based. This is because the idea of the given is that we acquire primitive and self-verifying factual knowledge just *by* observing some state, that is, in a way requiring no further evidence or background knowledge. This may, however, only appear to be the case when, in fact, it is not. It may seem that some knowledge is immediate (i.e., that we "just know" some facts) simply because we are not conscious of the implicit inferences and the automatic processing of relevant background knowledge involved in knowing such a fact.

If we are to avoid the notion of a given, all observational knowledge must involve background knowledge or some other evidence. At the same time, it is clear that there are many things we seem to know without any conscious deliberation, that is, things we seem to "just know." If Sellars wants to avoid the notion that these things are given to us, he must develop an alternative account of noninferential observational knowledge (particularly of our mental states). By saying that such knowledge is noninferential, Sellars simply means to say that acquiring such knowledge does not involve explicit conscious deliberation about premises or pieces of evidence and the laws governing their relations. Nevertheless, according to Sellars' view, a theory must be implicitly involved. In other words, such knowledge must be couched in the language of a theory, however naïve and commonsensical the theory might be, or else we have reintroduced the notion of a given. This is the burden we face in our interpretation of Sellars' work.

The Emergence of Inner Worlds

The idea that thoughts are like theoretical entities may seem counterintuitive because we are so familiar with our own experiences. It is perhaps easier to grasp this notion by considering the mind of another. It is natural to assume that our fellow human beings have minds, but we certainly do not have access to their thoughts in the same way that we have access to our own. We must rely upon publicly observable behaviors to support our assumption. As Sellars notes, behavior is the only intersubjective evidence for mental events (Wilfrid Sellars, "Mental Events," *Philosophical Studies*, vol. 39, 22). We can only infer and theorize what other people are thinking from their behavior, particularly their verbal expressions. Sellars writes:

> Overt speech is but the manifestation at the overt level of inner patterns and connections, but this is compatible with the idea that we conceive of these inner patterns and connections in terms of their manifestations. After all, we explain the behavior of perceptible things in terms of imperceptible objects (electrons, positrons, etc.); but this is compatible with the fact that we conceive of the imperceptible by analogy with the perceptible (Wilfrid Sellars, "Mental Events," *Philosophical Studies*, vol. 39, p. 58).

In other words, we explain the apparently intelligent behavior of other people by supposing that they are thinking beings, but we cannot directly observe their thoughts, so we conceive of their thoughts by using their behavior as the basis for constructing a model of their thoughts. When someone says, "Please give me some food," we can suppose that they are hungry and that they are thinking about eating. We assume that what they are thinking is roughly parallel to the linguistic expression "I am hungry." Thus, the overt behavior of others may actually be the expression of their thoughts, but we have knowledge of the overt behavior before we have knowledge about the inner processes that cause that behavior.

Behaviorism is one scientific approach to the study of mind which focuses primarily on studying publicly observable behaviors. On the

Cartesian view, the mind is utterly private and subjective, but such a view poses a problem for the scientific study of mind because the foremost principle governing the methodology of natural science is that of intersubjective verification. By "intersubjective verification," I mean confirming and testing observational data using as many iterations, experiments, and scientists as possible. The more a hypothesis has been tested by various researchers, the more certain it becomes. Physical science strives toward objectivity. Thus, if minds are purely subjective, private, and not publicly observable, it is impossible to study the mind using the methods of natural science or to accommodate minds within a physicalistic ontology. Behaviorism is a reaction against the Cartesian view, which would place the mind outside the bounds of scientific inquiry.

One rather extreme behaviorist who is largely responsible for the downfall of the Cartesian conception of mind was Gilbert Ryle. In his most famous work, *The Concept of Mind*, Ryle advanced a famous attack on the Cartesian construal of mind-body dualism (and mind-body dualism in general). He rejected the idea that the mind is an independent entity inhabiting and governing the body, and he coined his famous phrase, "the ghost in the machine," for describing this view. We can understand Ryle as arguing that the "ghost" or "soul" (as Descartes would say) was traditionally a sort of *virtus dormitiva* or homunculus used to explain intelligence, spontaneity, and various higher-level human cognitive functions. Ryle defended the idea that we must provide a meaningful interpretation of these higher-level, human cognitive functions without recourse to an abstracted or independent soul. According to Ryle, mind-body dualism was a piece of naïve literalism that carried over from an era before the biological sciences had fully developed. On his view, the proper function of mind-body language is to describe how organisms demonstrate resourcefulness, strategy, the ability to abstract, generalize, hypothesize, and so forth. He argued that we could understand these abilities by utilizing behavioral evidence and behavioristic language.

Ryle was committed to a complete rejection of the Cartesian concept of mind, and his work is perhaps an overzealous reaction to the longstanding dominance of the Cartesian view. He advocated a position called logical behaviorism, which is roughly the idea that statements describing mental or psychological phenomena can be translated, without loss of content, into a statement solely about behavioral and physical phenomena. Sellars believed that Ryle was on the right track but that he may have followed this track too far. Thus, Sellars disagreed with logical behaviorism almost as much as he disagreed with the Cartesian conception of mind. The goal of Sellars' work, throughout his career, was to find a middle ground between a radical, logical behaviorism, and the common-sense Cartesian view. To this end, he proposed a hypothetical story about how we developed conceptions of "inner psychological episodes," which is intended to offer an alternative to the Cartesian conception of inner episodes without thoroughly rejecting the idea that humans really do have a private, mental life which has significance for understanding and interpreting human behavior. Let us consider this story.

Sellars asks us to imagine a primitive community that does not yet have concepts of "inner psychological episodes." He names this community the "Ryleans" after the famous logical behaviorist. The vocabulary of the Rylean language is limited solely to descriptions about publicly observable objects, properties, and so forth. One day a member of the Rylean community named "Jones" attempts to explain the Ryleans' behavior by postulating "inner psychological episodes." Until this point, the science of psychology had been purely a study of observable behavior akin to logical behaviorism. In short, the Ryleans lived in a world in which everything was publicly observable, and they understood one another in terms of a theory of behavior rather than a theory of mind. (The precise conditions of being "publicly observable" are a matter for debate, but we should simply take this at face value for the time being.) Let us consider a hypothetical scenario intended to illustrate how Jones may have arrived at the idea of "inner episodes."

Imagine that the Ryleans can reliably detect the presence of water. They can observe water and respond with assertions such as, "There is water." One day, some sort of hallucinogenic substance is introduced into the community's water supply. Jones, who has been away for a while, returns to find his friends drinking mud. He is puzzled by this and says: "Well, everyone is behaving just as they always do; they are bending over to scoop something from the ground with their cupped hands and sipping from their hands. They are behaving as-if they were drinking water from the watering hole, but that is clearly mud. They must think that it is water."

Jones used overt assertions as a model for a certain kind of inner psychological episode which we typically refer to as a propositional attitude. In the example above, we noted that the Ryleans are capable of making the assertion that "There is water" as a response to seeing water. Beliefs or thoughts, in the Jonesean model, are the inner analogues of assertion; thus, Jones theorized that his fellow Ryleans were capable of thinking something that is roughly parallel to the assertion "There is water," even when they did not make this assertion "out-loud." The point of importance is that "thinking out-loud" and private thinking are indistinguishable semantic events. Just as the assertion, "There is water," was meaningful for the Ryleans and was a report about water, so the inner thinkings could be thought of as meaningful and about something in the world (i.e., as intentional).

Jones' psychological theory of "inner episodes" proved to be so useful that it became part of the Ryleans' ordinary discourse. The Ryleans found that Jones' theory of thoughts helped to explain all sorts of behaviors, so they developed a whole vocabulary of psychological concepts, such as believing, desiring, and so forth, which were modeled on linguistic propositions. They found that when their friends were drinking mud, the best way to explain their behavior was to suppose that they desired water and believed that the mud was water. They developed another class of inner episodes called sensory impressions (what we might call qualia), which were modeled on physical objects. This type of inner episode allowed them to explain perceptual mistakes. When somebody believed that mud was water, the Ryleans proposed that he was experiencing an inner representation that looked like water. In other words, they might suppose that he was having a qualitative experience that was similar to seeing water. Thus, the mud might appear to this person to be water. This helped the Ryleans explain how the person came to believe that the mud was water.

In this way, overt manifestations of intelligence are epistemically prior to their theoretical inner analogues, at least to third-person parties. To put this another way, a theory of behavior is necessarily prior to a theory of mind simply because overt behaviors are the grounds for applying a theory of mind. As we shall see in a moment, Sellars is suggesting that this is initially true for the first-person subject as well. By initially, I mean to say that the subject must first learn to use psychological language by observing overt behaviors, particularly verbal behaviors. Prior to the ability to conceptualize one's inner episodes, some sort of inner episode may be necessary for intelligence, but our concepts of these episodes will be modeled on their observable manifestations in the way discussed above, that is, by analogy with linguistic propositions. Similarly, we say that macroscopic objects are actually a bunch of microscopic particles, but we conceive of unobservable particles by using the analogy or model of observable macroscopic objects. For example, physicists sometimes describe molecules as behaving like billiard balls. Similarly, we might say that a sensory impression of a cow is analogous to a physical cow in some way, but we are not suggesting that there is actually a cow inside the thinker's head.

One possible Cartesian challenge to Sellars' hypothetical scenario goes as follows: If overt displays of intelligence are caused by thoughts, how could the Ryleans not experience inner episodes and be aware of them? (Willem A. DeVries & Timm Triplett, *Knowledge, Mind, and the Given*, 144) In other words, to use Sellars' terminology, if thoughts are prior to verbal behaviors in the order of being, how could they be subsequent in the order of knowing? The response to this is simply that the Ryleans have inner episodes, and these episodes play a role in governing their behavior, but they do not have knowledge of the fact that they have inner episodes. Before Jones proposed the concept of thoughts or inner episodes, his overt verbal performances stand in relation to some sort of inner state of his organism. Verbal acts are linked to thoughts even before we have psychological concepts. After Jones acquires psychological concepts, he comes to believe that verbal acts "express" these thoughts and eventually learns to ascribe thoughts to himself, as it were.

One may object to this response in the following way: According to the Cartesian view, we know our mental states or inner episodes directly, but this does not require us to hold that we additionally have immediate knowledge of the fact that we have inner episodes or that we know them. In other words, the Cartesian view holds that we have direct knowledge of what we are thinking, but this does not entail that we have direct knowledge of the fact that we are thinking. Descartes's foundational truth only shows that, when we do have knowledge of the fact that we are thinking, that fact is self-justifying and indubitable. This objection is an accurate portrayal of the Cartesian view, but it is not an appropriate response to Sellars' argument.

Sellars is arguing for two closely related points: (1) when we directly know what we are thinking, what we directly know is not an inner state but an object that is known via some inner state; and (2) we have knowledge about our inner episodes or the knowledge that we are thinking by deploying psychological concepts. When these two points are combined, we have the conclusion that being aware of inner episodes at all means having conceptual recognition of those inner episodes. In other words, we only know about our inner episodes in a conceptually mediated way. Hence, knowing about our inner episodes entails knowledge of the fact that we have certain kinds of inner episodes or that we know them.

This point is perhaps the most important point for understanding this paper, so let me repeat it: Because mental states are not directly present to the subject, the only way in which one ever knows about one's inner mental states is by deploying concepts of psychological phenomena, which are defined by analogy with phenomena that are directly present to the subject (e.g., physical objects and linguistic terms, according to the Jonesean theory). On Sellars' view, knowing about one's inner episodes is knowing that one knows or that one is thinking. This is because the concept of an inner episode is the concept of a thought. The most important point of discrepancy between Sellars' view and the Cartesian view is the claim that we are ever, in any way, directly aware of our inner mental states.

It should also be clear that, according to Sellars' view, acquiring psychological concepts does not create all inner episodes, none of which were previously there. It simply enables Jones to know that the inner episodes were always there, to conceive of his own thoughts and to become aware of his thoughts as thoughts, where "thought" is Jones' concept of "an inner episode that is analogous to verbal acts." It is actually quite simple: before we developed psychological concepts, we simply did not conceive of a distinction between inner and outer. This, I believe, is the best way to read Sellars' argument. After the development of psychological concepts, the Ryleans came to conceive of an inner world, not only within their fellows, but also within themselves. At this point, Jones began to report his own cognitive states.

From Theory to Observation Reports

The next step in the Ryleans' development is an important one. It is easy to believe that we must learn to infer one another's thoughts from overt behaviors. It is more difficult to accept that we must infer our own thoughts from our own behaviors. We often seem to know what we are thinking without much deliberation. This is, perhaps, one of the reasons for the Cartesian idea that we have immediate access to our thoughts. However, ease of access does not entail immediate access. Knowledge of our own thoughts involves psychological concepts, but we have learned to utilize these concepts without needing to draw explicit inferences. This entails that human infants, for example, have no factual, propositional knowledge of their own thoughts or experiences.

Knowledge of our own thoughts is not always inferred from overt behavior, yet the fact that we learned to infer thoughts (others' and our own) from overt behaviors is, according to Sellars, a necessary step in explaining how we have come to have noninferential knowledge of our own thoughts (Wilfrid Sellars, *The Structure of Knowledge*, 324). It should be clear that Sellars uses the term "noninferential" in order to exclude explicit inferences involving conscious deliberation. We could (and probably should) read Sellars as arguing that knowledge of our own thoughts usually involves automatic, unconscious inferential processes which produce conscious linguistic responses phrased in the vocabulary of a folk-psychological theory of mind. (As we shall see in a moment, language learning necessarily involves cases in which automated linguistic responses are not theory-laden, that is, are not inferences drawn in accordance with the framework of a theory.) In other words, there is nothing to suggest that

Sellars would disagree with the idea that we still draw automatic, uncon-scious, implicit inferences when identifying our mental states.

It is central to Sellars' account that theoretical terms, whose existence can only be inferred, must come to be utilized noninferentially in the sense discussed above. We can take this to mean that, by gaining expertise in using the language of psychological theory, we learn to deploy this lan-guage rapidly, automatically, and unconsciously; this enables us to use theoretical language in an observational way. Recall that Sellars is utiliz-ing the term "theoretical" to refer to unobservable explanatory entities; we should also recall that the boundary between theoretical and observational terms is flexible. At this point in Sellars' story, the Ryleans learn to issue observation reports about their own mental states without needing to draw explicit inferences about their mental states. Sellars' story goes:

> once our fictitious ancestor, Jones, has developed the theory that overt verbal behaviour is the expression of thoughts, and taught his compatriots to make use of the theory in interpreting each oth-er's behaviour, it is but a short step to the use of this language in self-description. Thus, when Tom, watching Dick, has behavioural evidence which warrants the use of the sentence (in the language of the theory) 'Dick is thinking "p"' (or 'Dick is thinking that p'), Dick, using the same behavioural evidence, can say, in the lan-guage of the theory, 'I am thinking "p"' (or 'I am thinking that p'). And it now turns out—need it have?—that Dick can be trained to give reasonably reliable self-descriptions, using the language of the theory, without having to observe his overt behaviour. Jones brings this about, roughly, by applauding utterances by Dick of 'I am thinking that p' when the behavioural evidence strongly sup-ports the theoretical statement 'Dick is thinking that p'; and by frowning on utterances of 'I am thinking that p', when the evi-dence does not support this theoretical statement. Our ancestors begin to speak of the privileged access each of us has to his own thoughts. What began as a language with a purely theoretical use has gained a reporting role. (Willem A. DeVries & Timm Triplett, *Knowledge, Mind, and the Given*, 269)

To understand how this transition occurs, let us first look at the case of perceptual knowledge. We must learn to identify objects as being of a certain kind. In other words, we must develop a concept of certain types of objects and learn to apply these concepts in the appropriate situations. This requires that we learn to master a certain set of inferences. DeVries provides the example of a bird watcher (Willem A. DeVries and Timm Triplett, *Knowledge, Mind, and the Given*, 153). Initially, the bird watcher has to learn to infer from a bird's features what kind of bird he is watching. For example, the bird watcher may think that, "This bird has a red breast; therefore, the bird is a Robin." Eventually, with practice and experience, the bird watcher is able to identify the bird's species without giving its features much conscious consideration. Of course, the bird watcher still notices features of the bird, but he does not have to think about them explicitly. He has developed a kind of procedural knowledge. In other words, he does not have to consciously deliberate and infer the bird's name from his observation of its features. He has developed some sort of situational recognition and can identify birds confidently. He knows that he is a reliable bird-detector. The bird watcher has learned to use appropriate words in certain perceptual situations and responds directly to the situation. Once the bird watcher has mastered the necessary inferences and features associated with a given concept, he no longer has to explicitly draw these inferences or consider the features of the situation.

We have seen how Jones and the Ryleans learn to apply psychological concepts to one another's behavior and further developed that with an illustration of how a bird watcher gains expertise. Just as the bird watcher gains situational experience in identifying birds, we gain expertise in identifying others' thoughts. It is probably easier for us to identify the thoughts of those who are close to us and with whom we spend a lot of time than it is to identify the thoughts of relative strangers. Thus, it is fairly easy to suppose that we are extremely well-qualified when it comes to identifying our own thoughts.

The Ryleans initially inferred their own mental states from their behaviors. In order for Jones to have noninferential knowledge of his thoughts, Jones must develop the capacity to infer what he is thinking. In other words, he must master a (possibly tacit) theory of psychology. Once he develops this capacity, he does not have to explicitly infer what he is thinking. We can imagine Jones as he is still developing psychological concepts, saying: "Well, I am probably thinking about food because my stomach is growling, and I am salivating, and so forth." Through practice, he masters certain inferential abilities and, in doing so, learns that he is a reliable thought-detector. Thus, it is possible that, just as the bird watcher learns to reliably identify birds as being of a certain kind as he gains expertise, so we learn to noninferentially monitor our own mental states as we gain expertise in this area.

Once Jones can noninferentially monitor most of his own thoughts, it is appropriate to say that the knowledge that began as theoretical and inferential has become observational and noninferential. According to Sellars, anything that we can report knowingly and without deliberation is essentially observable, but we should not think of reporting our psychological states as "observational" in the same sense as perception (i.e., as using an inner sense that is something like our five senses). One can imagine Ryle's reaction to the idea that we observe our mental states. This point will become important later.

One of the advantages of Sellars' account is that perceptual and introspective knowledge are acquired in the same way. Although there may be different underlying mechanisms involved in the development of these two kinds of knowledge, each adheres to roughly the same theoretical framework. Specifically, the acquisition of concepts pertaining to both physical and mental phenomena can be explained in terms of either (1) being told the rules governing a set of inferences associated with a particular concept (e.g., the rule that "Robins have red breasts") and mastering the use of this set of inferences, or (2) being trained, especially in early stages of development, to reliably respond to certain kinds of stimuli in the appropriate situations. Both of these amount to learning, in one of the above two ways, to issue observation reports automatically, that is, as a direct conceptual response that does not involve conscious deliberation. The second of these two options will be the focus of the following section.

To what are we responding when issuing observation reports in perception and in introspection? Are we responding solely to our overt behaviors? Is the only way we know about our mental states by observing our behaviors? Do we not directly feel and respond to our emotions, for instance? In the following section, we will discuss how we learn to identify the thought, "I am hungry," by directly responding to a feeling of hunger as well as by responding to overt behavioral symptoms (e.g., salivation). As I have said, Sellars wants to find a compromise between the Cartesian view and an overzealous logical behaviorist view. Accordingly, Sellars does not intend to diminish the importance of the first-person situation, but he also insists that the mind (and, in particular, conceptual thinking) is public in a strong and important sense. As Sellars says, his story of Jones:

> helps us understand that concepts pertaining to such inner episodes as thoughts are primarily and essentially inter-subjective, as inter-subjective as the concept of a positron, and that the reporting role of these concepts—the fact that each of us has a privileged access to his thoughts—constitutes a dimension of the use of these concepts which is built on and presupposes this inter-subjective status. My myth has shown that the fact that language is essentially an inter-subjective achievement, and is learned in inter-subjective contexts ... is compatible with the 'privacy' of 'inner episodes.' It also makes clear that this privacy is not an 'absolute privacy.' For if it recognizes that these concepts have a reporting use in which

one is not drawing inferences from behavioural evidence, it nevertheless insists that the fact that overt behaviour is evidence for these episodes is built into the very logic of these concepts, just as the fact that the observable behaviour of gases is evidence for molecular episodes is built into the very logic of molecule talk. (Wilfrid Sellars, *Science, Perception, and Reality*, 189)

Reliably Responding

We have discussed how knowledge of our psychological states may be seen as conceptually mediated. We have also seen that, on Sellars' account, we deploy these concepts in observation reports or "direct descriptive responses to a situation." Now it is time to look more closely at what is involved in learning to respond directly. According to Sellars, we have the ability to consistently exhibit a certain kind of response to our inner states without having the knowledge that these states are of a certain kind, that is, without having a concept of the kind of state in question. Similarly, we learn to reliably respond to certain kinds of environmental stimuli without an understanding of the fact that they are of a certain kind.

This helps explain how we might come to have an awareness of certain kinds of things without an innate awareness of facts, that is, without propositional knowledge that a certain stimulus is of a general kind that is denoted by a linguistic term and without propositional knowledge about the various inferential rules and features associated with that general kind (i.e., without a conceptual understanding of the stimulus). This is most clearly seen in the case of language learning. Daniel Dennett explains this point about general attitudes concisely:

> Consider that case of learning that all orange mushrooms are toxic. What the dog can learn, perhaps learning from training from its mother, is the disposition, whenever you see an orange mushroom, to shun it. That is, the disposition to acquire a particular 'this is toxic' belief, whenever encountering a particular orange mushroom. (Daniel Dennett, cited in Jay L. Garfield, et al., *Let's Pretend! The Role of Pretence in the Acquisition of Theory of Mind*, 27)

Thus, on Dennett's view, the dog learns to reliably respond to orange mushrooms before the dog learns that things with a certain shape or scent are "orange mushrooms" or that "orange mushrooms are toxic." Jay Garfield follows Dennett on this point:

An infralingual creature can surely reliably intend each member of some class on each occasion, and even be said counterfactually to do so. In one sense this might count as having a general attitude. But, as Dennett points out, this is a kind of amphiboly: it is instead generally true of such an animal that it intends each member in the same way. Generality emerges with quantification, and quantification is a linguistic device. (Jay L. Garfield, et al., *Let's Pretend! The Role of Pretence in the Acquisition of Theory of Mind*, 27)

Sellars explains this idea in terms of a distinction between rule-conforming and rule-obeying behaviors. Rule-conforming behavior describes pattern-governed behavior in which the behavior of individuals "just happens" to contribute to the realization of a complex pattern. One is conforming to rules when one is behaving "as-if" one has an understanding of these rules. In other words, rule-conforming means acting in accordance with a certain set of rules without an understanding that one is acting in accordance with these rules. Rule-obeying behavior is when an individual behaves in a certain way with the intention of fulfilling a certain role in a system. This still does not necessarily entail explicit knowledge of a system of rules, but it does entail the knowledge that one is involved in a larger social pattern and that one's behaviors are (more or less) consistent with whatever rules govern this pattern (Wilfrid Sellars, *Science, Perception, and Reality*, 325).

Rule-obeying behaviors often do not begin with rule-conforming behaviors, but it is important to Sellars' account that a certain number of them must begin in this way, specifically in the case of language learning. If all linguistic rule-obeying behaviors were learned by being told the rules of language, then learning a language would presuppose an understanding of language, which either results in an infinite regress or entails that we are born with innate knowledge of some rules of language (i.e., some sort of meta-knowledge of language). This latter possibility would introduce a new version of the given, according to which we have an innate knowledge of certain facts. This is not unlike the familiar versions of the given which grant us innate capacities for abstracting or recognizing certain facts (e.g., that sensation inherently delivers perceptual facts). If we are to avoid this conclusion, therefore, some rule-obeying behaviors must begin as rule-conforming behaviors. In other words, language must originate by being trained to consistently respond with verbal utterances to bodily and environmental stimuli without recognition that one's utterances are properly linguistic or are reliably adhering to the rules of language. Consider Sellars' account of a child learning language:

> We can imagine a child learning a rudimentary language in terms of which he can perceive, draw inferences, and act. In doing so, he begins by uttering noises which sound like words and sentences and ends by uttering noises which are words and sentences....in the earlier stage we are classifying his utterances as sounds and only by courtesy and anticipation as words. (Wilfrid Sellars, *The Structure of Knowledge*, 320)

We can now apply the distinction between conforming to rules and obeying rules to the case of issuing observation reports about one's inner states. Sellars gives us the example of a child learning to report his anger. By noticing the child's behavior, the child's parents infer that the child is angry. Through positive and negative reinforcement of some sort, the parents train the child to respond directly to the bodily states and dispositions characteristic of anger by uttering, "I am angry." They know the functions that linguistic utterances perform, and they ensure, perhaps without any knowledge of how they do so, that the child responds with verbal utterances which are appropriate to the circumstances (Wilfrid Sellars, "Behaviorism, Language, and Meaning," *Pacific Philosophical Quarterly*, vol. 61, issue 1-2, 11). Thus the child can learn to noninferentially report that he is angry by responding directly to his dispositions. Sellars describes the process this way:

> The functioning which gives the utterances of one who has learned a language their meaning can exist merely at the level of uniformities, as in the case of the fledgling speaker. Those who train him, thus, his parents, think about these functionings and attempt to ensure that his verbal behavior exemplifies them. In this respect, the trainer operates not only at the level of the trainee, thinking thoughts about things, but also at that higher level which is thinking thoughts about the functions by virtue of which first-level language has the meaning it does. In traditional terms, the trainer knows the rules which govern the correct functioning of language. The language learner begins by conforming to these rules without grasping them himself. (Wilfrid Sellars, *The Structure of Knowledge,* 321)

This example of the ability to respond directly to a situation with a linguistic utterance is important for understanding how we can come to issue noninferential reports of our mental states without directly observing them in a Cartesian sense (indeed, without even an understanding that they are mental states at all). It is important that this sort of response is an actualization of a disposition rather than a report about a disposition, although the utterance certainly provides evidence about the nature of the disposition in question. The child's profession of anger is an assertion that he or she is angry, and the cause of this assertion (if the child has learned to use linguistic utterances reliably, that is, in the appropriate circumstances) is the child's anger, but this does not entail that the child first observes this anger and then reports that he or she is angry. The case is quite the opposite; the child first responds with the appropriate utterance and later learns to recognize that he or she is angry as a result of "hearing" his or her own utterance. Thus, the child observes his or her anger indirectly by observing the verbal profession that "I am angry." The anger itself is never known directly but only indirectly as an analogical extension of linguistic utterances. As Sellars writes:

> Notice that the child isn't acquiring the propensity to say "I am angry," when he notices his anger. This would put the cart before the horse. The noticing simply is the actualization of the acquired propensity to say 'I am angry' as a direct response to the anger itself. (Wilfrid Sellars, "Behaviorism, Language, and Meaning," *Pacific Philosophical Quarterly*, vol. 61, issue 1-2, 11)

This may seem counterintuitive, especially in the case of sensory experiences. Clearly, it seems that we feel anger and then report this anger. The point of importance is that feeling anger does not entail one's recognition that one is angry, and recognizing that one is angry first requires the ability to respond directly (i.e., in a way not involving theory-laden inferences) to one's anger with verbal utterances. Paul Churchland puts the above point this way:

> [W]hile it is one thing to claim that all feelings are felt, it is quite another to claim that all feelings are conceptualized as such, are recognized as feelings, and as feelings of a determinate sort. For this latter claim is clearly false. An infant, for example, is presumably subject to a substantial range of sensations and feelings— bodily, sensory, and emotional. But being an infant he has yet to generate or acquire the conceptual framework necessary to judge that he is thirsty, to recognize that he is in pain, or to be aware that he is having a sensation of red. No doubt the infant feels thirst, suffers pain, and senses redly, but a judgement to any such specific effect is as yet beyond his capabilities….In sum, the difference between having a φ-sensation, and judging that one has a φ-sensation, shows up in the following way. The making of a judgement necessarily involves the application of concepts… whereas the mere having of sensations and feelings does not require the

application or even the possession of any concepts at all. (Paul Churchland, *Scientific Realism and the Plasticity of Mind*, 98)

There is a point here that should be clarified. If the child directly feels anger, is the child not responding to this anger when acquiring the concept of anger? In other words, it seems that the feeling of anger plays an important role in the development of a concept of anger. I said a moment ago that anger itself is first noticed indirectly by way of the relevant language, that is, that the child cannot notice his or her anger until he has learned to utter that "I am angry." I have just said that anger can be directly felt, and anger can be felt whether or not one possesses a concept of anger. Do these two claims conflict? No; they do not.

We begin to learn to use language by being trained to respond reliably to overt behaviors characteristic of anger. This is because this training is made possible by third-person reinforcement of the child's overt verbal behaviors, and third-person parties know whether to applaud the child's utterances or frown on them by observing the child's other overt behaviors, that is, by becoming familiar with the child's dispositions and patterns of behavior. On the first-person side of this story, however, the behaviors characteristic of anger (if the parents are doing their job well) coincide with a feeling of anger. Thus, the child is responding with an appropriate utterance and feeling anger. In this way, the child learns to connect the word, "anger," with the feeling of anger.

It is important, however, that these responses are, at least initially, reinforced according to the child's behavior and not according to the child's feelings. As Sellars says, "the fact that overt behavior is evidence for these episodes is built into the very logic of these concepts" (Wilfrid Sellars, *Science, Perception, and Reality*, 189). Thus, the child learns to recognize that his or her feeling is one of anger by first learning something about what anger is from a third-person perspective. This initial learning is accompanied by a feeling of anger, and the child can classify or identify this feeling as anger when he or she has begun to acquire some proficiency in using the appropriate conceptual tools. In a moment, I will argue that it is even later in the child's development that he or she learns to classify or identify the feeling of anger as a "feeling of anger." This requires that the child master the concept of a "feeling." I will shortly argue that mastering the concept of a feeling (at least a full-fledged concept of a feeling) requires the development of a theory of mind.

This idea can be confusing when it is combined with Sellars' attack on the notion of the given. The important moral of the story of the Ryleans is that all observational knowledge is in some sense theory-dependent. However, this claim does not entail that verbal responses to inner psychological episodes always involves theory-based inferences from data which provide inductive support for the report. In fact, such a claim would reintroduce the notion of a given because the data used in justifying one's report would have to be of a kind that can function as an inferential premise in the language of the theory. For something to function as a premise for theoretical inferences entails that the thing be known as of a certain kind.

There must be some cases in which reporting an inner psychological episode involves deploying psychological language in a way that does not require the possession of a psychological theory. On Sellars' account, the child first learns to exhibit the appropriate responses and only later acquires the theory behind them. Put another way, the child first develops implicit procedural knowledge concerning when it is appropriate to make a certain kind of response, and only later comes to recognize that he or she is responding appropriately. The question concerning such cases is that of whether a verbal response, in this sense, really qualifies as observational knowledge. Put another way, does the language-learner really know anything about that to which he or she is responding when "reporting" feelings and sensations in this sense of "report"? The answer is "no"; he or she does not yet understand the meaning of these responses.

The above should stand in opposition to a Cartesian model of introspection and language learning. According to the Cartesian view, we know and express what we are thinking by first observing some inner state and then expressing some fact about this inner state. In other words, we think about a thought and then express the thought. This situation is reversed by Sellars' account, according to which we learn to think about our thoughts or inner states by first learning to use verbal expressions, and then by learning to think of those verbal expressions as a result of some inner cause. The idea that these words express thoughts may, however, be misleading. We must remember that the utterances are sometimes thinkings in and of themselves, even though they are not conceived as such. This may allow us to see how directly and reliably responding to certain circumstances with the appropriate verbal utterances is the first step in learning to conceptualize and, hence, monitor our thoughts.

The Problem of Qualia

The idea that propositional thinking is conceived by analogy with language does not seem to bother too many people. This is probably why we often describe this form of thinking in terms of propositional attitudes. The debate becomes more heated when we try to suggest that experiences are conceived in just the same way, that is, by analogy with language. When we begin to discuss experiences, certain Cartesian intuitions come back to haunt us. Does it not seem that experiences are self-intimating? Can one be in pain and not know that one is in pain? Do we not know that we are in pain just by being in pain?

I will argue here that the answer is that we do not know that we are in pain just by being in pain. This argument has to do with two points: (1) an analysis of what it means to have knowledge about an experience, and this has to do with how we understand the semantics of the term "experience"; and (2) the distinction between recognizing that one is in pain and simply feeling pain and responding to pain. The second of these was alluded to above in the passage by Paul Churchland and our discussion of Sellars' account of a child's knowledge that he or she is angry. To restate my position on this point, knowledge that one is angry presupposes mastery of a concept, and the capacity to feel pain is independent of mastery of any concept. The first of these points will be the subject of the following section. This first point has to do with the nature of experiences and the consequences of our ontological and semantic account of "experience" for our epistemological account of what it means to have knowledge about an experience per se. Before we turn to an analysis of "experience," however, let us briefly lay out the dimensions of the problem.

The problem, in short, is that of how we explain appearances which do not match reality. The problem has two dimensions. The first is the problem of where we should locate these appearances in our ontological framework. The second is how we are to explain epistemological mistakes in cases of false belief. Let me begin by explaining the second of these. Recall the example in which Jones came home only to find his fellow Ryleans drinking mud. Let us consider three kinds of psychological explanation for the Ryleans' behavior. The first possibility is that we could view the Ryleans' error as a sensory error. According to this explanation, we would say that the Ryleans were seeing mud which appeared to them as water. In other words, they were experiencing some sort of sensory distortion or anomaly (e.g., perhaps something like seeing an oasis in a desert). The second possibility is that we could explain their behavior as a conceptual error. We could hypothesize that their sensory faculties were in working order, but, for some other reason, they arrived at the false belief that the mud was water. In other words, they were seeing a liquid with an opaque, muddy quality but, perhaps through some horrible error in reasoning, came to believe that it was water. The third (and most likely) possibility is that the Ryleans made a perceptual error, that is, an error which involved both a sensory and a conceptual error.

We could avoid the ontological dimension of the problem if we accepted a purely conceptual explanation of the kind mentioned above. In other

words, we could say that the problem is a purely epistemological problem in which one simply "believes that one saw something which did not
match reality." This, however, seems extremely unlikely and counterintuitive. Is it not evident solely from first-person phenomenological evidence
that we sometimes really see things which are not there? There seem to be
many cases of sensory anomalies. If we accept this, we have committed
ourselves to facing the problem of qualia. By "qualia," we are referring to
the phenomenal characteristics of experience and attempting to isolate this
aspect of consciousness.

The ontological problem of qualia is this: where in the world are we
to locate phenomenal appearances? There are four alternatives that come
to mind. The first is that the qualitative aspect of consciousness is simply
an awareness of the qualities of objects. In other words, we could say that
qualia are properties of physical objects. This is a notoriously inadequate
view for the simple reason that appearances do not always match reality.
How are we to explain cases in which we see something which is not
there? The second option is that qualia are mental states, that is, they are
appearances to the mind of objects in the world. This too is a mistake, but
the reason for rejecting this alternative is more complex and is addressed
in detail the following section. Essentially, the problem with this view is
that it renders the mind-body problem completely insuperable by creating
the problem of locating a "phenomenal appearance" in the mind or brain.
The need to reject the above two alternatives has led many philosophers
to a third option, which we will call qualia nihilism. If we are to accept
physicalism, this is the first option we have considered that has real merit.

There are many versions of qualia nihilism, and a thorough examination of this view is beyond the scope of this paper. Furthermore, I am not
concerned here with a thorough examination of the ontological dimension
of the problem of qualia, but it will be helpful to have some understanding
of this problem. Jaegwon Kim offers an excellent summary of the kind of
qualia nihilism to which I am alluding here:

> Proponents of this position argue that there "really" are no such
> things as qualia and that a close analysis of the concept of a quale
> will show qualia to be merely a piece of philosophical invention.
> Arguments for qualia nihilism ... typically begin with an enumer-
> ation of the properties usually associated with qualia, such as their
> infallible and incorrigible first-person accessibility, their ineffabil-
> ity and inaccessibility to the third person, and their intrinsicness.
> These arguments then attempt to show that either these concepts
> are incoherent or hopelessly obscure or that they are empty, ap-
> plying to nothing recognizable in our mental life. One problem

with many of these arguments is that they tend to exaggerate the epistemic and other properties some philosophers have claimed in behalf of qualia, with the unsurprising result that nothing could qualify as qualia. To believe in qualia, it is not necessary, for example, to insist on absolute first-person infallibility or third-person inaccessibility. And then there are the all too facile analogies advanced by qualia-phobes between belief in qualia and the discredited beliefs in witches, phlogiston, and magnetic effluvia. The idea is that belief in qualia will be discredited when neuroscience reaches the stage where it can explain human behavior without recourse to an inner mental life, just as belief in phlogiston was abandoned when the oxidation theory of combustion took hold. But such arguments depend on the premise that qualia are only theoretical constructs posited to explain human behavior, an assumption that will be rejected by those who take qualia seriously. (Jaegwon Kim, *Philosophy of Mind*, 179)

The problem with qualia nihilism is that such accounts tend to avoid or "explain away" the problem of qualia rather than solving or genuinely explaining the place of qualitative experience in the world. In cases where we see something which is not there, for example, a red after-image, this after-image must be somewhere in the world if we are to be realists about conscious experience. We cannot simply say that we do not have qualitative experiences because it is phenomenologically evident that we do have qualitative experiences. Consequently, we must locate this red after-image somewhere in the world; we cannot simply say that it does not exist.

The fourth option is the one I advocate. It is simply a compromise between the first two options. I view qualitative experiences as necessarily relational. My argument regarding the epistemology of introspection presupposes that, in the context of the philosophy of mind, the term "experience" should always be a verb and never a noun. (Although, as I have said, I provide further explanation and reasoning behind this presupposition in the following section.) Viewing "experience" as a noun means that we are interpreting experiences as particular things which are to be located in the world of things, rather than as continuous with other cognitive processes. In this sense, I may be advocating a form of qualia nihilism, but it is a fairly weak version of this view. I am suggesting that there are no qualia in that we should not view qualia as particular states.

If we are to understand qualitative experiences, we must recognize how inextricably they are intertwined in the processes involved in both organism-environment or sensorimotor interactions and in the conscious conceptual narrative characteristic of an organism's mental life. Isolating qualia as particulars and removing qualia from the context of such processes results in the terrible, ontological problem of qualia, which has significant consequences for our epistemological account of introspecting experiences. Again, my focus is on the epistemology of introspection, but it is important to have some ontological understanding of what it is that we are introspecting if we are to understand the epistemological dimension of this problem. We will return to this problem shortly, but, for now, let us consider what is involved in an account of introspecting experiences. It will then become clear why we must consider the location of experiences in the world if we are to understand what is involved in acquiring knowledge about our experiences.

Thinking about Experiencing

There is a temptation, especially in the case of sensory experiences, to model introspection according to what Sydney Shoemaker calls the "object-perception stereotype" (Sydney Shoemaker, "Introspection," in *A Companion to the Philosophy of Mind,* Samuel Guttenplan, (ed.), 397). This is essentially a two-stage model in which one is first aware of a non-factual experience, and it is by being aware of such non-factual experiences that one somehow derives facts about these experiences. By non-factual experience, I mean an experience which does not involve propositional thinking. Factual experiences are essentially perceiving that an object is a certain kind of thing, that is, they are experiences involving a propositional thinking. For example, when sensing a red ball, a non-factual experience is a purely qualitative awareness of a red-circular stimulus, whereas a factual experience is such a qualitative awareness accompanied by the propositional thinking that "There is a red ball."

We could, for example, read Churchland as saying that one first has a non-factual experience and then, as a result of having this experience, judges that it is a certain kind of experience by applying a concept to this non-factual experience. This interpretation can be subtly misleading in that it may tempt us to reintroduce the notion of an inner sense. By "inner sense," I mean a model of introspection in which awareness of or knowledge about one's mental states involves directly witnessing or observing one's mental states in a broadly Cartesian manner. In order to first observe a non-factual experience and then apply a concept to this experience, we must be able to observe our internal, mental states. The reason for this has to do with the semantics of the term "experience." We could say that experiencing essentially is observing or sensing an object. If we adopt this interpretation, however, then what we know is an object, e.g., a red ball, and not the experience itself. This is how we should understand the term "experience." Experiences are the processes by means of which we interact with objects in the world in a sensorimotor way.

Conceptualizing Intentionality

Conceiving of these processes, then, involves a conceptual thinking about inner processes which are not directly present to the subject. The task of judging that something is a certain kind of experience is a fundamentally different problem than that of judging that an object is a certain kind of object which has a certain qualitative character or "feels" a certain way. In other words, acquiring knowledge about the way something feels is fundamentally different than acquiring the knowledge that we know this by means of a feeling, sensation, or experience, specifically. This is because we can use our senses to observe an object, and we can then respond to this non-factual awareness of the object with propositional thinking. In the case of experiences, however, we do not have the means to observe our experiences in a non-factual way. This is because we have adopted an interpretation of the word "experience" according to which experiences are relations to objects in the world. In short, we have accepted that objects rather than experiences are directly present to the knowing subject.

Thus, in order to conceptualize or think about experiences, we must do so by analogy with language, specifically, by utilizing the representational function of language. The capacity to use the representational function of language is necessary for an understanding of our own intentionality or for understanding the mind-dependent nature of perceived objects. In other words, to conceptualize the experiential relation (or any relation between the mind and the world), we must have the knowledge that we are mental organisms, that is, we must have concepts of psychological phenomena. This is because what we understand when we conceive of mind's intentionality is that something inside (which is known by analogy with a word) stands for, which is to say, is of or about or represents, something outside in the world.

We can use language to represent or stand for things which are not directly present. It quite commonly agreed that the ability to use language to represent is necessary for thinking about something which is absent or distant (e.g., a unicorn or a positron). What I am arguing here is that our mental states are essentially absent in a similar way. (However, we should briefly recall that we can, in certain cases, "observe" absent phenomena by their effects, as in the case of "force" discussed toward the beginning of essay.) Thus, in order to conceive of a feeling or experience, we must be able to conceive of the relation between an inner experiencing (i.e., a mental state of the organism) and the objects which are felt or experienced.

Inner Awareness

If we say that we are directly aware of experiences themselves, we have conceded that we observe our experiences via an "inner sense" which is something like our ordinary sensory faculties. In other words, we accept that experiences are presentations of objects to the knowing observer, that is, they are inner replicas which mediate our detection of and interaction with objects. If we accept this model, then this is what we see when we see a red ball, that is, we see the red-ball experience and not the red ball itself. This, however, reintroduces the Cartesian model of introspection. Locke has a nice way of describing this model of introspection:

> Secondly, the other fountain from which experience furnishes the understanding with ideas is the perception of the operations of our own mind within us...which operations...do furnish the understanding with another set of ideas, which could not be had from things without. And such are perception, thinking, doubting, believing, reasoning, knowing, willing, and all the different act-ings of our own minds, which we, being conscious of and observ-ing in ourselves, do from these receive into our understandings as distinct ideas....This source of ideas every man has wholly in himself; and though it is not sense, as having nothing to do with external objects, yet it is very like it, and might properly enough be called internal sense. (John Locke, *Modern Philosophy: An An-thology of Primary Sources*, Roger Ariew, et al., (eds.), 276)

This view of introspection is particularly tempting in the case of phe-nomenal experiences. What makes the "inner sense" model irresistible is the object-perception model of visual sensations in which, for example, seeing a red after-image involves existence in the mind of something red. This view essentially says that perceiving or seeming to perceive an object involves directly observing phenomenal objects (i.e., qualia or sensory impressions) distinct from whatever external objects (if any) that might cause such experiences. We tend to think of phenomenal experiences as necessarily involving an awareness of the intrinsic character of the experi-ence. In fact, this intrinsic character is precisely the quality we are trying to isolate by using terms like "phenomenal experience" or "qualitative experience."

This can be problematic when combined with the idea that qualitative experiences are internal sensory states of an organism rather than the sensory processes via which we interact with objects and witness the qualitative character of objects standing in a certain relation to our organism, that is, as they are apprehended from a certain perspective of an organism endowed with the specific set of capacities which enable that organism's sensory or conceptual apprehension of the object. The combination of the idea that we are aware of the intrinsic character of qualitative experiences and the idea that these experiences are inner states of our organism inevitably leads us to the idea that we know these things through an "inner sense," which leaves us with the intractable problem of placing qualia in the physical world because we cannot and should not locate anything that is qualitatively like a red ball inside the mind or brain.

Why is this so? It is important that we do not adopt a Cartesian view of introspection. If we adopt such a view of introspection, then we directly observe our thoughts as the kinds of things they are. If our thoughts are observable in the Cartesian sense, there is no possibility of explaining how their intrinsic character can be other than the way in which we know them. In other words, if we directly observe our thoughts or experiences in the Cartesian sense, then there is no hope of explaining how thoughts might actually be states of our brain. This is because it is phenomenologically evident that we do not know thoughts or experiences as states of our brain.

Descartes famously argued that the mind cannot be physiological in nature because we can have direct knowledge of our thoughts without knowing that the nervous system even exists. Sellars' intention is, in part, to refute this view by arguing that we can introduce a new kind of direct knowledge of our mental acts. Sellars writes:

> What is, perhaps, new in the account I am proposing is the idea that direct self-knowledge may essentially involve analogical concepts, i.e., that the concepts in terms of which we have what is often called 'reflexive knowledge' of our mental acts are analogical extensions of concepts pertaining to the public or intersubjective world of things and persons. (Wilfrid Sellars, *Science, Perception, and Reality*, 48)

Sellars argues that it is possible have direct reflexive knowledge of our inner states, but he has a very different account of what it means to have "direct reflexive knowledge" of our inner states. In Sellars' usage, such knowledge is still noninferential, and so it is direct in this sense, but it is indirect in that it involves the noninferential deployment of analogical concepts. The important difference is that, if the concepts in terms of which we conceive and, hence, "observe," our mental states are analogical concepts, then it invites the possibility that mental states are, in propria persona (i.e., in a non-analogical guise), physical or neurological states.

In the case of "experiencing a red ball," it is tempting to say that something like a red-ball expanse appears to my mind (as though on a movie screen), and that this is what we call an experience. In calling this appearance to the mind an "experience," however, we have hypostasized the experience. We have isolated a particular and located it in the mind-brain, removing it from the context of the larger process in which it figures and in virtue of which it is an experience of a red ball. Experiencing a red ball is no longer conceived as standing in such-and-such perceptual relation to a red ball (or something that appears to be a red ball when we are standing in such-and-such a relation to that thing), and we instead think of experiencing a red ball as witnessing (in the Cartesian sense) a picture on a movie screen. We call this picture a red-ball experience (or quale), which we have isolated and hypostasized as a particular thing. Witnessing this experience, then, does entail that we know something (in whatever sense of "know") about the intrinsic character of the experience. This eliminates the possibility that the experience is intrinsically a series of physical processes or physical states of any sort (unless we can find some actual red expanse in a person's brain or eye, one which literally is the "what it is like" quality of seeing a red ball).

Many have succumbed to a strong tendency to think of phenomenal experiences not as the states and processes via which we perceive the qualitative character of objects but rather as an object or content of cognition. Even Sellars, whose work I have used as an inspiration for constructing a model of introspection, succumbed to this idea at times. It is quite strange that he spent most of his life prosecuting the falsity of this notion while at the same time wrestling with it. It is almost as if he knew it to be false, but could not bring himself to believe that it was actually false. The problem of qualia left Sellars speaking about the need to locate "ultimately homogenous" expanses in the brain and mumbling about pink ice cubes for the latter half of his life. Sellars writes:

> From this point of view, one can appreciate the danger of misunderstanding which is contained in the term 'introspection'. For while there is, indeed, an analogy between the direct knowledge we have of our own thoughts and the perceptual knowledge we have of what is going on in the world around us, the analogy holds only in as much as both self-awareness and perceptual observation are basic forms of non-inferential knowledge. They differ, however, in that whereas in perceptual observation we know objects as being of a certain quality, in the direct knowledge we have of what

we are thinking (e.g. I am thinking that it is cold outside) what we know non-inferentially is that *something analogous to and properly expressed by the sentence, 'It is cold outside', is going on in me.* (Wilfrid Sellars, *Science, Perception, and Reality*, 32)

Then, in almost the same breath, the language in which we talk about qualitative experience betrays him into actually believing that sensations present themselves in their qualitative character:

My strategy will be to argue that the difficulty…arises from the mistake of supposing that in self-awareness conceptual thinking presents itself to us in a qualitative guise. Sensations and images do…present themselves to us in a qualitative guise… (Wilfrid Sellars, *Science, Perception, and Reality*, 32)

I have been trying to point out that it is not sensations but sensed objects which have a qualitative character. Sensations are invariably of or in some way related to objects in the world, whereas sensations (i.e., inner states or processes) themselves are never known directly. Am I suggesting that the an itch sensation is of my sweater? No; my sensation is of an itch, which, importantly, is caused by or is a relation to a sweater, and my sensations are the inner states and processes by means of which I feel the itchiness caused by my sweater. In short, the qualitative itchiness is a relational property. It is a purely semantic point that the term "experience" or "sensation" should be reserved for denoting the whole process by which we know the qualities of objects, but it is a semantic point which seems to have caused a great deal of unnecessary philosophical confusion.

Sometimes the objects of sensations are distorted by standing in an abnormal perceptual relation to the object. At such times we might say that the object of one's experience is a hallucination, an after-image, or whatever kind of instance in which appearance does not match reality. We can note that imagined or remembered objects do not seem to have the same sort of phenomenal quality as distorted perceptions. This should offer prima facie evidence for the claim that phenomenal experiences are always relationships between object and organism. For in the absence of a physical object that is directly present to the perceiver by way of that perceiver's sensory processes (i.e., in the case of imagined or remembered objects), the phenomenal character of such contents of consciousness is diminished or completely lacking.

Conclusions about Experiencing

I am not suggesting that we do not have phenomenal experiences or that it is by virtue of having such experiences that we feel "what it is like" to see a red ball. Experience, however, is an abstract term denoting distributed processes or states which enable us to know "what it is like" to see a red ball. In Jonesean psychology (which is a basic and ultimately inadequate theory of perception), we may conceive of experience as an "inner" perceptual state. This might cause the problem under discussion, i.e., that we have isolated an inner representation of the red ball as the state we are observing when we perceive a red ball. Our perception of a red ball, our "experience" of it, should be conceived as a process or relation between an organism and a red ball (or some other object that might appear to be a red ball).

This process or relation is not a re-presentation or "inner replica" that is a secondary appearance in the mind of something which is first presented to our bodily sensory faculties. In short, when we know "what it is like" to see a red ball, what we know is not something about the intrinsic character of an experience but about a physical object (as seen from a certain perspective in certain circumstances, that is, in relation to ourselves). Intrinsically, the "experience" is the whole process by means of which we know about a red ball at a certain instance in a certain relation to our organism. The experience is of the instance of the-red-ball-in-relation-to-our-organism. Thus, the distinction between the "inner" and "outer" (i.e., the "mental" and "physical") components of experience cannot be clearly drawn in reality but only in theory or discourse, that is, in our conception of such a relation. In terms of the metaphor of mental representation, the conceived representational relation between signifier and signified (i.e., between a mental representation and its object or content) dichotomizes two aspects of a process which is fundamentally continuous. Experience is a communion of mental and physical processes, and we introduce a distinction between these two aspects of the process only in introspection or when we acquire a theory of mind.

The point of importance is that qualitative experiences are known in just the same way as any intentional mental state, that is, by analogy with language. We know our experiences indirectly by analogy with language, although we may experience objects directly and be aware of "what these objects feel like." I am not suggesting that experiencing does not have a qualitative character. I am only arguing that to conceive of our experience of objects as experiences involves the same kind of language involved in conceiving of any intentional mental state. We can view introspective knowledge of experience as involving three dimensions: (1) a nonconceptual sensory awareness of a stimulus; (2) conceptual knowledge about that stimulus, e.g., perceptual knowledge; and (3) conceptual knowledge about a psychological state which stands in relation to a concept of that stimulus. In other words, being aware of an object is not the same as having propositional knowledge about that object, but it is a far cry from having knowledge of the fact that we are experiencing that object, that is, from having knowledge about the experiential process or relation itself.

Conceiving of this relation involves relating a concept pertaining to an object and a concept pertaining to one's inner, mental states. This relation can be seen as a second-order relation which is a conception of a first-order relation between the physical states of an organism and its environment. In other words, we are drawing a distinction between intentionality and intentionality conceived as such, which is a higher-order form of intentionality. This higher-order form of intentionality is necessary for knowledge of the fact that we are thinking organisms and, hence, for acquiring introspective knowledge of our mental states.

Such higher-order intentionality is also necessary for knowing that what we are thinking about is "what we are thinking," that is, that what we are thinking about is a content of thought rather than a common-sense physical object. That is, the knowledge that one is a thinking organism is necessary for understanding "what's going on in one's mind" in the full sense of the phrase. In other words, knowledge about what one is thinking only counts as introspective when one conceives of this knowledge as the content of a thought, that is, when one can preface the thought with "I think that...." The conception of oneself as a mental organism is necessary for introspection.

As an aside, there is a point here that should be clarified. While it is one thing to suggest that experiences of objects in the world are relational, it may seem like another to suggest that feelings are relational. The feeling of anger, for example, may not seem to be related to an object in the world. Similarly, proprioceptive awareness of one's body, for example, the positions of one's limbs, may not seem to involve a relation to an object in the world. I would take issue with these claims. I would argue that feeling anger does necessarily involve a relation to objects in the world. It seems to me that the purpose of feeling anger is to influence one's responses to one's situation in the world. This does not necessarily mean that one must be aware of the worldly causes of one's anger, but it does mean that feeling anger is a result of causes in the world and that the purpose of this feeling is to play a role in governing one's interactions with the world.

Such an argument, however, is beside the point. I am arguing that experiences are relational in that they necessarily involve a relation between mental and mind-external states. Hence, a proprioceptive awareness of the position of one's limbs, for example, involves a relation between a conscious state and unconscious, bodily states. Thus, knowledge of the fact that one is experiencing the position of one's limbs still requires a concept of an intentional, mental state that is a related to a concept of an object (e.g., one's body). In such a case, we could still apply the three layers identified above in the following way: (1) a nonconceptual awareness of the position of one's limbs or of being angry, for example; (2) a concept of anger or of one's body; and (3) a concept of mental states such as feelings, sensations, or experiences, which stands in relation to the kind of concept described in (2). In other words, I am suggesting that a concept of "anger" is distinct from a concept of "feeling anger."

The concept of "anger" can be understood in terms of being angry as well as the overt behavioral symptoms that typically accompany being angry. The concept of "feeling anger" can be understood as a concept of a mental state or psychological episode, i.e., a "feeling" or "experience," which is the apprehension of "anger," as that anger is conceived. In other words, it is not necessary to conceive of anger as a kind of mental state or as a phenomenally conscious state. To do so requires a theory of mind and, specifically, a concept of something like "sensory impressions" or "qualia." Is it really possible to have a concept of "anger" without have the concept of a "feeling" (which I am taking to be a particular kind of mental state)? Yes. In the case of language learning, for example, "anger" may be conceived in terms of "waving one's fists and yelling." In other words, one may conceive of anger in terms of a theory of behavior rather than a theory of mind.

Talking about Experiences

In terms of the Sellarsian framework discussed earlier, what is involved in introspecting qualitative experiences in a way which does not involve a direct observation or witnessing of the experience itself? We have conceptual knowledge about our experiences by way of our verbal responses to these experiences. Noninferential responses to our internal states can be considered observational, but not in a Cartesian sense. They are observational in the same sense as perceptual observation reports. As Sellars uses the term, observation reports are verbal episodes which are a direct, descriptive response to a situation (Willem A. DeVries, *The Philosophy of Wilfrid Sellars*, 177). A perception, then, is the inner analogue of an observation report. This is, of course, only after Jones has introduced his theory of inner states to the Rylean community. In short, we can "observe" our mental states in the sense that we can directly respond to a situation with a psychological description (e.g., "I perceive that 'There is a red ball.'")

It is important that such descriptive responses do not necessarily involve a statement about our inner states, although the statement involves the language of Jonesean psychological theory. When one says that "I perceive a red ball," one may essentially be saying "There is a red ball." One may be making an assertion about the perceived object and not about the internal cause of this assertion or the nature of the perception itself. In many cases, the prefix "I perceive that..." could easily be omitted from the statement.

In Sellars' story of Jones, even prior to the moment when Jones introduced his theory to the Ryleans, the Ryleans were capable of making observation reports such as "There is a red ball." As a result of the way in which the language of Jonesean psychology became an integral part of ordinary discourse within the Rylean community, the Ryleans have simply learned to add the prefix "I perceive that..." to observation reports about physical objects. The fact that they use this prefix does not mean that every time the Ryleans use Jones' term, "perception," they are using the term in the same way the term is used in the context of Jones' theory. In other words, when they profess that "I perceive a red ball," it may simply be a matter of habit, of making automated responses to physiological and environmental cues, that they use the prefix "I perceive...."

The reason that the Ryleans have learned to add such a prefix is that, as a result of Jones' theory of psychology, they have realized that there are times when it is useful to make statements that are specifically about their inner psychological episodes. At dusk, the Ryleans may say that "I perceive a red ball," but they may use this phrase with a different illocutionary force, one that draws attention to the accuracy of their perception rather than to the red ball. They may be, in a sense, asking whether the ball really is red or whether the ball merely appears to be red, instead of making an assertion with the illocutionary force of "Look at the red ball!" or "Direct your attention to that red ball." In this case, they are making an introspective judgment; they are attempting to draw theory-based inferences about an "inner" perceptual episode according to the Jonesean theory of the conditions of perception.

The Ryleans may know that, at dusk, the environmental circumstances tend to alter the normal lighting conditions. As a result, they may infer that the ball is not actually red but merely appears to be red. In such a case, they are applying a theory about the circumstances of perception. It so happens that they are using the Jonesean theory, which happens to explain appearances through recourse to "inner" sensory states (something similar to what we call "qualia"). Thus, they are actually making a statement about their inner states, but they are doing so in terms of analogical concepts. They are inferring that "Something somehow like a red ball must be going on in me." They infer that this is the case because there is no red ball before them (perhaps they tried to grasp it, and it was not there), and they have adopted the Jonesean theory (which explains cases of false perception by postulating "inner appearances" called "sensory impressions") in order to explain such instances. They are drawing inferences about (not directly observing) the nature of this inner sensory appearance.

Over time, as we have said, they may become very good at using Jones' theory, in which case they may be able to know what is going on within them without drawing explicit inferences (i.e., without consciously applying a theory). They may become accustomed to making certain kinds of introspective judgments according to the tenets of the Jonesean theory, at which time they can simply assert that "There appears to be a red ball" or "I am perceiving a red ball" or "I am undergoing a red-ball experience" without deliberation. In other words, they may have noninferential, reflexive knowledge of their own mental acts. This does not mean that they have immediate access to their mental states, because such ease of access is only made possible by their mastery of the Jonesean theory and their development of a certain kind of procedural knowledge. Access to our internal states is always mediated by analogical concepts which are extensions of the public world, which, of course, involves our public language.

Thinking about Thoughts

We are now in a position to explain how observation reports or direct descriptive responses can allow us to think about our own thoughts. Now that we have an account of automated responses, we can see how thoughts can become objects of thought in an indirect way mediated by our automatic verbal utterances.

There are clearly cases when we have to infer what we are thinking or what drives our behavior. We often have unconscious motivations for our behaviors. For example, when we want to avoid doing something, we may find ourselves drifting into another activity (like watching television or playing music). Similarly, negative behavioral patterns are often repeated unconsciously and habitually. For example, an alcoholic may find himself walking home along a route that passes several bars, until he finally stops to get a drink. Later, the alcoholic might infer that the most likely explanation for his behavior is that he was taking that route home because he wanted to stop and have a drink. In the case of psychoanalysis, the analysand may come to consciously recognize beliefs of which he was previously unconscious. The idea that the mind is completely transparent to the first-person subject is clearly false. On the other hand, we cannot completely discount the Cartesian intuition that we sometimes know our mind quite intimately.

There are clearly times when we seem to know what we are thinking without any deliberation, evidence, or inference. In other words, there are cases in which we seem to "just know" what we are thinking. To explain such cases, we must account for the intuition that we seem to have direct access to our thoughts. We can avoid the notion of a given by accepting Sellars' account of direct access which does not involve an immediate awareness of our mental states or of facts about our cognitive processes. In short, it will help to develop an account of noninferential knowledge of our mental states which is conceptually mediated and fallible, but does not involve theoretical inferences. This will allow us to account for Cartesian intuitions about direct access while preserving the idea that our mental states are not immediately given to us. How can we have direct, noninferential knowledge about something which is not directly observable? This is where it becomes important to understand the denouement of the story of Jones, in which Sellars writes that: "What began as a language with a purely theoretical use has gained a reporting role" (Willem A. DeVries & Timm Triplett, *Knowledge, Mind, and the Given*, 269).

I think it useful to clearly distinguish the two kinds of cases mentioned above. Jay Garfield's distinction between professing and introspecting is useful here:

> [R]ecall that the model of thinking that **p** is saying that **p**; it is clear that there are two ways in which one could intend, "I think that **p**." One could, as a consequence of…observations of oneself and one's behavior, decide that the only plausible explanation for these observations is that one believes that **p** (as in the case of psychoanalytic explanation….) Or one could ascribe oneself the belief as a way of asserting **p**. For to believe **p** is, on this model, to assert **p** in foro interno. And if one endorses this model, asserting **p** is one way of expressing one's belief in its truth. (Jay Garfield, "The Myth of Jones and the Mirror of Nature: Reflections on Introspection," *Philosophy and Phenomenological Research*, vol. 50, no. 1, 13-14)

Profession of one's beliefs is a spontaneous belief assertion or a direct descriptive response to a situation in that it does not involve explicit inferences in accordance with a psychological theory. This is possible because profession is the product of the automatic, unconscious processes learned during acquisition of skill in utilizing psychological language. Profession is the kind of case when one's thoughts seem to "pop into one's head" or "suddenly enter one's mind" without any apparent cause or conscious deliberation.

Professions are assertions of the contents of one's beliefs, an endorsement of one's belief in the truth of that content, although these contents are expressed as the complement of a mental verb. Unless that content has specifically to do with the internal state of the believer, one is not making an assertion about one's beliefs or inner states. While terms in the vocabulary of one's folk-psychological theory are used as a prefix for asserting the content of one's belief, such terms are not being utilized in their theoretical context. In other words, one might profess that p by saying "I believe that p," but one is using the prefix automatically, without conscious consideration about its theoretical context. Garfield notes a confusion that could result from the notion of profession:

> This is not to say that observing or reporting thoughts is entirely non-conceptual. That would be to embrace givenness with a vengeance. Rather…the use of the concept of a thought in reporting one's inner states becomes non-inferential. The application of the predicate is spontaneous—caused by one's inner state, and not inferred from theoretical premisses plus observations issuing in perceptual beliefs couched in a different, less theoretical vocabulary. (Jay Garfield, "The Myth of Jones and the Mirror of Nature: Reflections on Introspection," *Philosophy and Phenomenological Research*, vol. 50, no. 1, 13)

Introspective judgments, by contrast, involve the conscious, deliberative application of a theory. As one develops expertise in making introspective judgments, however, certain cases can become noninferential in that one is capable of figuring out what one is thinking without much deliberation. At this point, what was once introspected can be professed, or, as Sellars puts it, what was once theoretical can be reported.

Introspection refers to cases in which we really have to figure out what we are thinking, when we draw inferences by utilizing a psychological theory. In such a case, we are trying to understand something about our inner, mental states, that is, we are utilizing a theory to help us understand something about the nature or internal causes of our professions. As we have noted, there are times when we clearly arrive at beliefs by considering evidence. We may observe our behaviors and conclude that the most plausible explanation is that we hold a certain belief or are having a certain kind of experiential episode. This is an introspective judgment. If the vocabulary of thoughts is embedded in a theory, something like Jonesean psychology, then there are times when we really utilize a

folk-psychological theory in order to draw inductive and deductive inferences from observational data. In such a case, professions are one of
the most important types of data. Using our professions as observational
evidence, we can infer that we must believe the content of the profession
or draw inferences about the inner causes of our professions.

Formulating introspective judgments essentially involves adopting a
third-person perspective on oneself. At no time do we directly observe our
mental states and then make a judgment about them. Rather, we respond
to our inner states and then draw theoretical inferences about these inner
states using our responses as evidence. By "theoretical inferences," I mean
that we use the vocabulary of a psychological theory in its theoretical context. We are applying the theory as a way of explaining observational data.
The important point is that the observational data is not any inner state
but our behaviors and professions, which are "observations" of our inner
states only in a very different sense of "observation," that is, a Sellarsian
sense in which an "observation report" is a direct conceptual response to
one's circumstances.

Professing our thoughts allows us to take thoughts as the objects of
thinking. Andy Clark has a nice way of putting this point:

> [A]s soon as we formulate a thought in words (or on paper), it
> becomes an object both for ourselves and others. As an object it
> is the kind of thing we can have thoughts about. In creating the
> object, we need have no prior thoughts about thoughts—but once
> it is there, the opportunity immediately exists to attend to it as an
> object in its own right. The process of linguistic formulation thus
> creates the stable structure to which subsequent thinkings attach.
> (Andy Clark, "Dealing in Futures: Folk Psychology and the Role
> of Representations in Cognitive Science," *The Churchlands and
> Their Critics*, Robert McCauley (ed.), 177)

Introspection involves taking a linguistic/symbolic representation of
a thought as the content of thought. In order for thoughts to be the object
of thoughts, one must be able to think about a linguistic term which represents or "stands for" a state which is not immediately present. This can
be seen as similar to the way in which an eye cannot see itself without a
mirror. In this case, cognition cannot intend itself without the "mirror" of
a linguistic representation. In other words, mind's intentionality can never
be directed upon or about mental states in a direct way; mind's intentionality can only be directed upon or about mental states derivatively, that is,
in an indirect way involving a mediating linguistic representation. The use
of linguistic representations which can stand for intentional mental states
requires mastery of theory of mind, which develops socially and involves

mastery of certain linguistic skills, particularly, sentential complementation.

Theory of Mind

This picture is supported by a wealth of recent research on children's acquisition of theory of mind. The de Villiers have demonstrated that sentential complementation (almost immediately) precedes a child's acquisition of theory of mind. De Villiers argues for a Strong Linguistic Hypothesis, according to which theory of mind acquisition can be attributed principally to linguistic maturation and, in particular, to mastery of complementation (Jill G. de Villiers, "Language and Theory of Mind: What Are the Developmental Relationships?" in *Understanding Other Minds: Perspectives From Developmental Cognitive Neuroscience* (2nd ed.), (Simon Baron-Cohen, et al., (eds.)). Children begin using mental verbs (e.g., think, know, etc.) around the age of three. These uses, however, are not genuine uses of the mental verbs. In terms of our earlier discussion of language-learning, we could say that they "sound-like" mental verbs, that is, that the children are using mental verbs in appropriate instances without conceptual recognition of the fact that they are using such verbs in appropriate instances and, hence, of what it means to use mental verbs.

Around the age of four, children then begin to understand that mental verbs can be used as a prefix for another sentence (i.e., a complement). For example, the child can learn to say that "Mom thinks that 'The shampoo is toothpaste'" (Jill G. de Villiers, et al., *Point of View and Theory of Mind*). They shortly learn that the embedded sentence (i.e., "the shampoo is toothpaste") can be true for mom but false from another's point of view. In other words, the child can begin to think of his or her mother's "mental world." Verbs of communication (e.g., say, tell, etc.) provide the basis for learning to use sentential complements for mental verbs. In other words, children first learn to say "Mom said that 'the shampoo is toothpaste.'" This should all provide prima facie evidence for the claim that children conceive of intentional mental states by analogy with verbs of speech.

This evidence can be combined with evidence for what Garfield, Peterson, and Perry term the Strong Priority Thesis, which states that "Public co-operative attitudes towards propositions are epistemically prior to private unobservable attitudes towards them" (Jay Garfield, et al., "Social Cognition, Language Acquisition and the Development of the Theory of Mind," *Mind and Language* 16, 10). They support this thesis by demonstrating that verbs of pretense arise first in social interaction. The grammar and meaning of phrases like "pretend that" allow children to learn, publicly and collectively, to reason about deliberately false beliefs. This kind of social interaction, combined with the ability to deploy sentential complements of mental verbs, is integral to the development of theory of mind. This should support the idea that we initially learn the language of theory of mind in a public sphere, through third-person reinforcement, and that we initially understand the meaning of mental verbs in terms of their publicly accessible properties. Similarly, I have suggested that we initially understand the meaning of "anger" in terms of overt behaviors.

This is consistent with the picture of language learning discussed earlier. We can view the developmental progression towards the language of theory of mind roughly as follows: We can assume that children already have the ability to make assertions about conditions in the environment. Children first learn to utter what "sound-like" mental verbs (in the sense discussed above). Children next learn to profess their beliefs using mental verbs as a prefix for an embedded sentence (and they do this by the analogy of verbs of speech and their complements). It is important to note that, at this stage, the profession is primarily an assertion of the embedded sentence. Eventually, the child can learn to assert the embedded sentence on behalf of another person, at which time they can learn to reason about the mental states of others and, hence, about their own mental states. In this way, introspection essentially involves adopting a third-person perspective on oneself.

This is consistent with Lev Vygotsky's view that language initially develops as social coordination and is later internalized as a "medium" for thought. The term "medium," however, can be misleading. Garfield puts the point this way:

> This pattern—the learning the relevant language preceding the ability to perform the reasoning; the precedence of mastery of reasoning regarding joint pretence over that regarding inner episodes—confirm the Vygotskyan intuition that representation is initially a public activity and that as the public representational medium of language is learned, it can scaffold autonomous thought and reasoning. The most plausible mechanism of this scaffolding is that our ability to intend is turned upon this representational medium, allowing us to make autonomous use of language. The representational weight is borne by language; the ability to make use of that power in thought requires our complex cognitive ability to intend—to engage cognitively with our environment. When that environment includes symbols, the magic of human thought occurs. (Jay Garfield, *Intention: Doing Away with Mental Representation*, 27)

According to the view I have put forth, introspection utilizes the same theory of mind, the same "scaffolding," that we use in third-person mental state ascriptions. Nevertheless, this is compatible with the idea that first-person professions of our beliefs carry a certain authority, but these professions should not be seen as introspective. For the normal, fully-developed human, belief profession is automatic but framed by the wealth of background knowledge involved in a theory of mind. Such background knowledge is available should we need to avail ourselves of this knowledge in formulating introspective judgments. Oftentimes, however, we simply profess our beliefs without much consideration of the fact that they are beliefs or of the causes of our profession. The important point is that the ability to profess the contents of one's beliefs and to profess these contents as the complement of a mental verb is prior to and, hence, not dependent upon a theory of mind. For this reason, profession should not be considered properly introspective.

Conclusion

The fact that we use language as a metaphor for our thoughts and that we do so without conscious deliberation can be misleading in several ways. It can lead to the belief that we actually think in language, not of or about language. In other words, we might suppose that language is the medium of thinking rather than among the contents of our thoughts. This is because we often conceive of our thoughts as being like sentences in a language. Similarly, we often conceive of our thoughts as being like images on a movie screen. It is important, though, that we are thinking about language, which, in certain cases, can be language intended to represent an inner thinking. This is just the way that the word "ball" symbolizes or represents an actual ball but is not an actual ball. To forget this is to confuse cognition's intentionality with the representational function of language, which is natural because the former is conceived in terms of the latter.

Part of the benefit of Jones' theory is that it employs the semantic feature of public language, that is, its meaningfulness, as a metaphor for the meaningfulness of thoughts. We may want to explain how thoughts are about things (i.e., how they are intentional) by using the metaphor of how language symbolizes things (i.e., the representational function of language). We should not, however, take this metaphor literally. If we do, we will confuse thoughts themselves (e.g., cognitive processes) with the objects about which we think (e.g., sentences in a public language). This will lead us to a skewed version of the notion of Mentalese or private language, one which does not recognize the essential publicity of the language in terms of which we conceive of and know our own thoughts. Hence, to the extent that we might say that we do think linguistically, it is important that Mentalese must be made of the same words and structured in the same way as our public and intersubjective language. Thus, the language in which we understand our own minds is public in principle and private only as a matter of practice (e.g., we may choose not to speak).

Taking the metaphorical concepts which allow us to conceptualize our mental states too literally may leave us searching for a "language in the brain" or "phenomenal expanses" in the brain. We might be led to think of a phenomenal experience as being like a picture on a movie screen, that is, an experience "inside our minds." If this were the case, then it would be true that we have knowledge about the intrinsic character of the experiences or thoughts themselves. In other words, viewing mind's intentionality as directed upon inner mental states can lead to the idea that we directly know the nature of our thoughts in propria persona.

We can note that, on the Cartesian view, the notion of "turning the gaze of mind's eye inwards" is prima facie awkward and problematic. If perception is mediated by the observation of internal ideas formed from sensations, then the mind's eye is already "turned inwards," that is, the observer is already watching its own internal ideas. Thus, we must wonder whether the mind's eye, which is already directed inwards, turns inwards on itself again to observe its own doubly-internal operations. In short, according to such a view, the idea that mind can "look inwards" seems to involve an equivocation on the term "intentionality," that is, on mind's directedness, which I have argued is always directed upon objects and never upon the mind itself.

By now, the reader will hopefully be convinced that such a view is either patently false or at least crippling to a scientific understanding of the mind. The rejection of such a view should lead us to the idea that mentality is distributed over the world rather than purely internal, private, and subjective phenomena. Experiences are essentially a communion of knower and known, of subject and object. Thoughts, also, are a communion of knower and known in which the known objects are terms in the public language that we use to understand the world, others' minds, and our own minds.

If introspection refers to the act of gaining knowledge about our mental states, it is important that we distinguish conceptual knowledge about our thoughts from knowledge about the objects that we are capable of thinking about. Thoughts themselves can only be the objects of thought indirectly, by way of symbolic representations. This is because we are now conceiving of mental states as unobservable, which is to say, theoretical, "inner" states of our organism, whose form is determined by the context of a particular theory, whether that is a neuroscientific theory or a common-sense, folk-psychological theory. When we master the use of such a theory, however, we can deploy such theoretical terms in an observational way (in the sense of "observation" discussed above). When this happens, it may appear that we "just know" our thoughts, and this may give rise to the unfortunate idea that we immediately or directly know our thoughts.

Consciousness

American Transcendentalists: Emerson's "Nature"

But when, following the invisible steps of thought, we come to inquiry, Whence is matter? and Whereto? many truths arise to us out of the recesses of consciousness. We learn that the highest is present to the soul of man, that the dread universal essence, which is not wisdom, or love, or beauty, or power, but all in one, and each entirely, is that for which all things exist, and that by which they are; that spirit creates; that behind nature, throughout nature, spirit is present; one and not compound, it does not act upon us from without, that is, in space and time, but spiritually, or through ourselves: therefore, that spirit, that is, the Supreme Being, does not build up nature around us, but puts it forth through us, as the life of the tree puts forth new branches and leaves through the pores of the old. As a plant upon the earth, so a man rests upon the bosom of God; he is nourished by unfailing fountains, and draws, at his need, inexhaustible power. Who can set bounds to the possibilities of man? Once inhale the upper air, being admitted to behold the absolute natures of justice and truth, and we learn that man has access to the entire mind of the Creator, is himself the creator in the finite. This view, which admonishes me where the sources of wisdom and power lie, and points to virtue as to

> *"The golden key*
> *Which opes the palace of eternity,"*
> *[Milton, Comus, II, 13-14]*

carries upon its face the highest certificate of truth, because it animates
me to create my own world through the purification of my soul.
                                        —*Ralph Waldo Emerson, "Nature"*

Though Ralph Waldo Emerson's *Nature* is a somewhat philosophical essay, Emerson does not present his views in a clearly delineated, formally structured argument. He relies rather on the beauty and impact of poetic language to appeal to the reader's own inner sense of spirituality and help the reader relate to his ideas. His writing is a sermon for the people, employing an inspiring tone and intended to romanticize lives. Using the image of nature as a symbolic representation of the divine nature, the author carefully portrays man in nature and, ultimately, identifies man and nature with spirit. Emerson uses language to render a vision of man's place in nature in which a man's microcosmic existence is identified with the macrocosm of divine nature.

The paragraph opens with interrogatives, immediately signaling to the reader that there is a question of what is real, that we are in search of something and that the answer lies within the mind. We are "following the invisible steps" as if we were tracking a creature that wasn't there. The choice of the word "invisible" makes this pursuit mysterious, and it is juxtaposed with the idea of matter, which is visible. The use of the phrase "steps of thought" seems to subtly, but not overtly, personify an immaterial substance, hinting at the idea that it is possible to transfer the mental into the material. Emerson implies here that to answer the questions of "Whence is matter?" and "Whereto?" we must go beyond mundane reality into the invisible recesses of the mind, and that through the mind we can understand how the material comes into being. The capitalization of the words "Whence" and "Whereto" further hint that we are dealing with a grand and supreme mystery through which things come into being.

Emerson then tells us what is revealed when we have found the truths that arise from the recesses of consciousness; we discover the soul of man. He uses "that" to preface a series of phrases with similar structures, all of which describe what spirit is. The use of parallel structure creates a tempo, which shortens as the phrases narrow down to what and where spirit is. He includes in this a catalogue which describes that spirit is not merely love or wisdom, but is "all in one, and each entirely." Indeed, spirit can also be the "dread universal essence." Emerson also uses a number of prepositions in these clauses intended to locate spirit in a spatial manner, which is clearly impossible with something that includes all and transcends mundane reality. He uses these words to describe that we exist both for spirit and by spirit, and to describe how spirit comes forth through us and is within us. In this passage, he takes many different ideas, for example, the idea that nature is a physical force that acts upon us and is separate from the mental, and simplifies them to the one truth that is, "that spirit, that is, the Supreme Being." The capitalization of this phrase makes the "location" of the "Whence" and "Whereto" of matter clear. All things are part of the Supreme Being.

After narrowing all these complex themes down to the one Supreme Being, Emerson releases the tightness of his tempo as the Supreme Being puts nature forth through us "as the life of the tree puts forth new branches and leaves through the pores of the old." This pair of similes comparing man to a tree is central to this paragraph. Through this comparison to living growth, Emerson makes the somewhat dead language in this passage come alive. The language that was mysterious, abstract, and confusing is now clearly rooted in an image that is very much alive. It is growing, nourished by "unfailing fountains" and "inexhaustible power." The fact that it is the "life" of the tree that puts forth new branches gives the tree itself an animating spirit, which is associated with the spirit of man via simile. The soul draws from the earth, which, when viewed symbolically, is the living "bosom of God." This begins to hint again at the idea of personifying and animating matter, since matter is now seen to be an outgrowth of spirit.

Then Emerson asks another question; he asks: "Who can set bounds to the possibilities of man?" This question of a "who" is the question unasked at the beginning of the paragraph. It has been shown that matter exists in the mind and comes into being through the mind. So whose mind is it? Here, Emerson explains that man is the creator of the finite and has access to the entire mind of the Creator. The "who" is the Supreme Being, putting itself forth through the microcosm of a man's world, which is not at all separate from the macrocosm of the Supreme Being. Nature, man, and spirit are identified with one another. At this point, Emerson personifies the constructions of his mind explicitly. He says that "his view...carries upon its face the highest certificate of truth, because it animates me to create my own world through the purification of my soul." This gives his thoughts the ability to have a face and to create a world by way of the soul. This idea is the heart of the paragraph.

Emerson is implying that we are all personifications of spirit, that all of nature is a symbol of spirit. All his language leads to this conclusion. In the phrase "inhales the upper air," for example, "air" could almost be seen as a use of metonymy, for this word refers to the whole of spirit. The tree accesses the whole of spirit and is inseparably rooted in it, just as man is inseparable from spirit. Each image or symbol is the face of spirit itself.

Two Accounts of Mystical Experience

Early American advocates of the perennial philosophy, which examines common themes present in world religious experiences and beliefs, were motivated by the notion that the diverse accounts of mystical experience found in the world's various religious traditions could be different descriptions of identical experiences. Constructivism has since become a paradigm for modern science and philosophy as growing emphasis has been placed on social theories of development. The constructivist holds that mystical experiences are shaped by a given mystic's beliefs, practices, and cultural background. The best way to resolve the debate between the perennialists and constructivists is to find a compromise between the two views, which holds a weaker version of each thesis and allows for the two schools to co-exist.

There are many intricate forms of perennialism and constructivism, but each has basic claims and ideas. The simple version of the constructivist thesis is as follows: "The [mystical] experience itself as well as the form in which it is reported is shaped by concepts which the mystic brings to, and which shape, his experience" (Robert K.C. Forman, "Introduction: Mysticism, Constructivism, and Forgetting," in *The Problem of Pure Consciousness*, R.K.C. Forman (ed.), 10). A certain set of beliefs, intentions, cultural tools, memories, and autobiographical information is involved in the conscious content of the experience or directly shapes the content of the experience. The complete constructivist, who holds the strongest and most pure version the thesis, claims that all mental content of mystical experiences is drawn from and shaped by this set of preconceptions. Robert Gimello, for example, writes that mystical experience is just the "psychosomatic enhancement" of one's religious beliefs (Robert K.C. Forman, "Introduction: Mysticism, Constructivism, and Forgetting," in *The Problem of Pure Consciousness*, R.K.C. Forman (ed.), 13).

The perennialist claims that mystical experiences are transculturally homogenous (Robert K.C. Forman, "Introduction: Mysticism, Constructivism, and Forgetting," in *The Problem of Pure Consciousness*, R.K.C. Forman (ed.), 3). People with unique sets of preconceptions, memories, and beliefs can have the same experience, but will report it in different ways. The mystic's subsequent conception and report of the experience (at least a large portion of it) is determined by the mystic's set of beliefs. For example, a Buddhist may describe the experience as "Buddha-mind." A Christian mystic may describe it as "Christ-consciousness." In the perennialist's view, the mystical experience is direct contact with some universal and absolute principle that is defined in various ways, depending upon an individual's frame of reference. In other words, perennialists generally believe that there is some kind of god or divine force that humans can know experientially. If the constructivists are right, humans cannot directly experience the divine, and all accounts of divinity are purely speculative.

If the perennialists are right, it is possible to have some kind of "raw experience" that is free of concepts, beliefs, self-awareness, and cultural influence. If an unmediated moment of consciousness could be isolated, it could be studied independently of other brain processes, such as those involved in producing abstract thought or language, and without referring to social theories of development. According to the constructivism, social and linguistic theories are inextricably intertwined with the study of consciousness. Constructivism is not only intended to provide a theory of mystical experiences, but of mental experiences in general. If constructivism cannot explain mystical experience, it may become significantly easier to argue that constructivism is false in other cases as well.

The debate between the perennialists and constructivists can be applied to normal, waking mental states. Pain, for example, may be a fundamental type of mental state that all humans experience. Is the experience of pain mediated by an individual's beliefs and cultural background? In other words, do people with different beliefs have different experiences of pain as a result of their beliefs? A perennialist would claim that there is some raw experience of pain that has basic similarities for people across cultures. Two people's conception of the pain or reaction to the pain may differ, but the pain experience itself can be identified as a certain kind of mental event that occurs in people with basically similar brain structures. According to the constructivist, the experience of pain is not only conceived of differently, but is actually altered by these conceptions. There is not an identifiable type of experience called "pain" that can be found in different people; every pain experience is determined by the overall context in which it is experienced.

The best resolution for this debate comes from weaker forms of perennialism and constructivism. One weaker interpretation of the perennialist thesis concedes that only certain experiences (i.e., mystical experiences) can be freed from mediation through mental practice. This version of the thesis allows constructivism to play a role in the study of normal, waking mental states, suggesting that there is a spectrum of experience ranging from mediated to unmediated. Ninian Smart suggests another compromise of the perennialist position. Smart suggests that two mystical experiences can be fundamentally similar yet have slightly "different flavors" (Robert K.C. Forman, "Introduction: Mysticism, Constructivism, and Forgetting," in *The Problem of Pure Consciousness*, R.K.C. Forman (ed.), 13). The flavor comes from the individual's conception of the experience. Smart's notion of perennialism allows both constructivism and perennialism to be true, though it may be difficult to clarify the implications of such a claim or how this position could be practically applied. Smart's view is consistent with incomplete constructivism, which holds that some mental content comes from the individual's set of beliefs, while some content comes from elsewhere (e.g., raw sensory input). These weaker versions of the two positions allow for the two schools to be reconciled.

I advocate incomplete constructivism or something similar to Smart's "incomplete" perennialism. It seems clear that there are specific, identifiable types of experiences. Pain, for example, results from certain types of neurological processes that are similar in all humans with basic brain structures. This claim is supported by the fact that most humans have basically similar brains and report basically similar experiences (i.e., we all talk about pain). For a weaker version of perennialism to be true, raw experiences need be identical, only similar in certain, fundamental ways (though it is not clear exactly what fundamental similarities should be criterial).

In normal, waking states of consciousness, these "raw" or "baseline" experiences cannot be separated from the overall context in which they are experienced. Experience occurs as a jumble of data such that the subject cannot separate the raw pain state from background, autobiographical information. This seems self-evident, but is certainly supported by a broad range of evidence. The diversity and similarity in verbal reports suggest that this could easily be true. Most people talk about pain, but provide slightly different details in telling the story of their pain experience. Many neurological theories of consciousness also support this idea (e.g., Antonio Damasio's notion of the extended self, which places experience in a biographical context).

My position does not exclude the possibility that, through practice, mystics can learn to limit the contents of consciousness such that they could have only the "raw" experience. It does not seem impossible that self-awareness could be minimalized by focusing attention on certain input. If one focused only on the sensation of a steady pain for years, it seems possible that one could experience only that pain state or know the "pure" sensation of pain. I do not hold that perennialism is true, only that it could be true. The evidence for this claim is that complete constructivism cannot be proven to be true. Constructivists have criticized perennialists for using verbal reports as evidence that there is a single, perennial experience. Similarly, constructivists should be criticized for using verbal reports as evidence that there is not a single, perennial experience. The debate remains open because the available evidence does not conclusively show what phenomenal experience is like. Therefore, the best position to adopt is one that allows either possibility to be true, or a position somewhere between perennialists and constructivists, something like incomplete constructivism.

I am basically an incomplete constructivist.

1) I hold that there are basic kinds of neural events (i.e., pain) which could be studied in an unmediated form. This is supported by the fact that most people have basically similar brain structures. These may not be identical: your red may not be exactly like my red because we have retinas with a slightly different shape, but they are close. Our concept of red and associations with red are mediated by the set of beliefs (e.g., one person may have a propensity for roses, another, blood).

2) In normal experience however, these baseline kinds of experiences such as pain/joy cannot be separated from the overall context of the experience, which means, the background of the self. In Damasio's view, this would mean that experience is contextualized by the extended, autobiographical conception of self, as supported by Damasio's neurological explanation of consciousness. It also seems to be self-evident.

3) I do not exclude the possibility that, through mental practice, it is possible to minimize self-awareness such that one could experience a mental state, the contents of which are "pure" experience, e.g., in the case of pain this would be the immediate sensory experience of pain. In the case of mysticism, the only content may be something like a conception of nothingness or infinite space, whatever content defines the state. The evidence suggesting this consists largely of verbal reports and whole traditions to verify them. But my argument is not that perennialism is true, only that it *could* be true, which does not require evidence for perennialism as much as evidence to disprove perennialism—and there is none, because phenomenal states are personal and can only be verified by experience. If mystics say they know they have had the same experience, who can prove them wrong?

4) I also will allow for kinds of mystical mental states. Within just the Buddhist tradition, there are many types of practice that are intended to yield various mental states. I am a perennialist because I do not preclude the possibility that a given meditation system can produce the same mental state in various people. This does not mean there has to be the *one* perennial experience. My evidence for this is based again on the reports of mystics and the design of meditation systems that have been studied experientially

by monks for thousands of years. Again, if these monks say they have different mental states as a result of different meditation practices, who is to say they are wrong, just as people who train in logic or science tend to arrive at similar conclusions and explanations, which may differ as well, but seem to be easily brought into dialogue? Buddhists are trying to perfect methods for attaining given states, which are verified in the best way they could be.

Culturally Common Mythological Archetypes of the Collective Unconscious

There are various systems of dream interpretation, most of which address dreams from the perspective of an individual dreamer within the context of their specific cultural background or personal history, from which the dreamer seemingly draws images and associations. While it is true that any given image or symbol may hold totally different meanings in various contexts, it is also true that every human being shares a commonly patterned experience of growing up and passing on the common bond of being human, of universal human experiences such as birth, love, parenthood, sickness, and death, which puts the experience of any dreamer in a universal context that applies across cultures and individuals. It is possible then for the dreamer to draw associations from these universal human patterns and events, though the details of each image may be specific to the dreamer's personal experiences. Carl Jung speaks to this idea in great depth, labeling these universal patterns of common human notions as "archetypes." He claims that certain images in dreams cannot be understood merely from personal associations produced by the dreamer, and that these archetypal images are primordial, structural elements of the human psyche.

Jung originally developed the idea of archetypes from work with his colleague and close personal friend, Sigmund Freud, who also found that certain elements of his patient's dreams could not be derived from the dreamer's history. "These elements, as I have previously mentioned, are what Freud called 'archaic remnants'— mental forms whose presence cannot be explained by anything from the individual's own life and which seem to be aboriginal, innate, and inherited shapes of the human mind"

(C. G. Jung, *Man and His Symbols*, 67). Jung developed this idea much further over the course of his life.

Carl Gustav Jung was born in Switzerland in 1875, the son of a local pastor. Given such conservative origins, one would imagine him to be amongst the more staid and conservative thinkers in modern times, and his ideas did stay more closely in line with typical Western psychology for years, but then became progressively more radical. Eventually, a schism began to form between him and Freud, his long-time mentor. While Freud continued to view the unconscious as personal, Jung developed the concept that there is both a personal and collective unconscious. His tendency toward this world view may be in part explained by his involvement with Toni Wolff, who introduced him to Buddhist thought and more Eastern views on dreaming and the unconscious. Jung writes:

> The dream is a little hidden door in the innermost and most secret recesses of the soul, opening into that cosmic night which was psyche long before there was any ego-consciousness, and which will remain psyche no matter how far our ego-consciousness may extend. For all ego-consciousness is isolated: it separates and discriminates, knows only particulars, and sees only what can be related to the ego. Its essence is limitation, though it reaches to the farthest nebulae among the stars. All consciousness separates; but in dreams we put on the likeness of that more universal, truer, more eternal man dwelling in the darkness of primordial night. There he is still the whole, and the whole is in him, indistinguishable from nature and bare of all egohood.

> It is from these all-uniting depths that the dream arises, be it never so childish, grotesque, and immoral. So flowerlike is it in its candor and veracity that it makes us blush for the deceitfulness of our lives (C.G. Jung, *Collected Works* Vol. X, par. 304-5).

This quotation is evidence of a transpersonal world view, and one can clearly see the influence of Eastern thought. Jung was a rare breed of psychologist who tried to integrate spirituality into his theories. He claimed "[t]he collective unconscious contains the whole spiritual heritage of mankind's evolution, born anew in the brain structure of every individual" (C.G. Jung, *Collected Works* Vol. VIII, par. 342). Since the body has an evolutionary history and is based on the anatomical patterns of its predecessors, it should seem natural that the mind develops in a similar way. If this is the case, then a more primitive and ancient psyche is the basis of our mind. It is through this foundation that Jung believed archetypes were perpetuated in the mind of each individual.

Archetypes are closely related to the primal, instinctual mind. "Here I must clarify the relation between instincts and archetypes: What we properly call instincts are physiological urges, and are perceived by the senses. But at the same time, they also manifest themselves in fantasies and often reveal their presence only by symbolic images. These manifestations are what I call archetypes. They are without known origin; and they reproduce themselves in any time or in any part of the world" (C.G. Jung, *Man and His Symbols*, 69).

If archetypes are deeply connected with instincts, then they are rooted in the survival mechanisms of an organism. They have a double nature; they are deeply connected to our primal needs, but recognizing their existence and influence also gives us a potential means to transcend instinct and make choices based on our own will and mental order, which form from our experience of the imaginary and spiritual as they manifest in archetypes, consciously or unconsciously. According to Jung, "[a]rchetypes are systems of readiness for action, and at the same time images and emotions.... They represent, on the one hand, a very strong instinctive conservatism, while on the other hand they are the most effective means conceivable of instinctive adaptation. They are thus, essentially, the chthonic portion of the psyche ... that portion through which the psyche is attached to nature" (C.G. Jung, *Collected Works* Vol. X, par. 53). These ideas are consistent with the Buddhist distinctions between body, mind, and spirit, where mind is the link between the experience of body and spirit. If this is the case, the power of dreams can become divine; the manifestations, however, remain specific to the individual and the details of the dreamer's physical life.

There is a distinct difference between an archetype and an archetypal image. An archetype is a basic universal pattern or motif from the collective unconscious after which specific life experiences of many different individuals are patterned. An archetypal image is the form or representation of an archetype in consciousness; the basis for the image comes from the collective unconscious while the specific details of the image come from the personal unconscious. Archetypes appear to the dreamer in the context of his or her life and can manifest both on a personal level and collectively, as characteristics of whole cultures. Jung believed that each age, if not every person, ought to learn to understand anew the contents and effects of each archetype in relation to its specific culture and time. Such basic notions and lessons are certainly valuable to the progression of any society. These are the sort of lessons and ideas behind fables and myths, which are another classic expression of the archetypes. The similarity between myths in different cultures is one of the primary reasons why Jung came to believe so strongly in archetypes. While the details of archetypal images come from specific aspects of the dreamer's mind, the basic patterns and notions behind these images remain common across cultures.

According to Jung, dreams are spontaneous manifestations of the personal or collective unconscious. Not all dreams hold archetypal significance. Some rely solely on the mundane, consisting of personal associations and day-to-day emotions or experiences. One must keep in mind that, while archetypal patterns sometimes surface from the collective unconscious, the dream is still an experience had by the dreamer and the dreamer alone. Jung writes: "The whole dream-work is essentially subjective, and a dream is a theater in which the dreamer is himself the scene, the player, the prompter, the producer, the author, the public, and the critic" (C.G. Jung, *Collected Works* Vol. 8, par. 509). If one interprets dreams on a subjective level, images can be seen as symbolic representations of elements in the dreamer's own personality. Manifested in this symbolic form, dreams allow us to look at the current situation of the psyche from the viewpoint of the unconscious. Jung claims that "[d]reams are neither deliberate nor arbitrary fabrications; they are natural phenomena which are nothing other than what they pretend to be. They do not deceive, they do not lie, they do not distort or disguise.... They are invariably seeking to express something that the ego does not know and does not understand" (C.G. Jung, *Collected Works* Vol. 17, par. 189). If this is true, then dreams have a clear clinical purpose and could be used to learn more about oneself.

Jung thought the mind regulated itself by a process called compensation, a natural process that helps establish or maintain balance in the psyche. This process uses the unconscious as a mirror to examine and balance out consciousness. In writing about dreams, Jung focused not only on their symbolic content, but the way in which that content serves a compensatory role in the self-regulation of the psyche by serving as a link between the conscious and the unconscious. Jung notes:

> The activity of consciousness is selective. Selection demands direction. But direction requires the exclusion of everything irrelevant. This is bound to make the conscious orientation one-sided. The contents that are excluded and inhibited by the chosen direction sink into the unconscious, where they form a counterweight to the conscious orientation. The strengthening of this counter-position keeps pace with the increase of conscious one-sidedness until finally ... the repressed unconscious contents break through in the form of dreams and spontaneous images.... As a rule, the unconscious compensation does not run counter to consciousness, but is rather a balancing or supplementing of the conscious orientation. In dreams, for instance, the unconscious supplies all those

contents that are constellated by the conscious situation but are inhibited by conscious selection, although a knowledge of them would be indispensable for complete adaptation (C.G. Jung, *Collected Works*, vol. 6, par. 694).

Dreams reveal some aspect of the dreamer's self that is not present consciously. Jung says that "[i]n this regard there are three possibilities. If the conscious attitude to the life situation is in large degree one-sided, then the dream takes the opposite side. If the conscious has a position fairly near the 'middle,' the dream is satisfied with variations. If the conscious attitude is 'correct,' then the dream coincides with and emphasizes this tendency, though without forfeiting its peculiar autonomy" (C.G. Jung, *Collected Works*, vol. 8, par. 546). The compensatory functions of the mind, such as dreaming, are a primary guiding force in ego-development and the formation of the psyche. If there is a collective unconscious, which is ethereal, ancient, and a part of nature, then this guiding force becomes very powerful and intimately involved in the order and harmony of our existence. Jung believed very strongly in finding balance with the unconscious and designed an exercise called active imagination, the power of which he describes:

> The judging attitude implies a voluntary involvement in those fantasy-processes which compensate the individual and—in particular—the collective situation of consciousness. The avowed purpose of this involvement is to integrate the statements of the unconscious, to assimilate their compensatory content, and thereby produce a whole meaning which alone makes life worth living and, for not a few people, possible at all (C.G. Jung, *Collected Works*, vol. 14, par. 756).

Active imagination is a method of assimilating unconscious contents like dreams and fantasies into consciousness through some form of art, self-expression, or creative self-exploration. The object of this exercise is to get in touch with some part of the personality, especially the shadow and the anima, which one is not usually in touch with, thereby establishing a connection to the unconscious. Jung believed that the process of creation helped effect the transformation of consciousness and, therefore, experience. The first stage of active imagination, in which one envisions the creation or "chooses a dream," as Jung says, is much like a waking dream formed from one's unconscious. Jung writes:

> ... you choose a dream, or some other fantasy-image, and concentrate on it.... You can also use a bad mood as a starting out point, and then try to find out what sort of fantasy-image it will produce,

or what image expresses this mood. You then fix this image in the mind by concentrating your attention. Usually it will alter, as the mere fact of contemplating it animates it. The alterations must be carefully noted down all the time, for they reflect the psychic processes in the unconscious background, which appear in the form of images consisting of conscious memory material. In this way conscious and unconscious are united, just as a waterfall connects above and below (C.G. Jung, *Collected Works*, vol. 14, par. 706).

Accessing the unconscious mind helps teach us how to deal with and peacefully live our lives. While all dreams come from the unconscious mind, some compensate for day-to-day anxieties and others compensate for deeper, more spiritual levels of our experience, or help us to find direction from basic universal patterns stored in the collective unconscious. Jung saw these elements in dreams as primordial images or archetypes. The lessons and notions we get from these archetypes are the precursors and progenitors of mythological representations or motifs. In their mythic form, the archetypes are an expression of the culture in which the myth originated, but in Jung's view, the archetypal image is larger than any individual or cultural expression of it. Archetypal imagery applies timeless patterns in the collective unconscious applicable to a specific culture or life situation. According to Jung, one of the primary expressions of this is myth:

> The collective unconscious ... appears to consist of mythological motifs or primordial images, for which reason the myths of all nations are its real exponents. In fact, the whole of mythology could be taken as a sort of projection of the collective unconscious.... We can therefore study the collective unconscious in two ways, either in mythology or in the analysis of the individual (C.G. Jung, *Collected Works*, vol. 8, par. 325).

The interpretation of dreams is a valuable tool for exploring an individual's psyche, whether in a personal endeavor or a clinical analysis. Dreams, however, are intensely personal, and while many share similar patterns and experiences, any archetypal imagery is often mixed with details from the personal unconscious. Looking at archetypes in dreams, especially from a cross-cultural perspective, becomes difficult because there is so much personal interpretation involved. Since many dreams do not have archetypal significance, finding clear examples of the archetype becomes a somewhat subjective matter.

Archetypes, as a direct manifestation of the collective unconscious, can perhaps be more clearly seen by looking at mythology from a cross-cultural perspective. Dreams, mythology, and active imagination or art are all closely linked, because they share roots in the collective unconscious, yet are influenced by the personal unconscious and therefore serve as expressions of both the individual and his or her culture. Because these modes of expression are all based on the archetypes of the collective unconscious, it is possible to see a great deal of similarity across cultures. If these similarities and universal patterns could be identified and understood, it would give us a universal system for analyzing and interpreting dreams, myths, works of art, life patterns and transitions, and many other things. Jung identified many archetypes in pursuing this line of thought, but was primarily a psychologist.

Joseph Campbell, a mythologist who was strongly influenced by Jung, continued Jung's classification of the archetypes. Campbell studied how the unconscious manifests itself in mythology through basic life patterns; he writes: "... through dreams a door is opened to mythology, since myths are of the nature of dream, and that, as dreams arise from an inward world unknown to waking consciousness, so do myths: so, indeed, does life" (Joseph Campbell, *The Mythic Image*, xi). Mythology captures the most classic human values and experiences, giving us basic lessons about life, death, rites of passage, and other things which are common to people of all cultures. Along these lines, Campbell studied myths across many different cultures and found some striking similarities. This is a study of great importance in understanding how universal, archetypal patterns resurface in the context of a specific culture and time as well as in some of the dreams analyzed by Jung.

Many of the archetypal patterns noted by Campbell center around life's milestones or cyclic "great events," birth, childhood, puberty, love, marriage, parenthood, illness, and death. Others are of religious significance in many cultures, such as sacrifices, sacred places, and themes of resurrection and rebirth. Powerful emotional experiences, including rage, fear, grief, desire, hunger, thirst, joy, and jealousy are incarnated in myths across cultures. All such things are universal notions in human experience.

In writing about the archetypes in dream symbolism in his book, *Man and His Symbols*, Jung focuses on a set of dreams by an eight-year-old girl which comprised, he said, "the weirdest series of dreams" (C.G. Jung, *Man and His Symbols*, 59) he had ever seen. Most focused on images of death or of being attacked and devoured by animals, and, uncannily, within a year after giving her dream journal to her father, the dreamer fell victim to an infectious disease and died. Other dreams from this journal depict animals killed by an "evil animal" and revived by God, which Jung describes as the general image of Christ the Redeemer which:

belongs to the world-wise and pre-Christ theme of the hero and res-
cuer.... When and where such a motif originated nobody knows....
The one apparent certainty is that every generation seems to have
known it as a tradition handed down from some preceding time.
Thus we can safely assume that it "originated" at a period when
man did not yet know that he possessed a hero myth; in an age,
that is to say, when he did not yet consciously reflect on what he
was saying. The hero figure is an archetype, which has existed
since time immemorial. (C.G. Jung, *Man and His Symbols*, 61).

The myth of the hero is one Campbell addressed in a ground-breaking
work which was also one of his earliest, *The Hero With a Thousand Faces*.
In *The Mythic Image*, Campbell reflects on *The Myth of the Birth of the
Hero*, a work of psychologist Otto Rank (one of Jung's contemporaries)
in noting the common features of the exiled hero archetype. Common features of the hero myth as catalogued by Rank include the hero's birth to
noble or divine parents, threats and persecution of the young infant in
his earliest days, the infant's physical exposure or homelessness, and the
hero's return to either depose and supersede the father or take the father's
place and continue his mission. These features figure prominently in many
paramount religious myths and classical Greek myths. For example, the
Hindu god Krishna and the Buddha were both descended from noble parents, and Jesus was, of course, God's son. Krishna, Jesus, and Zeus were
prophesied to overthrow the current ruler; both Krishna's cousin Kansa
and Zeus' father Kronos systematically killed all the children of the hero's
mother, while Herod set about a methodical genocidal extermination of
male infants across the land. Famous mythological characters such as Mo-
ses, Oedipus, and Romulus and Remus were exposed and left to die, then
subsequently rescued and raised by strangers or animals. All of these are
cross-cultural expressions of a powerful and universal human archetype
that surfaces in both myth and dream. The fact that myths from very different cultures bear such striking similarity in their basic themes and patterns
is some of the most promising evidence that there are indeed common
human notions that are rooted in our very nature and experience.

Archetypes provide one of the most powerful systems for the interpretation of dreams as well as any other myth or art form. Though free-asso-
ciation often is needed to identify details from the personal unconscious
that surface in dreams, the archetypes allow us to understand the deeper,
timeless lessons of the collective unconscious, a force Jung believed guided us throughout our lives. Jung claimed that the sort of morbid, archetypal imagery the dream journal of this eight-year-old child depicted was
preparation for her death. In this way, our collective unconscious prepares

us for all major life events and rites of passage, and also endows us with inspiring, human stories from which to learn about life.

Jung found great comfort in believing that there is a collective unconscious that holds some basic, underlying order which applies to human beings of any culture. To me this means that, when we don't know where we're going, at least *something* does. I find this thought very comforting as well, and feel that it is right.

Dreams and Sleeping Consciousness

Are dreams conscious experiences that occur during sleep or stories that enter consciousness upon waking? In *Dreaming Souls*, Owen Flanagan reconsiders this classic problem from the perspective of a contemporary theory of dreams informed by a broad range of recent scientific research, and concludes that the available evidence strongly suggests that dreams are sleep-time experiences. Years earlier, in an article entitled "Are Dreams Experiences?" Daniel Dennett argued against proponents of the "received view," who hold that dreams are experiences that occur during sleep. Dennett concludes that the question remains open until a well-confirmed theory of dreams can be developed. According to Flanagan, the naturalistic theory of dreams he proposes is "enough of a well-confirmed theory" that can make us "confident, if not absolutely certain, that the received view is true" (Owen Flanagan, *Dreaming Souls: Sleep, Dreams and the Evolution of the Conscious Mind*, 178). Although Dennett is correct in claiming that the received view could be false, Flanagan's natural method alleviates such skeptical worries and places them in the background of modern dream research.

The received view states that dreams are thoughts, sensations, or otherwise conscious states that occur during sleep, often arranged in coherent narratives that are recollected upon waking. On Dennett's account of the received view, dreaming usually involves a presentation process and a recording process. Presentation refers to the conscious experience of dreaming that occurs during sleep. In order to explain this process, a theory of dreams should be able to systematically correlate neural events with phenomenal events that occur in the dream (Daniel C. Dennett, "Are Dreams Experiences?" *The Philosophical Review*, vol. 85, no. 2, 152).

Recording is the process of storing dream experiences into memory such that the dream's content can sometimes be reported upon waking. A related memory-loading process is responsible for recalling stored content in the morning. Dennett emphasizes that recalling dream content is similar to the recall of memories in general. As we remember, we also revise and rewrite the story—memory recall is a process of composition (Daniel C. Dennett, "Are Dreams Experiences?" *The Philosophical Review*, vol. 85, no. 2, 154).

Dennett's argument is intended to call the received view of dreams into question, claiming only that the received view could turn out to be false. He argues that dream reports cannot be confirmed; therefore, correlations between sleep-time neural events and any sleep-time experiences cannot be confirmed, nor can the claim that sleeping subjects are even conscious. Dennett proposes a thought experiment, describing a dreamer whose memory of a dream is replaced with the memory of a different dream. Upon waking, the dreamer reports a dream that he or she did not have (Daniel C. Dennett, "Are Dreams Experiences?" *The Philosophical Review*, vol. 85, no. 2, 156). This anecdote is intended to show that memory is fallible and that dream reports are unreliable. Dennett argues that, since the subject's report of dreaming is unreliable, there is no clear evidence about what the phenomenal experience of dreaming is like, if there even is such an experience. All we have is what Flanagan calls the "morning story," the report of what the subject thinks the dream was like upon waking (Owen Flanagan, *Dreaming Souls: Sleep, Dreams and the Evolution of the Conscious Mind*, 178). It cannot yet be shown that neurological and physiological observations necessarily correlate with conscious activity or any kind of phenomenal experience because there is no definitive account of the experience. One must admit that the received view could be false, as Dennett describes: "dreams, it might turn out, are not what we took them to be—or perhaps we would say that it turns out that there are not dreams after all, only dream 'recollections' produced in the manner described in our confirmed theory, whichever it is" (Daniel C. Dennett, "Are Dreams Experiences?" *The Philosophical Review*, vol. 85, no. 2, 158). If this is true, dreams are no more than a memory, and it is possible that we are unconscious when asleep.

Dennett introduces several alternatives to the received view, focusing on what he calls the "cassette" model. The cassette theory states that "all dream narratives are composed directly into memory banks; which, if any, of these is available to waking recollection depends on various factors" (Daniel C. Dennett, "Are Dreams Experiences?" *The Philosophical Review*, vol. 85, no. 2, 159). In this view, there are many memories stored in the brain, which could be recalled in different ways depending on surrounding circumstances. The idea behind the cassette theory is that there is a recording/memory-loading process without a sleep-time presentation process. The process of recording and composing these narratives could occur during the night, during the day, or over a period of years—it is probably an ongoing process. According to Dennett, this is because the composition process is entirely unconscious. If composition is viewed as a sleep-time process, then cassette theory accounts for dreaming in the same way as the received view but for one crucial difference: "the process of dream-memory production is entirely unconscious, involves no awareness or experiencing at all" (Daniel C. Dennett, "Are Dreams Experiences?" *The Philosophical Review*, vol. 85, no. 2, 160).

The question at stake in the debate between the received view and cassette theory is that of whether dreams are experiences. On the cassette model, dreams are not like anything at all; dreams are nothing but an unconscious composition and memory-loading process. Dennett compares this to the example of learning from subliminal audio tapes during sleep. People who listen to audio tapes while sleeping sometimes report that they have learned something new upon waking, but they cannot describe what it was like to learn this material during sleep. The learning process is unconscious. Dennett suggests that the case of dreams may be similar, that dreaming may not be a form of consciousness.

Dennett's ulterior motive is to bring the term "experience" into question by introducing doubts about the relationship between memory and experience. According to Dennett, a Nagelian (i.e., one who holds that there is something called "experience" and that the term refers to all states which have the subjective quality of "what it is like") must grant that a subject's subsequent report of an experience is not an authoritative description of the actual experience (Daniel C. Dennett, "Are Dreams Experiences?" *The Philosophical Review*, vol. 85, no. 2, 166). A Nagelian also holds that objective observations do not provide definitive evidence about subjective phenomena. As there does not seem to be any definitive evidence about phenomenal experience, Dennett suggests that experience may not be a useful term to use in scientific explanations (Daniel C. Dennett, "Are Dreams Experiences?" *The Philosophical Review*, vol. 85, no. 2, 171).

Dennett's argument that dreams may not be experiences can be applied to almost any experience. The only evidence we have about experience (other than one's own, immediate experience) is based on observation. There is no observable sign of a subject's experience itself, only *indications* that the subject is experiencing. These indications, however, are not definitive. From the skeptic's point of view, it is not only possible that dreams do not actually occur during sleep, but also that none of our memories are accurate. Perhaps our memories of the past were implanted by some scientist or Descartes's deceiver. (Descartes describes this supposed deceiver as "some malicious demon of the utmost power and cunning [who] has employed all his energies in order to deceive me" such that Descartes cannot rely upon his own mind or senses (*The Philosophical Writings of Descartes*, John Cottingham, et al. (eds.), 316). This argument also applies to peripheral consciousness and begins to introduce what later becomes Dennett's Multiple Drafts Model of consciousness. In Dennett's view, some peripheral data is not consciously experienced as it occurs but has a subliminal effect on short-term memory that can be experienced as a "recollection-production" or a rewritten memory. For Dennett, the boundary of conscious experience (i.e., the distinction between conscious and unconscious states) is so vague and jumbled that "experience" is not the best term to use in scientific discourse.

Flanagan addresses this question in *Dreaming Souls* and acknowledges that there is no certain answer to Dennett's skepticism. Flanagan discusses the claim that the received view could be false because memory is unreliable (Owen Flanagan, *Dreaming Souls: Sleep, Dreams and the Evolution of the Conscious Mind*, 175). According to Flanagan, this is reason to take the problem seriously. Flanagan agrees that there is no way to be sure that dream reports are accurate. Though he argues that the best explanation for what he calls "morning stories" is that some kind of sleep-time experience occurred, this does not mean there is any reliable correlation between the recollected story and the sleep-time experience (Owen Flanagan, *Dreaming Souls: Sleep, Dreams and the Evolution of the Conscious Mind*, 178). This is why Flanagan believes in the natural method.

Flanagan compares evidence from all fields of study in order to draw the best possible inference. The staples of Flanagan's natural method are phenomenology, psychology, and neuroscience. Though these may be the focus, Flanagan abides by the principle that no piece of evidence or field of study should be ignored. He also examines work in philosophy, evolutionary biology, anthropology, sociology, and other disciplines. Flanagan's argument is that, though there is no definitive proof that the received view is true, using the natural method to compare all the available evidence will allow us to make a reasonably "well-confirmed" conclusion. Reports alone do provide a definitive account of dream experiences, but when phenomenological evidence is consistent with neurological and psychological evidence, it strongly suggests that the received view is true. Flanagan's theory of dreams tries to weave all these pieces of evidence into a coherent theory in order to get the best possible picture of what is going on in the mind during sleep. After weighing all the evidence, he concludes that the received view of dreams is almost certainly true.

Dennett raises skeptical worries, which are important and justifiable. Flanagan makes a good point, however, in saying that these worries can be appeased by modern science and ought to recede into the background of modern dream research. Flanagan is correct in claiming that, regardless of whether dreams occur during sleep, there is something called a dream—dreams are real phenomena that ought to be explained by any comprehensive model of mind. Furthermore, it seems that (and I must appeal to authority here) when one attempts to construct a well-informed theory of dreams that incorporates data from many fields of research, one will encounter evidence indicating that there is some type of mentation during sleep, that these neural processes resemble certain waking processes associated with some aspect of waking experience (e.g., vision), and that these processes often seem to correlate with phenomenological and psychological evidence.

The question of whether dreams are sleep-time experiences may be an open theoretical question, as Dennett claims, but Flanagan has formulated an outstanding and coherent answer using a method that is open to evidence gathered in all fields of study. As in the case of many theories, it seems like there can be no certainty. While Flanagan seems right in claiming that, when large bodies of data gathered in many different fields lend support to a coherent theory, it is fair to say that the theory is worth investigation, even if it is later shown to be inaccurate. Scientific progress often requires that scientists infer the most likely explanation for a given set of data. Often, all one can do is make inferences, trying only to develop theories that are consistent with, seem to follow from, and best explain whatever data is available.

Perception

When we perceive an object visually, our mind imposes form and order on the image before it enters our visual consciousness. The raw image is a jumble of incoming sensory data representing various properties of the image being perceived. Different properties, such as form, motion, color, and distance, must be separated and sent to different areas of the brain to be processed. The image we see is a product of our mind recombining the various properties in a coherent image, meaning that objects are distinguished from their backgrounds, incomplete objects such as apple behind a leaf are still recognized and distinguished, and in actuality, all properties are attached to their corresponding objects. The process of visual cognition is a very intricate and complicated process that has evolved over history. It has a deep evolutionary background and therefore must have some basic evolutionary advantages.

Ultimately, the purpose of sensory perception is to have awareness of our surroundings so that we can perceive threats or desirable objects and react accordingly. The most important thing about sensory data (in terms of survival, not aesthetics) is how the organism acts in response to it. This means that the organism with the quickest and most accurate reaction is the most likely to survive. A human being's reaction to his or her surroundings is based on other more complicated cognitive processes, but begins with perception. The quicker we are capable of perceiving a threat, the more likely we are to survive it. The first time we perceive something, we may have to explore it or test it a bit to decide how we want to act in response to it, but as we learn what objects or organisms represent a threat or represent a source of food, we can respond to them immediately. The quickest way to identify a stimulus or some aspect of our surroundings is to rely on bottom-up processes, meaning processes based on data retrieval. Once we have learned what an apple is, there is no need to think about it. We can simply and immediately recognize it as an apple, which frees up attentional resources in the brain to perform other higher-level cognitive processes, such making the decision to eat the apple. If we did not rely on bottom-up processes to sort out sensory data, we would have to rely on top-down processes, which would involve us consciously sorting out the jumble of information we perceive. We might see an obvious threat, such as an oncoming truck, and have to spend a moment or two registering the scene, identifying the object and its location and direction, and finally reacting to it a moment or two too late. Since we have an advanced visual memory, we can immediately register the object as the front of a truck and react to it quickly. It would be completely inefficient to live our day-to-day lives without relying on our sensory memory to inform our perception; we would spend all day trying to process incoming stimuli and sorting them out. We would be constantly processing on a sort of sensory delay, trying to keep up with what was going on around us, while we would have little room in our mind for the higher level cognitive processes that determine our behaviors.

The disadvantage of this is that we often can make perceptual mistakes. We might perceive something that isn't there. This process is very similar to word recognition in reading. Often people overlook minor misspellings or mistake similar words because they are relying on a bottom-up process of word recognition, but this is an advanced reading ability, because it frees attentional resources which allow us to actually comprehend what we read, especially when dealing with long passages, or make an assumption based on our sensory memory that is not accurate. For instance, we might only soften minor visual mistakes. We do this at times, but these instances usually result in slight visual illusions or perhaps mistaking a word for a homonym. We therefore tend to read any word that is similar to a word stored in memory as the word we know. And while this process may result in a few minor mistakes, it is still often a characteristic, and it also increases reading speed and efficiency. In dealing with our world, recognizing sensory stimuli is the first fundamental step, just as word recognition is in reading; it must be performed quickly and automatically so that the higher level processes, such as comprehension and resulting action, may be carried out. Any minor disadvantages of this system are vastly outweighed by our need for speed and efficiency in perception.

There is also a long-standing debate between whether language comes first in labeling things, as opposed to awareness of things "as the things they are," and it's very complicated. In the case of a table, for example, of course you'll see the brown structure that's hard, square, has legs, etc., first, but to be aware of it as "a table" then requires conceptual labeling, which requires the *concept* of a table.

Often people differentiate between perception versus sensation, sensation being conscious awareness, which comes first, and is then labeled linguistically in a conceptual way that is then called "perception."

The question is the process of how this happens. Do we first see a bunch of tables and then learn that they all behave in a certain way and group them together in our brains (i.e., neural connections) to form a concept? Behaviorists and developmental psychologists often think that's what happens when children first learn language.

Perception: Relativism or Realism?

Is our perception proof of realism, or only of relativism? Any proof of the external world is based in some way on perception; the direct realist must rely on something real and perceivable to prove his position. Perception, however, occurs only within our organism, which means it is not proof of an external world. Also, perception relies on a perceiver, which means that it is not proof that there is a world independent of us. Furthermore, any statement we might make about the real world as we experience it is entirely relative and dependent upon a number of factors, cultural and cognitive, which inform our experience. Relativism is intrinsic to any statement made or position held by an individual, because the individual makes the statement from his own relative viewpoint in a specific context or framework. The relativist, however, does not make any definitive claim regarding an external world that exists independently of us, because he grants that his claim is based on his frame of reference and, therefore, not independent of us. Any knowledge of a world that exists independently of us cannot be known without becoming dependent on us and interpreted by us. Therefore, I conclude that any truth about a world that exists independently of us or external to us is not perceived in the world we know, which is based on internal functions of the body and mind and is entirely relative to and dependent upon its relationship to the specific conceptual framework which informs our perception and perspective at any given time.

Humans experience life in an individual consciousness, which is isolated in so much as we have a sense of self that applies only to knowing the state of our own personal organism: the state of our mind, body, and experience. The sense of self is a very elaborate conceptual framework that is being formed in the mind from birth till death as the result of a number of different factors ranging from culture to body size. Anything we perceive, whether it is direct sensory information or the verbalization of someone else's thoughts, is perceived through the interpretive processes of our mind and experienced relative to our organism. Cognitively speaking, processes in the brain are interpretive; our minds automatically perform many functions that modify our perceptions. We distinguish properties of an object as relating to the object (i.e., light radiating from a lamp); we distinguish objects from their background (i.e., stars from the night sky). Furthermore, any stimulus we perceive is perceived only in relation to our organism, meaning that we cannot separate our perceptions from the specific body position, place, time, emotional state, etc., in which we perceived them. In much the same way, any new concept introduced to us is integrated into the framework of concepts and beliefs we are developing from our experiences, relationships, environments, thoughts, education, and any number of other factors. All the factors that make up the sense of self at a given moment create a conceptual framework that is the basis to which we relate everything. If we claim that we know the way the world is because we have direct perceptual access to it, we are advocating some form of relativism, because perception is inherently relative. We must concede that, if the world can in fact be known through the senses, it can only be known relative to a specific perceiver, and therefore, it is not the same world for all of us. Perception and awareness, however, are clearly based not only on apprehending in general, but on apprehending some object or stimulus. This raises questions about the nature of these objects or stimuli and the nature of the world in which we perceive.

Everything that we call the real world, any perception of object or stimulus or any knowledge of anything, is internal. Perhaps, these internal phenomena could be based on some external world, but that world is only known internally, after interpretation. There is no way for us to know the precise nature of the external world, if there is such a thing. The world we know is the one we perceive and interact with on a daily basis; our reality. This reality or experience of a world exists to us in the same way a direct realist describes: through the senses. We can learn about our reality by looking at it, touching it, rolling in it, studying it empirically, interpreting it creatively, experiencing it from new perspectives (which are actually part of a singular, continuous, and constantly changing perspective), discussing and relating our views to one another, and generally living our lives. Every self-proclaimed relativist accepts their reality, whether they claim to or not, by the simple act of making a claim, but that does not say anything about a reality that exists independent of or external to us. Addressing the issue of a reality independent of the individual, nothing can be said by any individual because it poses a simple contradiction. When a direct realist claims that there is a real world which we have direct perceptual access to, this claim seems to be indestructible, because every relativist accepts their reality. It is only reasonable. I am writing on a page; the page, of course, exists to me. It exists to me in the way I perceive it through my senses. In our day-to-day lives, we act as though we are in a world where simple principles like the correspondence theory of truth—the idea that truth corresponds to fact and accurately describes the world— are held to be true. We all accept this. It is undeniable, but it is also dependent on perception. By relying on perception, our argument is limited to the perceived world, and cannot go beyond our sense of perception relative to the self to make any sort of statement about a world that exists independently of the individual.

The question of whether there is an absolute, external reality that exists independently of us cannot be answered, because any answer subscribes to an individual's relative perspective in the context of a conceptual scheme. We cannot know the nature of external reality, only the nature of our perceptions. The cognitive process of perception requires a sense of self, because objects can only be perceived in relation to the self. Without the sense of self, there is no sense of the world. Metaphysical realists understand this point but still make the claim that there is a real world that exists independently of us, though we cannot know it. If we cannot know the world, there is no way to show that it exists or that it does not exist. Furthermore, if it cannot exist in the world we know, then does it really matter in a discussion about the world we know? In discussing philosophy or reality, we deal with many worlds known to many different people that are all relative to a conceptual framework. The notion of an external world that is not knowable or perceivable in the known world is not particularly relevant to anything, especially not to a debate that deals with the knowledge of the individuals involved.

Damasio on Consciousness

The neuroscientist Antonio Damasio defines consciousness as "the sense of self in the act of knowing" (Antonio Damasio, *The Feeling of What Happens: Body and Emotions in the Making of Consciousness*, 308). According to Damasio, consciousness requires interaction between an object and the perceiving organism—all conscious experiences are centered around the self and all objects are perceived in relation to the self. Mystics write narratives describing states of consciousness that have no object or observer. The sense of self, the sense of an observer, is only an object of awareness (i.e., self-awareness). In a "contentless" state, the sense of self disappears along with all objects experienced in relation to the self—all objects of awareness are gone. In Zen Buddhism, such states are called "no-mind." From a scientific perspective, it seems that such a state would be unconscious. Can consciousness without content be a form of consciousness at all?

Damasio makes the claim that consciousness is not a monolith. By this he means that human consciousness can be separated into core and extended consciousness. He bases this claim primarily on his experience studying patients with neurological disorders who retain core consciousness in cases where extended consciousness is suspended. The most compelling example of this is the editor's account of an episode of transient global amnesia. It is clear from this explanation that the patient had very little or no knowledge about her past experience or future plans. She did not even remember what manuscript she was in the middle of reading, yet she was fairly lucid and definitely present, though perhaps a little confused. She could write clearly how she felt at any given moment and was capable of producing a very coherent record of her experience and state of mind. All her explanations, however, were confined to the specific moment in which she was writing them. This finding is consistent with Damasio's claims regarding core and extended consciousness because her sense of present was retained, which, according to Damasio, is evidence of core consciousness, yet her more elaborate sense of self and of her place in her life was suspended, including most autobiographical information (even her name was hard to remember). Human consciousness is more than just a basic sense of knowing that you and your body exist as the perceiver of your environment. We have a personal history that profoundly affects our sense of coherence in our life, and when that is suspended, we find ourselves at a loss. Clearly, episodes like this patient's support the idea that core consciousness can exist without the more elaborate aspects of consciousness and therefore core consciousness is divisible from extended consciousness, meaning that core consciousness does not depend on extended consciousness, though it certainly feeds off it.

There are several other neurological disorders which provide evidence that core consciousness can be retained while extended conscious is suspended. One such disorder is Anosognosia, in which patients cannot record the body component of the autobiographical self and their extended consciousness becomes impaired along with the inaugural proto-self. The patients are still capable of creating the second order neural patterns necessary for core consciousness. Another such example is Asomatognosia, a disorder which effects a patient's ability to feel aspects of their own body. Patients with this disorder develop a disorder of the autobiographical memory because they cannot integrate their perception with the proto-self and therefore cannot properly store memories of an autobiographic nature (autobiographic memories being centered on and experienced from the self). The patient still retained certain information about the proto-self, specifically the most crucial information about the state of the viscera and the internal milieu which are necessary for core consciousness, or the "sense of being" the patient maintained.

The idea is also supported simply by how well it works with Damasio's other findings, particularly his explanation of how consciousness evolved or emerges in a human life. Look at animals, specifically the great apes, who appear to have the beginnings of consciousness, one can see that human consciousness has a deep evolutionary history. The development of consciousness did not occur overnight. The first organism that became aware of itself, that knew that it knew what was going on around it, probably did not have a very elaborate sense of self. According to Damasio, consciousness was initially developed so that an organism could know its emotions and react to them. This is one of the primary functions of consciousness that probably was apparent early in the history of consciousness. The more elaborate aspects of consciousness, such as conscience, are unique to human consciousness. Core consciousness developed first, and from that basis extended functions developed as we evolved. It is unreasonable to think that these extended functions of consciousness are crucial to the basic processes of core consciousness. Though these two parts of consciousness are very much related, they can also be distinguished from each other.

Extended consciousness can also be impaired by defects in working memory. In such cases, the number of images or pieces of information that can be held in memory is so limited that extended consciousness is compromised, though usually retained in part. Whether or not all of these examples provide solid evidence for the separation of consciousness is questionable, but they certainly point in that direction.

Consciousness must be separated into core consciousness and extended consciousness in order to discuss the two aspects. The nature, function, and role they play in our life is very different and must be addressed as such. The situations in which they exist and the criteria necessary for their existence are also different. When discussing animals who may or may not have consciousness or have a limited level of consciousness, we must make it clear that we are talking about core consciousness. In Damasio's book *The Feeling of What Happens*, he discusses in great detail the different aspects of these two types of consciousness. There is also neurological and evolutionary evidence that one can exist without the other; core consciousness can exist without extended consciousness. Extended consciousness is built upon core consciousness, and the two are directly connected; they feed off one another, enhance one another, and work together to organize our experience of our life. There are so many instances where one form of consciousness has to be addressed specifically without addressing the other that a distinction must be drawn, if only for the purposes of discussion, but it is clearly a warranted and reasonable distinction that allows us to more clearly define different aspects of consciousness and helps us when discussing neurological disorders or circumstances of limited or impaired consciousness.

Block's Distinction: Access Consciousness and Phenomenal Consciousness

The philosopher Ned Block believes that consciousness is often treated as "mongrel concept." He argues that philosophers ought to recognize a distinction between two different types of consciousness, which he calls access consciousness (A-consciousness) and phenomenal consciousness (P-consciousness), when constructing their theories and arguments about consciousness.

Block defines phenomenal consciousness as experience. He alludes to Thomas Nagel's notion of "what it is like to be" the subject who is experiencing mental phenomena (Thomas Nagel, "What Is It Like to Be a Bat," *Philosophical Review*, LXXXIII (1974), pp. 435-450). According to Block, phenomenal consciousness must be defined in a circular way, and Nagel's definition must be taken for what it is. The controversial claim that Block makes about phenomenal consciousness is that phenomenal properties are distinct from any cognitive, intentional, and functional properties of consciousness, which are properties of access consciousness. A state is A-conscious if it is "...poised for direct control of thought and action" (Ned Block, et al., *The Nature of Consciousness: Philosophical Debates*, 382). This conception of consciousness is based on the information-processing model of mind, which views mind as functionally organized representational system. All information in access consciousness is representational, rather than phenomenal, and can therefore be defined formally and used in reasoning or guiding action.

Block notes that many phenomenal states are also representational. In such cases, it is by virtue of the state's phenomenal aspect that it is P-conscious, and it is by virtue of its representational aspect that it is A-conscious. The idea that a state can have multiple aspects may also begin to explain how P-consciousness and A-consciousness interact, as Block suggests they do. This may also provide an interesting account of psychophysical causation in that it links P-consciousness into the functional network of the brain. A-consciousness is a functional process, describing the informational relations among various modules of the system. It is a process based on the overall functional organization of the system's modules and has nothing to do with what goes on inside the modules. P-consciousness, on the other hand, describes what is going on *inside* a module; therefore, P-consciousness can only play a functional role in the system insofar as its content may be transferred outside of the module (i.e., becomes A-conscious and can be used in reasoning or action).

Block applies this distinction to what he calls the "target reasoning" in order to show how it may be useful. He draws on various examples that exemplify this reasoning. One such example is that of blind sight. According to Block, people often draw the conclusion that, since blind sight patients are not conscious of objects in the patient's blind field of vision and also do not use such information in guiding their actions, one function of consciousness must be to make information available for reasoning and guiding action. Block claims that the fallacy in this reasoning is that it is not clear what kind of consciousness is missing. The patient is clearly not A-conscious of objects in the blind field, but there is no way to prove that he is not P-conscious of this visual field. The fallacy, therefore, is jumping to the conclusion that P-consciousness has a certain function when only functions performed by A-consciousness can be seen to be missing. In other words, since the missing functions are all performed by A-consciousness, there is nothing to suggest what the function of P-consciousness may be. According to Block, thirsty blind sight patients will not reach for a glass of water in their blind field because they lack A-consciousness of the glass, which does not clearly reveal their phenomenal experience, but only shows that they do not report any visual information.

Scientific conceptions of consciousness are based on empirical study. This form of inquiry is based on objective observation, however, and may not be able to study phenomenal experience directly. In other words, the only way to study experience is to make inferences based on what appear to be physical displays of mentality. Evidence may include behavioral observations, verbal reports, and psychological/neurological analysis, but cannot cite experience itself. Scientists like Bernard Baars and Alan Baddeley define consciousness in much the same way as Block defines access consciousness, because this definition renders consciousness empirically observable. Phenomenal information that cannot be portrayed in verbal/behavioral reports and does not reach the system of A-consciousness cannot be studied objectively because it has no observable effect or function. There is no way to be sure that the blind sight patient is totally unconscious of information in the blind field (i.e., has no phenomenal experience of anything in this field) without leaving an explanatory gap. Even if one could show that certain brain functions were not present, this would still not prove that phenomenal experience is totally absent, that the patient is not at all P-conscious, because there is no way to certainly correlate the mental with the physical. Only those aspects of consciousness that produce observable, physical effects (i.e., A-conscious states) can be studied empirically as of yet. Therefore, even if A-consciousness and P-consciousness are empirically inseparable, Block's argument holds because it cannot be proven that they are *always* inseparable, only that there is no observable separation that can be studied empirically.

Though he cites empirical evidence suggesting that these forms of consciousness may occur separately in certain circumstances, Block's argument is primarily philosophical. It cannot be proven that Block's two types of consciousness are inseparable using available empirical evidence, and Block only claims that it is *possible* that they are separable (i.e., he does not claim that the two forms of consciousness are *necessarily* inseparable). His argument holds true on purely philosophical grounds, that is, independently of empirical evidence.

It is important to clarify the distinction that Block proposes, but it is perhaps even more important to understand why he believes that employing such a distinction will help to expose a crucial and common philosophical error. Block distinguishes various forms of consciousness in order to discredit vague accounts of mind, accounts of the sort people may ordinarily give. He exemplifies the layman conception of consciousness using John Searle's account, which describes consciousness as "...those subjective states of awareness that begin when one wakes in the morning and continue...until one falls into a dreamless sleep, into a coma, or dies or is otherwise, as they say, unconscious" (Ned Block, et al., *The Nature of Consciousness: Philosophical Debates*, 399). According to Block, the problem with this definition is that it views consciousness as an internal, entirely mental reality. Experiential states, however, cannot be objectively defined or directly correlated with claims about the physical functions of consciousness because of the infamous "explanatory gap" (i.e., the problem of explaining psychophysical interaction). Though Searle's account grows more complex, providing for "degrees" of consciousness and acknowledging the problem of discerning when a person is totally unconscious, Block believes that his distinction makes clear exactly what is known about consciousness and will prevent people from making claims that they do not know to be true, or, more specifically, from attaching uncertain claims about subjective experience to an argument about the externally observable functions of consciousness.

Bruner: Two Approaches to the Unconscious

The psychologist Jerome Bruner introduces a distinction between two modes of thought in his book, *Actual Minds, Possible Worlds*. These two modes, which he terms the narrative and the logico-scientific modes, describe two forms of cognitive functioning that Bruner claims are irreducible to one another. Applying Bruner's distinction to the study of the unconscious can help elucidate whether psychoanalytic and cognitive theories of the unconscious should be brought into dialogue. Cognitive and psychoanalytic approaches to the study of the unconscious can be seen as different modes for investigating the same phenomenon and are, therefore, reconcilable and complementary.

The logico-scientific or paradigmatic mode aims to explain reality in terms of a formally defined system. The domain of logico-scientific theories is limited by observations that correspond with its basic elements and the logical implications of the principled hypotheses that explain the relationships among these elements (Jerome Bruner, *Actual Minds, Possible Worlds*, 12). In other words, logico-scientific theories strive to correspond with observation and to be logically consistent in explaining these observations. Truth is established through empirical verification or formal proof. Personal opinions are overruled by observable facts and verifiable theoretical principles that govern the domain.

Unlike paradigmatic truth, narrative truth is determined by an individual's experience of the narrative rather than objectively verifiable observations. The narrative mode does not have clearly delineated governing principles. Good stories do not have to be logically consistent or factually accurate. There is no set method for creating or evaluating narratives because narrative truth is personal. In Bruner's view, the criterion for verifying narrative truth is verisimilitude or lifelikeness, that is, how much resonance the narrative has for a given reader (Jerome Bruner, *Actual Minds, Possible Worlds*, 11). Verisimilitude does not require that the specific, formal elements of the story resemble the reader's own life, only that the reader's interpretation of the story relates to his or her own life. Readers can empathize with characters in different places and times by recognizing some common theme of human experience. Narrative truth is whatever meaning an individual finds in the story.

Bruner argues that these two modes are irreducible to one another because the functioning and purpose of one mode cannot be encompassed in the domain of the other. The two modes have a different set of goals, principles, and criteria for verification. Moreover, the narrative mode does not have an explicit set of governing principles. It is extremely difficult, therefore, to explicitly define the manifold purposes of narrative such that they could be included in a formal system of the kind used in paradigmatic thought. The specific criteria and values of the narrative mode are determined by an individual's beliefs, desires, and intentions, rendering the task of formulating consistent and comprehensive laws for theoretical reduction nearly impossible. Any attempt to include the laws of one mode within those of the other will "inevitably fail to capture the rich diversity of thought" (Jerome Bruner, *Actual Minds, Possible Worlds*, 11). The two modes are engaged in fundamentally different projects.

The creation of meaning is a narrative process that reflects the internal life of an individual. Freud remarks that "…the act of composition is, after all, an act of decomposition: the artist's separation of his own internal cast of characters into the characters of the story or play. The plot then becomes a hypothetical actualization of the reader's own internal 'psychodynamics'" (Sigmund Freud, quote in Jerome Bruner, *Actual Minds, Possible Worlds*, 28). In Freud's view, the reader identifies with the characters in a story, projecting themes in his or her own life onto the story (Jerome Bruner, *Actual Minds, Possible Worlds*, 29). Freud's account of the interaction between person and text is rooted in his theory of the unconscious. In Freud's view, the "internal cast" is primarily unconscious content, much of which caused problems in the patient's mental life and has therefore been repressed by the patient. The goal of Freud's psychoanalytic theory is to enable the patient to become conscious of latent content, to help them understand the meaning of the story.

Psychoanalysis is a function of the narrative mode of thought. In other words, psychoanalysis treats the patient at the psychic level, addressing problems in the patient's internal, mental life by discussing and interpreting mental content. This contrasts with fields like pharmacology, which attempt to correct mental problems by altering the patient's physiological functions. Like narrative, psychoanalysis deals with human intentions. Psychoanalytic models provide a framework for developing "good stories" that can be verified by the patient and do not have to be verified empirically. Basic themes described by the theory inform the therapist's interpretation of specific elements of the patient's mental life. Dreams, for example, can be interpreted according to Freud's theory and "narrated" in terms of latent sexual desires and various psychological complexes that are identified by the theory. The therapist's story is then tested by whether it resonates for the patient, that is to say, a psychoanalytic theory is verified by helping a patient understand and cope with mental life.

Psychoanalytic theories will be misunderstood if they are viewed as logico-scientific theories and assessed by the kind of empirical verification procedures used in the paradigmatic mode. Clearly, Freud's topographic and structural models of the unconscious do not provide a factually accurate picture of unconscious processes in the brain. From the perspective of a cognitive psychologist, neuroscientist, or any practitioner of the logico-scientific mode, Freudian interpretations should only be taken as phenomenological evidence. Freud's methods are verified by narrative reports and can be taken as evidence that these methods work and produce similar results in many patients. Scientists ought to attempt to explain why Freudian theory works and why people participate in psychoanalysis. The fact that Freudian theory works for some people is a narrative truth that has already been verified by verbal report.

Cognitive psychology and psychoanalysis are different modes of study, one logico-scientific and the other narrative. Accordingly, they have different criteria and practice a fundamentally different kind of discipline. It is less problematic to compare research in different fields of study if the two programs are both a logico-scientific kind of discipline (e.g., cognitive psychology and neuroscience). Nevertheless, narrative and logico-scientific theories can be reconciled, at least in the case of cognitive psychology and psychoanalysis.

Each discipline can help the other achieve its respective goals. Research in cognitive psychology will obviously be useful for psychoanalysts in that it can explain how a patient's mind works. Information about cognitive processes can help psychoanalysts develop methods for treatment and models of mind that are supported by empirical research. Knowing how the mind works will help them understand what they are treating and how the treatment affects the mind. Empirical data is clearly beneficial to the practice of psychoanalysis. If, for example, the cause of patient's illness is a chemical imbalance that disrupts certain processes in the brain, medication and physiological data about the patient will be extremely helpful in treatment. Psychoanalysis is one way of putting cognitive and neuroscientific theories into practice.

The goal of cognitive psychology is to explain the processes of the brain-mind. In order for cognitive psychologists to develop a complete picture of processes in the brain-mind, physical events in the brain must be systematically correlated with certain types or kinds of mental events. This will require phenomenological evidence that can be compared with empirical observations. Psychoanalytic models that prove to be effective work for a broad cross-section of patients. In this sense, psychoanalysis provides a forum for verifying a systematic phenomenological explanation or a testable set of general laws and observations about a specified type of mental phenomena, such as a repressed memory coming to consciousness after therapy. Psychoanalysis provides one method for developing a comprehensive folk-psychology and phenomenology, an account of the mental that should be explained in terms of physical processes and used to help explain the processes of the brain-mind.

Many of the specific motivations for the development and practical application of psychoanalytic and cognitive theories differ, but one goal remains the same: the understanding of the human mind. Although cognitive and psychoanalytic theories of the unconscious are built with different kinds of data, both are trying to develop a picture of the unconscious mind. These two pictures can be seen as complementary. The best way to understand the function of the unconscious is to look at pictures taken from every angle, cognitive or phenomenological, and infer the best possible explanation for the role of the unconscious. Owen Flanagan suggests the natural method, which is to compare cognitive psychology, neuroscience, and phenomenology in order to develop the best overall picture of the brain-mind. Each of these respective disciplines provides a limited picture of the mind, modeling only one "level" of the mind. If all these pictures could be woven together, it may be possible to develop a complete picture that systematically correlates the hierarchical levels.

A Behaviorist Examines Automatic Writing

The source of poetry is not clear and is probably different for each poet, perhaps each poem. For centuries, poets have been trying to find the best way to access or channel whatever it is that causes the human soul to make the non-linear, intuitive leaps that let us feel the sense of what sometimes seems senseless. Poets have attributed their abilities and unique ways of knowing the world to just about every source one could imagine, ranging from a god to a muse, from the conscious to the unconscious mind, from an alternate self to communion with the inherent spirit of matter and earth. Each of the sources to which a poet attributes his work provides insight into that person's poetry, that is to say, a poem can involve anything and come from anywhere the poet finds poetry. On one extreme, some poetry is strictly cognitive, meant to impart logical ideas and no more; it is very deliberate and done consciously. This end of the spectrum is not the poetry in question. The meaning of such poetry can be understood with reason and does not carry with it the deep-felt element of mystery or touch of the mystical that probably will never be explained by humans yet is felt at times by most people and often connected with the essence of life. Generally speaking, cognitive poetry is poor poetry, because it lacks feeling and goes against the very nature of the poetic, which is human. Poetry is about expressing, whether in feelings between words or in direct language, a part of the human experience or a sense of the relationship of an individual to his reality. This life, all the loves and erratic passions, tragedies and uncertainties, twists, turns, and cups of tea, makes no clear sense except the sense felt through the experience of living in and of itself. It is this essence, known only from the feeling of being inside a world of intricate beauty and unfathomed magnificence, that we call the sacred fire in our lives. It is the expression of how it feels to be immersed in this mystery, this essence, that inspires truly great poetry. For a young poet, the question becomes: how does one write poetry if it is to come without reason, without being ordered by the known, with the intention of discovery and innovation? Where does a poet find this ability to write the random yet find coherence in it? In examining these questions, let us start with the place where such words apparently originate: the human mind.

From a psychological perspective, one must look at the factors which influence the formation of poetry in the brain. According to B.F. Skinner, this, along with all other human behaviors and abilities, is caused by an interaction of our genetic and environmental history. In his essay, "A Lecture on 'Having' a Poem," he asks the question: "Does the poet create, originate, initiate the thing called a poem, or is his behavior merely the product of his genetic and environmental histories?" (B.F. Skinner, "A Lecture on 'Having' a Poem," in *Cumulative Record: A Selection of Papers*, Ch. 23). Of course, the poet is nothing more than a personality formed from an interaction of his original organism, which is nothing more than his biological and genetic self, and his environment. It follows, therefore, that any creation on the part of the poet results from an interaction of his genetic and environmental histories, but what exactly does that entail? What unfathomable forces compose our environment, and with what capabilities is our organism endowed in terms of interacting with that environment? What is the nature of this interaction, and to what extent does an individual being, if any such thing even exists, play a role in that interaction? Along these lines, the possible explanations are as endless as the questions, all of which are complex to the point of being unanswerable (at least by mankind). Ultimately, it comes down to the age-old debate between free will and determinism, which holds little bearing on our lives, does not really change anything, and brings us no closer to understanding the source of poetry.

Accepting a behaviorist perspective, Skinner compares the way fragments of original thought come through a poet to the way a baby comes into the world through a mother, meaning that the poem forms inside the poet as a result of his personal history and then emerges, in contrast with a poet himself truly creating an original thought. This process is in large part unconscious. "The poet often knows that some part of his history is contributing to the poem he is writing.... But it is quite impossible for him to be aware of all his history, and it is in this sense that he does not know where his behavior comes from.... And because the poet is not aware of the origins of his behavior, he is likely to attribute it to a creative mind, an 'unconscious' mind, perhaps, or a mind belonging to someone else—to a muse, for example, whom he has invoked to come and write his poem for him" (B.F. Skinner, "A Lecture on 'Having' a Poem," in *Cumulative Record: A Selection of Papers*, ch. 23). This explanation brings us back to the question at hand regarding the source of poetry. Regardless of whether a behaviorist approach is the correct method for analyzing the birth of a poem, the fact that a poet cannot be aware of all the factors that influence his ability to originate a poem or his apparent predisposition to having a poem originate inside him leads us into the realm of the unconscious mind.

The degree to which the unconscious mind plays a role in the formation of a poem depends upon the poem. The poetry of B.F. Skinner, for example, is very conscious, and any role the unconscious mind plays is indirect, meaning that its effects are seen only as they affect the formation of conscious thoughts. The other extreme, however, is harder to examine and more difficult to isolate. Writing that is totally unconscious is probably impossible because the author would have to be comatose. The most extreme example of unconscious writing, however, is found through experiments in spontaneous automatic writing. Gertrude Stein and several colleagues conducted such experiments designed to examine the limits of motor automatism and the potential for developing in normal minds a "second personality" similar to those seen in certain cases of hysteria, though any secondary personality that could be deliberately developed would obviously be incomplete. The experiments focused on learning to write automatically while directing attention elsewhere. They were fairly successful: "The unconsciousness was broken into every six or seven words by flashes of consciousness, so that one cannot be sure but what the slight element of connected thought which occasionally appeared was due to these flashes of consciousness. But the ability to write stuff that sounds all right, without consciousness, was fairly well-demonstrated by the experiments" (B.F. Skinner, "Has Gertrude Stein a Secret?" in *The Atlantic Monthly*, January, 1934, 51). Furthermore, most of the flashes of consciousness described by the subject which were even remotely related to the words she was writing on the page were caused by a reflexive recognition of muscle memory, that is to say, any "conscious flashes" related to the words on the page contained nothing more than information obtained from the arm through the automatic recognition of a given motion sequence, for example, the arm movements involved in writing the letter "m." This means that any conscious knowledge of the words on the page could only be obtained several seconds after having written them.

B.F. Skinner later used these experiments as a basis for comparison in his analysis of Gertrude Stein's writing. He writes, "No one who has read *Tender Buttons* or the later work in the same vein can fail to recognize a familiar note in these examples of automatic writing. They are quite genuinely in the manner that has so commonly been taken as characteristic of Gertrude Stein" (B.F. Skinner, "Has Gertrude Stein a Secret?" in *The Atlantic Monthly*, January, 1934, 52). This is quite a good point which, assuming that there is indeed truth in it, brings us much closer to identifying the role of the unconscious mind in writing. Though there is no way to be sure that the samples of automatic writing and the strange prose of *Tender Buttons* originate from the same source or to know exactly how much Miss Stein's consciousness affected either work, it would be a mistake to discredit either point. The source of Miss Stein's automatic writing could be from a number of places other than the unconscious mind, including outside stimuli, especially verbal ones, and the flashes of consciousness Miss Stein retained, but the fact remains that the words were written unconsciously. It is also hard to deny the stylistic similarities (and thus the similarity of origin) between a sample of Miss Stein's automatic writing, "When he could not be the longest and thus to be, and thus to be, the strongest" (B.F. Skinner, "Has Gertrude Stein a Secret?" in *The Atlantic Monthly*, January, 1934, 51), and her later, less intelligible work in *Tender Buttons*, "Within, within the cut and slender joint alone, with sudden equals and no more than three, two in the centre make two one side" (Gertrude Stein, *Tender Buttons*, in *Modernism: An Anthology* (L. Rainey, ed.), 379). One could argue that the similarities in style and origin only demonstrate that they are both originated by Gertrude Stein in her own characteristic style, but this argument is not sufficient when one considers the extraordinary differences in style that Miss Stein demonstrates from book to book. Furthermore, there remains the question of how Miss Stein originates her writing.

The available evidence and observations that might shed light on the source of Gertrude Stein's unusual words—whether it be an inference drawn from the results of psychological experiments, a cohesive analysis formed from a careful reading of *Tender Buttons*, a comparison focused on the presence of a "second personality" in her various works as the degree of such a presence relates inversely to the apparent intelligibility of her writing, a psychological analysis of that "second personality," or the personal accounts of the author herself—all suggest that a theory of automatic writing is the correct one, that is to say, the inspiration for Gertrude Stein's more experimental writing is primarily originated in her unconscious mind, though it may well be directed, connected, edited, and formatted consciously.

It seems fairly true that, upon reading *Tender Buttons*, one would readily agree that the source of Gertrude Stein's writing is not only her conscious mind. It seems impossible that anyone could consciously think such odd thoughts, especially without forcing them and making the flow of thoughts totally unnatural. Gertrude Stein writes these thoughts with, above all else, a very natural flow. In fact, I often think that part of the reason she allows herself to go so far out there is so that she can maintain the flow of thoughts, meaning that she will go wherever the flow takes her. Gertrude Stein herself backs up this point: "... let it take you and if it seems to take you off the track don't hold back, because that is perhaps where instinctively you want to be...." (Linda Simon, *Gertrude Stein Remembered*, 155). Furthermore, in looking at the presence of a "second personality" in her various works, it is clear that this personality grows continuously more dominant in her work, culminating in *Tender Buttons*. Her earlier work, such as the *Autobiography*, shows much more evidence of the author's personality as it is formed from her life experiences, meaning that the book contains more biographical information and more correlation to her personal experiences as well as the touch of a personality, that is to say, the narrative creates a clearer voice, showing the characteristics of someone with a past history and specific point of view, someone who probably went to grammar school and lived part of her life in California. The *Autobiography* shows evidence of a deeply-felt, primary personality and is quite intelligible. *Tender Buttons*, however, is much less intelligible and also shows evidence of another Gertrude Stein, best described (from the standpoint of a theory of automatic writing) as an unconscious version of herself deliberately separated from her conscious self. This personality has no personality really, but is merely a vessel through which words flow. As Skinner describes, "It is intellectually unopinionated, emotionally cold, and has no past" (B.F. Skinner, "Has Gertrude Stein a Secret?" in *The Atlantic Monthly*, January, 1934, 53). This second personality, if one accepts the distinction, is obviously similar to the alternate personality (which isn't a true personality) described by Miss Stein in her experiments with automatic writing.

Ultimately, the most convincing proof of the theory of automatic writing comes from the testimony of Miss Gertrude Stein herself. In an interview conducted by John Hyde Preston, she says in very clear correlation with B.F. Skinner's explanation of her writing and his analogy between giving birth and creating a poem:

> You will write if you will write without thinking of the result in terms of a result, but think of the writing in terms of discovery, which is to say that creation must take place between the pen and paper, not before in a thought or afterwards in a recasting. Yes, before in a thought, but not in careful thinking. It will come if it is there and if you will let it come, and if you have anything you will get a sudden creative recognition. You won't even know how it was, even what it is, but it will be creation if it came out of the pen and out of you and not out of an architectural drawing of the thing you are doing. Technique is not so much a matter of form or style as the way that form or style came and how it will come again. Freeze your fountain and you will always have the frozen water shooting into the air and falling and it will always be there to see—oh, no doubt about that—but there will be no more coming. I can tell you how important it is to have that creative recognition. You cannot go into the womb to form the child; it is there and makes itself and comes forth whole—and there it is and you have made it and have felt it, but it has come itself—and that is creative recognition. (John Hyde Preston, "A Conversation," *The Atlantic Monthly*, August 1935, 188)

One can see how Gertrude Stein works by comparing her explanation with that of B.F. Skinner. In this interview, she describes explicitly the way in which words must come on their own, "... not in careful thinking" (John Hyde Preston, "A Conversation," *The Atlantic Monthly*, August 1935, 188). By this I can only assume that the words come from somewhere other than her conscious thought processes, and that means the words come from her unconscious mind, unless of course Miss Stein's arm is being moved by the grace of some higher force or being, and I do mean physically moved by this force, not simply moving in coincidence with some ability Miss Stein has to tap into this higher force with her mind or in expression of some gift Miss Stein's mind has been endowed with by such a higher being. I will assume by the virtue of science that poetry comes from the poet's mind and that the role any mystical force plays in inspiring poetry (just as in all other instances where a mystical force might be credited) is only seen insofar as it affects, controls, contributes to, forms, or causes some real phenomenon that can be studied empirically, though not necessarily explained scientifically. By this I mean that if a mystical force is responsible for Gertrude Stein's work, then it is only because it is responsible for and the cause of her mind and her environment.

As an aside, this again raises the question of what causes Gertrude Stein's words and perspective. Skinner claims that all that is Gertrude Stein is caused by an interaction of her original genetic makeup as it goes through and is affected by her environment. This simply must be true because there isn't anything else involved in Miss Stein's life other than herself and the surrounding world. What then is Miss Stein? What forces are at work in her environment? The nature of both of these factors and the complexity of their interaction is unfathomable, just as Skinner's theory is all-inclusive but does not answer any of the questions Miss Stein is searching to answer. The depth and complexity of our environment appears mystical simply because it is beyond us, just as Skinner claims, and we credit the mystical because we do not know the causes of our behavior, but that does not bring us any closer to knowing the mystery of life, knowing what is inside the interaction between Miss Stein and her environment. That is a mystery which can only be felt and known by Miss Stein herself. Skinner's theory, therefore, correctly identifies the source of poetry: Miss Stein's words come from her life. Living is an ongoing interaction of the self, including all the unknown aspects of oneself, and the environment, including any and all forces, whether numinous or phenomenal, knowable or unknowable, which affect the workings of the universe. One might as well say that the formation of our minds and all our behaviors comes from nothing less than a complex interaction of all of reality. Any mystical force that might be involved, if it can only be known through its presence in reality, can still be termed part of the cosmos or the environment.

Skinner's theory presents us with a very meaningful duality that is the cause of all things which we know or experience in life, including poetry. Life is an experience of the tension between an individual and his reality. Art is about exploring what this tension feels like and what it means to us, because it is a mystery. We experience the mystery; our experience affects and connects us to it in ways we will never know, as Skinner says "... it is quite impossible for him to be aware of all his history...." (B.F. Skinner, "A Behavioral Model of Creation," in *The Creativity Question* (A. Rothenberg, et al. (eds.), 271). Along these lines, it seems that much of the history which is unknown to us and much of the way we feel about our life is registered unconsciously, as it clearly affects us, but we are not consciously aware of all the effects it has. It seems that an artist like Gertrude Stein is trying to look into her unconscious mind, trying to unveil or shed light on a part of her mystery. This being said, there remains only one more question I have to ask: "How on earth does she do it?"

Looking at Miss Stein's explanation of how she lets writing flow from her, especially when viewed with the perspective of Skinner's theory on automatic writing, it seems clear that she draws a great deal from her unconscious. When she lets her writing flow, she seems to be in a semi-meditative state, much like the state she describes when misdirecting her attention for the purpose of automatic writing. In this sense, as she herself describes, her writing is much like having a baby in that, "You cannot go into the womb to form the child; it is there and makes itself and comes forth whole" (John Hyde Preston, "A Conversation," *The Atlantic Monthly*, August 1935, 188). She continues, however, to say, "Of course you have a little more control over your writing than that; you have to know what you want to get; but when you know that, let it take you...." (John Hyde Preston, "A Conversation," *The Atlantic Monthly*, August 1935, 188). This aspect of her account, the idea that creation can come "... before in a thought, but not in careful thinking" adds an element of consciousness to her creative process (John Hyde Preston, "A Conversation," *The Atlantic Monthly*, August 1935, 188). Amidst her unconscious words, there are flashes of consciousness. These flashes are necessary for Skinner's theory of automatic writing to hold true, but they also hold implications about the purpose of her unconscious writing.

Skinner argues that Miss Stein's unintelligible work holds little or no importance because it is merely unconsciously formed gibberish of no more importance than the samples of automatic writing. The difference between the two, however, is the depth of conscious direction. In the samples of automatic writing, Miss Stein was not trying to get at something or to get an end product. In her literature, however, Miss Stein *is* consciously trying to get at something, something she doesn't quite know yet, but that, when she gets into it, will be a process of discovery that brings her new knowledge. To discover the unknown, however, one cannot remain only in the realm of the known. It seems to me that Miss Stein uses consciousness to direct her unconscious writing and, with her highly developed sense of what she calls "creative recognition," she is then capable of identifying what the unconsciously written passages mean in terms of the direction she is going (John Hyde Preston, "A Conversation," *The Atlantic Monthly*, August 1935, 188). She lets herself be taken by the current, popping up for air once in a while to keep herself oriented. It is this post-creation creative recognition that seems to be the key sense which makes her able to sense her right meaning in the senseless flow of thoughts. Then, having recognized something which she did not before, she redirects herself and goes under again into the unconscious flow of thoughts. The sense of creative recognition she has developed makes her able to recognize and ultimately know meaning in a sense which Skinner cannot, which is why I discount Skinner's suggestion that Miss Stein's writing holds no importance. He is in no place to judge this; I've read his poetry. In fact, I would argue that Miss Stein is the only one who can truly know whether the work is meaningful to her journey. Skinner greatly adores the parts of Gertrude Stein's work which are intelligible, but "I do not believe in the importance of the part of Miss Stein's writing that does not make sense.... I welcome the present theory [of automatic writing] because it gives one the freedom to dismiss one part of Gertrude Stein's writing as a probably ill-advised experiment and to enjoy the other and very great part without puzzlement" (B.F. Skinner, "Has Gertrude Stein a Secret?" in *The Atlantic Monthly*, January, 1934, 57). He says that his theory of automatic writing suggests that there is no meaning present in Miss Stein's senseless words, which may be true in cases of purely automatic writing. I would argue, however, that one cannot simply dismiss the parts of Miss Stein's writing that don't make sense simply because they aren't easily intelligible. Intelligibility is only the sum of the known. For Miss Stein, writing is an ongoing process of discovery, and I would argue that one cannot detach the unintelligible portions of her writing from the intelligible ones any more than one can separate the reasoning behind a conclusion from the conclusion itself. Writing the unintelligible portions of her work has probably helped Gertrude Stein lead herself to where she is and helped her to write many of the intelligible words she has written, and vice versa. All that she has done is part of her journey and is important as such. Surely, some steps may have been wrong turns that served no more importance than to teach her not to go in that direction, but she herself accredits her senseless writing as one of the most important aspects of her work.

By directing oneself consciously, then letting the unconscious take control, it is possible that writers are able to reveal to themselves new depths of their perspective. She is "... gradually growing and becoming steadily more aware of the ways things can be felt and known in words" (John Hyde Preston, "A Conversation," *The Atlantic Monthly*, August 1935, 194). Her writing is about discovery, and since the result deals with the unknown, it may or not make sense by itself. In the context the writer views it, however, it fits simply as an unlimited flow of expression that has been focused on going deeper or exploring new ways of knowing the writer's relationship through experience to some given aspect of the writer's life. This holds meaning by itself, that, just like life, can only be known in and of itself, from inside the perspective of the knower. Miss Stein believes that her writing justifies itself. She writes in *An Elucidation*: "If it is an event just by itself is there a question/Tulips is there a question/Pets is there a question/Furs is there a question/Folds is there a question" (Gertrude Stein, "An Elucidation," *transition*, April, 1927, 258). The idea here is that one simply knows, for instance, a tulip. There is no way to make the sense of knowing a tulip intelligible without actually being alive and knowing a tulip. At the same time, however, being alive and knowing a tulip is a sense that cannot be pinned down. One can know a tulip in many different ways, in many moments, in many contexts. Upon seeing a tulip, one can draw associations and metaphors from anywhere that are not any more logical than the sense a knower has of knowing of a tulip. The same holds true for any experience of a relationship between an individual and his reality. If Miss Stein, for example, holds a tulip, the meaning of holding that flower at that moment in her life could be anything, and if she draws unintelligible words from that experience, it only means that she is not confining this new instant of knowing to her rational mind, but is instead suspending the limitations of reason and stretching out into the reaches of her mind to find all the ways that moment of holding that tulip resonates in her being. Then, because she has deeply developed sense of creative recognition, she can realize by examining the results what implications her creation might hold and what it means to her in terms of finding her direction. I would argue, then, that the liberated flow of unconscious creation that might be unintelligible by ordinary standards is not only important (as such passages are clearly important to Gertrude Stein), but is the poet's path into the unknown and can lead to true innovation, provided that the writer is well attuned, meaning they are capable of recognizing what they've done and incorporating it fluidly into the direction and ongoing journey of their work. Becoming attuned, however, is the secret; the only way to learn this is to immerse oneself in the mystery.

Therefore, while I support Skinner's explanation that the birth of a poem is caused by an interaction of genetics and environment (though those two terms could include almost anything), as well as his application of a theory of automatic writing to work of Gertrude Stein, I disagree with his answer to the question he poses in the title of his essay. He asks "Does Gertrude Stein have a secret?" His answer to this is that she does not, that she is just a talented novelist who likes to experiment with automatic writing. He claims that, while these experiments may be useful in psychological studies of motor automatism, they hold no place in literature because they are "unintelligible" and therefore hold no meaning or importance. "I regret the unfortunate effect it has had in obscuring the finer work of a very fine mind" (B.F. Skinner, "Has Gertrude Stein a Secret?" in *The Atlantic Monthly*, January, 1934, 57). To this I say, first, that what is or is not intelligible is very much relative to a specific intellect, just as importance and meaning are, and second, that she certainly does a secret. It is a secret so secret that even she does not know it completely. Her secret is one of method; she is discovering how to discover the mystery of herself. She has developed the ability to know the unknown by a completely intuitive process of exploration. Developing this mysterious sense of creative recognition gives her the ability to feel her way through a chaotic journey and come out with newfound knowledge of what was once unknown to her. She is continuously uncovering the many secrets she has forming and growing inside her. In fact, I'm quite sure Miss Stein would say that understanding the secret in intelligible terms would end her writing because, for her, writing is the process of discovery.

About the Author

Ryan Farley was born in New Orleans in 1983. He loved the city's food, festivals, and culture, especially Mardi Gras parades, Jazz Fest, the New Orleans Saints, and "laissez les bons temps rouler," letting the good times roll. Ryan attended Hampshire College in Amherst, Massachusetts, with a National Merit scholarship, earning a bachelor of arts in philosophy with a concentration in philosophy of mind and Buddhist philosophy. After losing his home in New Orleans during Hurricane Katrina, he relocated to Portland, Oregon, where he graduated from Oregon Health & Science University with a bachelor of science in nursing and became a hospice nurse. He loved the natural world, especially backpacking, rock climbing, and downhill skiing. Ryan died in 2022.

Made in United States
Troutdale, OR
12/02/2024

25689026R00195